T0368958

An Age of Transition

An Age of Transition:
British Politics 1880–1914

Edited by

E.H.H. Green

Edinburgh University Press
for
The Parliamentary History Yearbook Trust

© 1997 Edinburgh University Press

Edinburgh University Press
22 George Square
Edinburgh

Transferred to digital print 2004

Typeset in Bembo by WestKey Limited, Falmouth, Cornwall

Printed and bound by CPI Antony Rowe, Eastbourne

A CIP record for this title is available from the British Library

ISBN 0 7486 0926 1

CONTENTS

PREFACE

This present collection of essays on *An Age of Transition: British Politics 1880–1914* is the fourth in a series of special volumes sponsored by the journal *Parliamentary History*, and published by Edinburgh University Press for The Parliamentary History Yearbook Trust. The series will consist of volumes on particular topics as well as collections of essays covering specific periods (like the present one). The fifth in the series to be published in early 1998 will be on 'Parliament and Locality' from the seventeenth to the twentieth centuries. Further volumes are planned on the Church and Parliament and on Ireland and Parliament.

In the footnotes, the place of publication is London unless otherwise stated.

As editor of *Parliamentary History* I would like to thank the editor and contributors to this volume, and to Alasdair Hawkyard who compiled the index.

Clyve Jones

General Editor

LIST OF CONTRIBUTORS

Frans Coetzee teaches in the History Department at George Washington University. He is the author of *For Party or Country: Nationalism and the Dilemmas of Popular Conservatism in Edwardian England* (Oxford, 1990), and co-editor of *World War I and European Society* (Boston, Mass., 1995) and *Authority, Identity and the Social History of the Great War* (Providence, R.I., 1995).

Sandra den Otter, Assistant Professor of History at Queen's University, Kingston, Ontario, is the author of *British Idealism and Social Explanation: A Study in Late Victorian Thought* (Oxford, 1996). Her current work addresses the ways in which mid-century social theorists interpreted law, community and the individual via their engagement with British India

E.H.H. Green studied at University College, London, and St John's College, Cambridge, and is currently Fellow and Tutor in Modern History at Magdalen College, Oxford. He is the author of *The Crisis of Conservatism: The Politics, Economics and Ideology of the British Conservative Party, 1880–1914* (1995), and has also published a number of articles on late nineteenth- and early twentieth-century British politics and political economy.

Jane Elliott is a Research Fellow at the University of Manchester. Her research interests include the analysis of large and complex datasets, and combining qualitative and quantative methodologies in the social sciences. She is currently working on an E.S.R.C.-funded project entitled 'Putting Qualifications to Work'.

Claire Eustance is a Research Fellow in the School of Humanities at the University of Greenwich. She is co-editor of *The Men's Share? Masculinities, Male Support and Women's Suffrage in Britain, 1890–1920* (forthcoming), and is currently working on a book on the Women's Freedom League, based on her University of York D. Phil. thesis.

Jon Lawrence is Lecturer in Modern History at the University of Liverpool. His publications on late Victorian and Edwardian popular politics include articles in the *Journal of British Studies* and *English Historical Review*. His *Speaking for the People? Party, Language and Popular Politics in England, 1867–1918* will appear from Cambridge University Press in 1997.

Margaret O'Callaghan studied at University College, Dublin, and St John's College, Cambridge, and is currently Lecturer in Politics at Queen's University, Belfast. She is the author of *British High Politics and a Nationalist Ireland: Criminality, Land and the Law Under Forster and Balfour* (Cork, 1994), and has published a number of articles on Irish politics and questions of Irish cultural identity in the late nineteenth and twentieth centuries.

Duncan Tanner is Professor of History at the University of Wales, Bangor, and Head of the School of History and Welsh History. Publications include *Political Change and the Labour Party, 1900–18* (Cambridge, 1990).

An Age of Transition: An Introductory Essay

E.H.H. GREEN

Magdalen College, Oxford

Historians are constantly discovering crises, watersheds, climacterics and turning points. Less charitable commentators might say that they are always *inventing* them, and that an historian of the Fall would probably seek to present the departure from Eden as 'an age of transition'. So what is it about Britain in the late nineteenth and early twentieth century, and British political developments in particular, that justifies the title of this collection?

In 1880 Britain's position in the world, its social and economic structures and its political institutions and practices would have been quite familiar to a time traveller from the 1840s. In international terms Britain had retained and strengthened its imperial presence, but when in 1883 J. R. Seeley noted that Britain had 'conquered and peopled half the world in a fit of absence of mind'[1] he was drawing attention to the unspectacular nature of British imperial expansion. The Empire had grown over 40 years, but largely through a gradual accretion of territories and informal influence of the kind that had characterized the earlier part of the century.[2] Britain in 1880, as had been the case in the 1840s, possessed a vast and expanding Empire, but, as Seeley implied, it was difficult to detect British imperia*lism* as a self-conscious ideology or guiding policy, and, equally important, the Empire had rarely been at the centre of political debate. Likewise Britain's diplomatic outlook was very similar to that of the earlier part of the century. From the vantage point of 1880, the Crimean entanglement could only seem an aberration in terms of Britain's international relations since the end of the Napoleonic Wars. With the Royal Navy's unquestioned supremacy providing a basic guarantee against potential aggressors, as well as ensuring the security of international and imperial trade, Britain's avoidance of continental alliances seemed both understandable and entrenched.

If Britain's international position in 1880 appeared to be as, if not more, secure than it had been in the 1840s, and based on similar premises and policies, Britain's domestic social and economic scene would also have been familiar to our time traveller. In the 1840s Britain was the most industrialized and urbanized nation in the world, and its manufacturers, merchants, shippers and bankers were the dominant force in international trade and commerce. In the early 1880s this was still the case. Britain had a 41 per cent share of international trade in manufactures, produced 26.6 per cent of the world's manufactured goods and 34.7 per cent of world iron and steel

---

[1] J. R. Seeley, *The Expansion of England* (1884, 1887 edn), p. 10.
[2] For the best recent survey see P. Cain and A. Hopkins, *British Imperialism* (2 vols., Harlow, 1993), I, *Innovation and Expansion, 1680–1914*.

output. In 1880 Britain had not only retained but extended its role as the world's banker and shipper. Britain's overseas investment assets totalled over £1 billion by the late 1870s, more than three times that of its nearest rival France. The British merchant marine made up 38 per cent of the world's tonnage, and 25 per cent of the world's trade went through Britain's ports.[3] This continuing process of industrial and urban development had altered Britain's economic and social structures in the third quarter of the century, but there were still important aspects of continuity. In 1841 Sir Robert Peel had argued that the die was cast in relation to Britain's economic development, in that the predominance of agriculture had passed and the balance had tipped towards industry and the towns. Yet, in 1881 agriculture continued to contribute 15 per cent of Britain's G.D.P. and provided a livelihood for 1.5 million people. Agricultural workers were, at almost 900,000, the largest labouring group in a single trade, and the arable sector continued to account for 40 per cent of agricultural production.[4] In spite of fears that the repeal of the Corn Laws would destroy British agriculture, especially the arable areas, the period from the late 1840s to the early 1870s had proved to be a golden age for British farming. Britain in 1881 *was* a more industrial and urban nation than it had been 40 years earlier, but the pace of change had been and remained gradual.

In the political sphere there were also marked continuities with the earlier period. The general election of 1880 saw the old Peelite Gladstone replace the old spokesman of Tory protectionism Disraeli as Prime Minister. The chief offices of state and the front benches of both major parties were filled by Britain's aristocratic *élite*, and the House of Commons was still dominated by landed M.P.s. Moreover, high political life continued to keep time with the rhythms of aristocratic and landed life – with the parliamentary timetable in step with the London season, the races and the grouse moors. The electorate had been extended to a large section of the urban working class in 1867, but British politics in town and country was still very much a 'politics of local notables' – at both the centre and periphery of politics the parties were largely reliant upon informal (i.e. non bureaucratic) social and associational forms of organiz-ation.[5] Likewise the 'stuff of politics' – the issues which dominated political debate – displayed marked continuities with the earlier period. Reform of the administrative machinery of the state, the nature of local government in urban centres, the governance of Ireland, and confessional questions concerning the role of the Anglican Church and the provision of education, had provided the main points of controversy in Parliament and the localities from the mid 1840s to the late 1870s. The issue of the franchise had been prominent in the mid 1860s, but it could hardly be said that there was an continuing clamour for further reform in the 1870s. Following the collapse of Chartist agitation in the late 1840s and early 1850s there were few signs of social and political unrest amongst the lower echelons of British society. The fear of a class

[3] See F. Crouzet, *The Victorian Economy* (1982), pp. 342–80; R. Floud, 'Britain 1860–1914: A Survey' in *An Economic History of Britain Since 1700*, eds. R. Floud and D. McCloskey (2nd edn, 3 vols., Cambridge 1994), I. 1–28.

[4] See C. O'Grada, 'British Agriculture, 1860–1914' in Floud and McCoskey (eds.), *Economic History of Britain*, II, 145–72.

[5] See H. J. Hanham, *Elections and Party Management* (Brighton, 1974).

polarization of British politics, a spectre that had haunted many contemporaries in the late 1830s, had been assuaged in the 1850s and 1860s as political allegiances settled into patterns of cross-class confessional alignment. This in turn seemed to have confirmed and reinforced the primacy of constitutional, parliamentary procedures as the basis of political action. Extra-parliamentary agitation and violence were confined to the margins of British political life, with Ireland proving the only significant, but also easily contained, exception. As a consequence the legitimacy of British political institutions, the ordering of social relations, the basic security of the rights and privileges of property, and the prevailing distribution of wealth, secured in the late 1840s, were seemingly entrenched in the late 1870s.[6]

Another crucial area of continuity concerned the function of the British state. The climax of 'economical reform' in the 1840s,[7] in particular the reintroduction of the income tax, the reduction of indirect taxation and the stabilizing of the banking and currency structure, had seen a general acceptance of a classical liberal model of the role of the state. The triptych of free trade, the gold standard and balanced budgets formed the basis for a restricted role for central government in the social and economic spheres. It has long been recognized that to characterize mid-Victorian Britain as 'an age of laissez faire' is in many respects simplistic, given that important areas of industrial and social life were policed by central and local government.[8] However, it is also clear that the prevailing assumption was that agencies of civil society rather than the state should be responsible for social and economic development. The Poor Law devolved responsibility for social distress onto local bodies, whilst private philanthropy, the churches, and agencies of self-help such as the friendly societies were expected to provide any additional provision of support for those individuals unable to support themselves. Social legislation from the 1840s to the 1870s emphasized the role of *enablement*, whereby civic institutions were granted powers to implement improvements in their social infrastructure, and *inspection*, as a means of ensuring conformity to certain basic standards. It was also accepted that the state should play a minimal role in the economy, as evinced by Disraeli's celebrated remark that protectionism was not only 'dead but damned' and by the broad (restrictive) fiscal consensus that marked budgetary policy under both Gladstone and Disraeli.[9] By the late 1870s the 'minimal state', essentially constructed in the 1840s, was regarded as the basis for relations between the state, civil society and the individual.

Underpinning the minimal Victorian liberal state was an emphasis on the personal responsibility of individuals for their social, economic and even moral improvement.

[6.] For the continuities of early and mid-Victorian political life see E. Biagini, *Liberty, Retrenchment and Reform* (Cambridge, 1991); J. Parry, *Democracy and Religion: Gladstone and the Liberal Party, 1867–1875* (Cambridge, 1986); idem, *The Rise and Fall of Liberal Government in Victorian Britain* (New Haven, 1994); M. Taylor, *The Decline of British Radicalism* (Oxford, 1995); M. Finn, *After Chartism* (Cambridge, 1993); T. Nossiter, *Influence, Opinion and Political Idiom in Reformed England* (Brighton, 1975); P. M. Gurowich, 'Party and Independence in the Early and Mid-Victorian House of Commons' (University of Cambridge Ph.D., 1986).

[7.] See P. Harling, *The Waning of Old Corruption* (Oxford, 1996), for a recent discussion placing Peelite reform in the context of earlier administrative reform.

[8.] The best summary is A. J. Taylor, *Laissez Faire and State Intervention in 19th-Century Britain* (1972).

[9.] H. C. G. Matthew, 'Disraeli, Gladstone and the Politics of Mid-Victorian Budgets', *Historical Journal*, XXII (1979).

This did not, however, mean an unattenuated individualism based on market relations.[10] A crucial assumption of the liberal state was that personal responsibility included a sense of civic responsibility, which meant an interest in the welfare of others.[11] The rationale for keeping state action and expenditure to a minimum, and thereby allowing money to 'fructify' in the pockets of individuals, was not simply that this would free 'wealth creators' from the trammels of taxation and allow prosperity to 'trickle down' through society. The proper enjoyment of wealth and prosperity was taken to imply an unselfish, responsible use of its benefits. For the very prosperous this civic mindedness meant, for example, engagement in the proper functioning of local government and philanthropic activity. But the less prosperous also had their civic duties to perform, principally pursuing a thrifty life-style which would enable themselves and/or their families to avoid becoming a charge on the community. The Victorian concept of the independent individual carried an unavoidable paradox insofar as it assumed the existence of others who were in various ways and to varying degrees dependent. But the important point was that this 'dependence' was personal and based on assumptions of good neighbourliness informed by notions of Christian duty to one's families and fellows. This sense of duty and responsibility had to be discharged on an individual basis, albeit perhaps mediated through associations such as charitable organizations or mutual aid societies. The impersonal state could not perform or substitute for the duties of individuals without eroding the reciprocal responsibilities which formed the basis of civic life.

One particularly significant manifestation of the independence/dependence paradox was the gendering of social, economic and political life through the pervasive notion of 'separate spheres' – the idea of a masculine public sphere of work, civic association and politics and a feminine private sphere of domesticity.[12] This meant that 'independence' was an intrinsically masculine quality, insofar as women, as daughters, sisters or wives, were dependent on the participation of their fathers, brothers or husbands in the public sphere.[13] The laws of marriage and married property, the idea of the family wage, religious teaching, the mores of sexual behaviour and, most obviously, the exclusion of women from the franchise provided a legal and cultural apparatus that valorized and policed a conception of gender roles that circumscribed female participation in the public sphere. That many working-class women were participants in the labour market did not serve to disrupt, and in some ways reinforced, the notion of women as dependents. Female wage rates were generally set at low levels on the assumption that they were supplementing a household income dominated by male earnings. Moreover, the hierarchical structuring of factory work and domestic service (the latter a key area of female employment) typically placed women in

---

10. A stimulating collection of essays which explores this issue is *Victorian Values*, ed. T. C. Smout, (Oxford, 1992).

11. See G. Finlayson, *Citizen, State and Social Welfare* (Oxford, 1994), pp. 19–106

12. The literature on this question is extensive. Particularly helpful are L. Davidoff and C. Hall, *Family Fortunes* (1987); A. Digby, 'Victorian Values and Women in Public and Private' in Smout (ed.), *Victorian Values*, pp. 195–216; M. Poovey, *Uneven Developments* (1989); *Suffer and Be Still*, ed. M. Vicinius (Bloomington, Indiana, 1972); *Fit Work for Women*, ed. S. Burman (1979); *Labour and Love*, ed. J. Lewis (Oxford, 1986).

13. See K. McClelland, 'Masculinity and the Representative Artisan in Britain, 1850–80' in, *Manful Assertions*, eds. M. Roper and J. Tosh (1991).

subordinate, non-supervisory roles. The architecture of this sexual division of life and labour, principally constructed in the late 18th and early 19th century, had been well established by the 1840s.[14] By the 1870s the 'masculinist' conception of gender relations was simply regarded as the 'natural' order of things.

In order to pre-empt any vulgarization of the argument at this point, it must be stressed that this essay is not seeking to contend that Britain's social, economic and political structures were wholly unchanged between the 1840s and 1880. Obviously this was not the case. It is the *degree* of change that is at issue here. The question posed is whether our time traveller from the 1840s would have felt at home in 1880 – whether they would have found clearly recognizable social, economic and political landmarks and landscapes – and on this basis it is difficult to see that they would have suffered any large-scale sense of disorientation. But the same thing could not be said if our time traveller was then taken forward to 1914.

Between 1880 and 1914 Britain's global position underwent major changes. The Empire was still intact and expanding, but whereas in 1880 Britain had enjoyed an unchallenged imperial supremacy the 1880s and 1890s saw the emergence of rival colonial powers, with in particular Germany, France, the United States and Russia posing problems for Britain. In these new conditions Britain's diplomatic isolation appeared less splendid, especially when at the turn of the century the Boer War 'revealed the unpleasant fact that Great Britain had scarcely a foul-weather friend in the civilized world'.[15] The realization of Britain's vulnerability in a changing world prompted a re-evaluation of its diplomatic and imperial outlook. The assumption that Britain could afford to stand aloof from alliances was questioned, particularly given that the Royal Navy's mastery of the seas was rendered less secure by the development of both rival, large-scale fleets and new naval technologies.[16] On the foreign relations front the net result of this re-evaluation was the British 'diplomatic revolution' of the Edwardian period, which saw Britain engage in a Pacific alliance with the Japanese in 1902, pursue an *entente* with France and, finally, form a defensive alliance with France and Russia in 1907. Having avoided formal engagement with other powers since 1815 Britain tied itself to a 'continental commitment' which was to help propel it into the Great War in 1914.[17]

At the same time as Britain's relations with other powers were reconsidered there were also important changes in Britain's imperial role. From the incursion into Egypt in 1882–3 to the Boer War of 1899–1902 Britain was a major participant in the 'Scramble for Africa'. Prompted in part by the 'fear of the closing door' as rival, protectionist powers carved out territorial possessions in Africa, British imperial policy became more assertive.[18] In the period up to the 1880s British imperial expansion

[14.] See in particular Davidoff and Hall, *Family Fortunes*; D. Wahrmann, *Imagining the Middle Class* (Cambridge, 1995), pp. 377–408.

[15.] L. J. Maxse, 'Episodes of the Month', *National Review*, CCLXXVII (Mar. 1906), p. 8.

[16.] See A. L. Friedberg, *The Weary Titan* (Princeton, 1988); P. Kennedy, *The Rise and Fall of British Naval Mastery* (1976); J. Sumida, *In Defence of Naval Supremacy* (1989).

[17.] For a summary of these developments see Z. Steiner, *Britain and the Origins of the First World War* (1977); M. Howard, *The Continental Commitment* (1972), pp. 9–30.

[18.] For the fear of the closing door and its impact on attitudes to Empire see W. G. Hynes, *The Economics of Empire* (1979).

conformed to the formula of 'trade with informal control where possible: trade with formal control where necessary'.[19] However, the large-scale formal acquisition of territory in the last quarter of the century serves to indicate that formal control was deemed much more 'necessary' in the new global climate.[20] In this respect Britain's participation in the 'new imperialism' was based on concern, even anxiety, about the implications of the new, more complex and increasingly tense international situation: an acknowledgement of the fact that Britain was no longer alone or unchallenged.[21]

The growing external challenge to the Empire was matched by changes in the internal make-up of the imperium. In particular the self-governing settlement colonies of the old Empire began to develop increasingly independent positions, especially in the realm of trade policy where Canada, New Zealand and the Australian territories all introduced high tariff regimes against both foreign and British goods.[22] This economic nationalism in the self-governing colonies and dominions reflected a more general 'rise of Colonial nationalism' in the old Empire, and gave rise to concern that the Empire might disintegrate spontaneously as its constituent parts went their own ways. In turn this led to the emergence of organizations such as the Imperial Federation League, founded in 1884, and various campaigns to bring about more formal bonds, both economic and political, within the Empire, culminating with Joseph Chamberlain's great crusade for imperial tariff preference inaugurated in 1903.[23]

The extension of the Empire in the late 19th century, and the changing relationship between Britain and the old colonies, ensured that imperial issues were, unlike in the mid-Victorian era, well to the fore of political debate. That the Liberal writer L. T. Hobhouse could describe the Boer War as 'the test issue of this generation'[24] sums up the new prominence of imperial questions in British politics. That imperial issues took on this significance was only in part due to the fact that there were major new developments and challenges to be confronted in the governance and defence of the Empire. Equally important, late Victorian and Edwardian arguments for restructuring the Empire generated a number of questions which had implications far beyond the realm of imperial policy. One of the main reasons Seeley had discerned 'absence of mind' in Britain's imperial enterprise was because he failed to detect a systematic imperial policy at the centre of government. He was right, insofar as successive British governments, mindful of the costs of imperial defence and administration, had been 'reluctant imperialists'. Until the last quarter of the century the preferred government approach to Empire was to devolve responsibility onto private bodies, with the actions

---

[19] This classic formulation is taken from J. Gallagher and R. Robinson, 'The Imperialism of Free Trade', *Economic History Review*, 2nd Ser., VI (1953).

[20] See D. C. M. Platt, 'Economic Factors in British Policy During the New Imperialism', *Past and Present*, No. 29 (1968).

[21] For a useful summary see B. Porter, *The Lion's Share* (1975), pp. 74–192.

[22] For a case study of the most important colonial market See R. C. Brown, *Canada's National Policy* (Princeton, 1964). A helpful collection of essays which covers this ground is *The Rise of Colonial Nationalism*, eds. D. Schreuder and J. Eddy Sydney (1988).

[23] For these developments see E. H. H. Green, 'The Political Economy of Empire, 1880–1914: The Limits to Constructive Imperialism' in *The Oxford History of the British Empire*, ed. W. R. Louis (6 vols., Oxford, forthcoming).

[24] L. T. Hobhouse, *The Nation*, 30 Mar. 1907, cited in P. Clarke, *Liberals and Social Democrats* (Cambridge 1978), p. 68.

of Cecil Rhodes's British South Africa Company and George Goldie's Royal Niger Company being prime examples of the partition of Africa 'by company'.[25] However, in the 1890s, particularly after Joseph Chamberlain became Colonial Secretary in 1895, there was a marked trend towards direct state control of imperial activity. Chamberlain's desire to 'improve the great estates' of Empire through state or state-sponsored development of colonial infrastructure were largely thwarted by the Treasury's parsimony, but there was a distinct shift towards an acceptance of state responsibility for colonial development.[26] Chamberlain's desire to break from a *laissez faire* approach to the Empire was underscored by his proposals for imperial tariff preference. The underlying rationale of both colonial development programme and trade preference was that Britain needed to 'systematize' the Empire and bring a coherent form to an as yet amorphous entity.[27] These ambitious schemes for planned imperial economic development and trade demanded positive and extensive state action and, crucially, a break from free trade. Changes within and debate about the Empire thus raised a range of questions about the role of the British state.

Concerns about the future of the Empire were themselves a sub-set of a more general anxiety about Britain's condition that emerged in the late nineteenth and early twentieth century. The onset of the series of cyclical downturns once known as the 'Great Depression' in the mid to late 1870s, and the parallel growth of foreign competition, began a debate as to whether the British economy was showing signs of 'decline'. There is no doubt that Britain's economic circumstances did change significantly in the period 1880 to 1914. There was a slow-down in the rate of British economic growth, and Britain moved from first to third place in terms of world share of manufacturing output, trade in manufactures and output of iron a steel.[28] Certain areas of British manufacturing, notably the metal trades of the Midlands and Black Country, saw foreign import penetration pose problems, and the textile districts of Lancashire and Yorkshire found many of their older markets in Europe and the United States closed by tariffs. Furthermore British agriculture, especially the arable sector, was faced with a massive inflow of imports from the Americas and Eastern Europe.[29]

Recent reassessments by economic historians have concluded that Britain's economic performance between 1880 and 1914 was quite respectable. But if the British economy is not seen as being in decline it is pictured as undergoing structural changes as adjustements were made to an increasingly competitive international economy. This process of adaptation witnessed the British economy moving towards a concentration on those areas where it enjoyed a comparative advantage, namely in the old staple industries of coal, textiles and heavy engineering and above all in banking and traded services. This process of adaptation was slow and painful for the British

---

[25]. J. Gallagher and R. Robinson, *Africa and the Victorians* (1961).

[26]. R. M. Kesner, *Economic Control and Colonial Development* (1981); M. Havinden and D. Meredith, *Colonialism and Development* (1993), pp. 70–90.

[27]. See Green, 'Political Economy of Empire'.

[28]. For the performance of the British economy in the late nineteenth century see in particular S. B. Saul, *The Myth of the Great Depression* (1972); Floud, 'Britain 1860–1914'; S. Pollard, *Britain's Prime and Britain's Decline* (1988); Crouzet, *Victorian Economy*, pp. 371–422.

[29]. O' Grada, 'British Agriculture'.

economy, made more so by the fact that in the period of the mid-Victorian boom
Britain had been a major producer and exporter of most manufactured and consumer
goods. As one commentator has put it, the main change for the British economy was
that it had enjoyed a 'free lunch' in the 1850s and 1860s which was taken away in
the last quarter of the century.[30] Thus the cyclical downturns that characterized the
period from the mid 1870s to the mid 1890s hit Britain harder than other countries
because its position as the leading manufacturing and trading nation made the British
economy more vulnerable. Similarly the emergence of strong foreign competition
and the revival of protectionism also hit Britain harder because of its reliance on
international trade. The verdict of economic history is that by 1914 Britain still had
a powerful position in the world economy, but that the nature of that position had
changed considerably over the previous 30 years in response to shifting market
conditions.

The social ramifications of the structural changes taking place in the British economy
were significant. The most marked effect was on the balance of the rural and urban
sectors. In 1880, as noted above, British agriculture and the rural population still
made a major contribution to Britain's G.D.P. and its social structure. But by 1914
agricultural production, hit hard by foreign competition, represented only 7 per cent
of G.D.P, and less than 10 per cent of the population lived and worked on the land.[31]
The way in which the rural population had voted with their feet in the last quarter
of the century was reflected in the rapid and deep urbanization of British society.
Whereas in 1881 only 36.2 per cent of the population had lived in towns of over
100,000, by 1911 this had risen to 51 per cent, and smaller townships had also been
growing in size.[32] Although the 'classic' period of urbanization is often seen as the
early nineteenth century, when the 'shock of the new' made it appear very dramatic,
in fact it was the late nineteenth century which saw Britain having to come to terms
with the rapid and permanent decay of the rural economy and the most accelerated
growth of urban conglomerations.

The depopulation of rural Britain made an important contribution to the debate
over the 'condition of the people' that was such a feature of late-Victorian and
Edwardian Britain. The growing concentration of Britain's population in towns and
cities was regarded by many as literally an unhealthy development, in that it placed
pressure on the sanitary infrastructure of urban centres, caused overcrowded housing
conditions, and glutted the urban labour market. Concern about urban living conditions
produced sensationalist accounts such as Andrew Mearns' *Bitter Cry of Outcast London*,
essays in persuasion such as William Booth's *In Darkest England*, and 'scientific' works
such as Charles Booth's survey of East London, Seebohm Rowntree's study of York
and A. L. Bowley's examination of a number of Britain's mid-sized towns.[33] This

[30.] D. McCloskey and C. K. Harley, 'Foreign Trade, Competition and the Expanding International
Economy' in *An Economic History of Britain Since 1700*, eds. R. Floud and D. McCloskey (1st edn, 2
vols., Cambridge, 1980).

[31.] O'Grada, 'British Agriculture'.

[32.] C. M. Law, 'The Growth of Urban Population in England and Wales, 1801–1911', *Transactions
of British Geographers*, XLI (1967).

[33.] J. Treble, *Urban Poverty in Britain* (1976); K. Williams, *From Papuperism to Poverty* (1981), pp.
309–68.

'discovery' of poverty in the 1880s and 1890s was underscored by revelations about the health (or lack of it) of potential recruits for the army during the Boer War.[34] As Britain entered the twentieth century the 'fitness' of its people in the 'urban rookeries' of its major cities and towns was much in question.

The combination of Britain's loss of its imperial and industrial hegemony and the rising tide of concern over the condition of the people placed question marks against the established orthodoxies of Victorian political economy and social philosophy. The Fair Trade agitation of the 1880s and 1890s and the tariff reform campaign of the early twentieth century questioned the wisdom of Britain's unilateral adherence to free trade.[35] The gold standard came under assault from the advocates of bimetallism in the 1880s and 1890s.[36] Balanced budgets became more difficult to achieve as the day-to-day costs of administering Britain's maturing urban society increased, and they were further threatened by the growing demands of imperial defence and social expenditure.[37] In short the Victorian 'minimal state' was challenged by a variety of problems and by increasingly vocal and numerous critics. The idea that all Britain's farmers and businessmen needed was 'fair field and no favour' lost much of its lustre in the glare of increased foreign competition. Likewise the notion that local civic institutions and voluntary associations could cope with the social consequences of a mature industrial and urban society appeared questionable, especially in the light of revelations about social conditions and the increasing financial problems faced by collective self-help agencies.[38] Britain's economic and social fabric had changed, and this led to doubts as to whether the economic and social policies and institutions that had been established and entrenched in the second and third quarters of the nineteenth century needed to be adjusted or even abandoned.

By the time Britain entered the Great War most of the social and economic attitudes of the mid-Victorian period had been questioned or significantly amended. The gold standard had been successfully and relatively easily defended. Free trade, however, had faced a more severe test and would never again possess the inviolable, quasi-religious quality that it had enjoyed in the mid nineteenth century: doubts had been raised, and doubt is the first sign of a weakening faith. More important the defence of free trade as a commercial policy had not been accompanied by an equally vigorous or successful defence of the state's minimal role in the domestic social sphere.[39] The social legislation of the 1906 to 1914 Liberal governments was particularly important in this respect. The provision of subsidized meals for schoolchildren in 1906, followed by old age pensions in 1908, medical and dental inspection of schools in 1908–9, regulation of the sweated trades in 1909, the establishment of labour

[34.] For the general impact of this revelation see G. R. Searle, *The Quest For National Efficiency* (Oxford, 1972).

[35.] B. H. Brown, *The Tariff Reform Movement in Britain, 1880–95* (Columbia, 1945); A. J. Marrison, *British Businessmen and Protection* (Oxford, 1996); E. H. H. Green, *The Crisis of Conservatism* (1995).

[36.] E. H. H. Green, 'Rentiers versus Producers: The Political Economy of the Bimetallic Controversy, 1880–98', *English Historical Review*, CIII (1988).

[37.] J. Cronin, *The Politics of State Expansion* (1991), pp. 50–4; A. Offer, *Property and Politics* (Cambridge, 1981), pp. 201–41; Green, *Crisis of Conservatism*, pp. 48–53.

[38.] S. Yeo, *Religion and Voluntary Organizations in Crisis* (1976) offers a useful case study. E. Hopkins, *Working Class Self-Help* (1995), pp. 53–70.

[39.] Finlayson, *Citizen, State and Social Welfare*, pp. 107–200.

exchanges in 1909 and the introduction of national health and unemployment insurance legislation is 1911, ensured that the British state was given a role in the economy and social policy which would have been unthinkable 30 years earlier. This extended level of state activity was achieved without abandoning a balanced budget, but this had only proved possible as a result of the introduction of innovatory taxation schemes, culminating with the 'People's Budget' of 1909. The steeply-graduated progressive rates of income tax, a super-tax on very high incomes, and taxation of land values – the key elements of the fiscal regime introduced in 1909 – may have preserved the Victorian balanced budget but they did so at the expense of another central Victorian notion, that of a socially 'neutral' fiscal structure.[40]

The Edwardian break from the precepts of the Victorian minimal state carried with it an implicit redefinition of the nature of citizenship. The notion of personal responsibility was by no means abandoned.[41] The Poor Law remained in place, and the distinction between the 'deserving' and 'undeserving' poor was maintained by all engaged in both the discussion and implementation of the new social legislation.[42] National Insurance was based on contributions, and private industrial insurance companies and friendly societies were integrated into the administration of the scheme.[43] Moreover, registration at a Labour Exchange was necessary before insurance benefits could be claimed, ensuring that unemployed individuals were actively seeking to re-enter the labour market. Yet, there was also an acceptance that there were *systemic* social and economic problems which no amount of individual 'character' could overcome, and that these social evils required a social solution organized by society's collective expression, the state. On grounds of ethics and efficiency poverty was deemed not only detrimental to the poor themselves but to society as a whole – a hindrance to an individual's ability to achieve their own potential and therefore a blow to society's ability to reach its highest goals. Society was defined as more than simply a sum of its individual components, and the good of the individual and the good of society were seen as organically related. Such was the thinking which justified the regulation of sweating and old age pensions, measures which, by supporting *adults*, eschewed Victorian limits on the category of non-voluntary assistance that could be made available. Moreover, even those measures which were aimed at children broke new ground insofar as school meals legislation, and other measures of child benefit, represented a new form of contract between the state and parents. The state had taken on a large degree of responsibility for child development, a clear difference from Victorian legislation which had policed or prevented child labour but had not provided positive benefits. In Edwardian Britain the boundaries of the state were redrawn in many crucial areas.

[40.] H. V. Emy, 'The Impact of Financial Policy on British Party Politics', *Hist. Jour.*, XV (1972); B. K. Murray, *The People's Budget* (Oxford, 1982).

[41.] J. Harris, *Private Lives, Public Spirit* (1993), pp. 180–250, provides an excellent survey of areas of continuity as well as highlighting the key changes in attitudes towards social problems and the role of the state.

[42.] A. Macbriar, *An Edwardian Mixed Doubles* (Oxford, 1986), illustrates the common ground shared by those supposedly implacably opposed couples the Webbs and the Bosanquets.

[43.] B. B. Gilbert, *The Evolution of National Insurance in Great Britain* (1966); E. P. Hennock, *British Social Reform and German Precedents* (Oxford, 1986); *Lloyd George's Ambulance Wagon*, ed. H. N. Bunburb (1957).

Before one can have policy one must have politics. That the direction of Britain's foreign, economic and social policy changed markedly in the period 1880 to 1914 was in large part due to the fact that changes in Britain's international and domestic situation affected and were in turn affected by changes in British politics.

The Third Reform Act of 1884 ushered in a new era of mass politics. The franchise was extended to rural householders, adding 1.76 million new voters to the electorate and giving two-thirds of adult males the vote.[44] That the new voters were for the most part agricultural labourers was important, in that for the first time the electorate in both borough and county seats was dominated by the labouring classes. All political parties after 1884 had to be, in some form or another, working class parties in order to survive.

The sheer size of the post-1884 electorate had important implications for the nature of British politics. Political parties had, perforce, to become quite different institutions. Mobilizing a large vote required mass communication and thorough organization. Mass canvassing and expert knowledge of electoral law were essential to local party organizations in order for them to identify voter allegiance and to ensure that supporters were placed on and, if possible, opponents struck off the electoral register. This meant that bureaucratic party structures, employing professional electoral agents, were a vital supplement to informal associational and kinship ties as the core of local party political activity. Clubs, social gatherings and the enthusiasm of local members were continued to be important, but these efforts had to be systematically organized to achieve maximum political/electoral effect. Hence at the centre of politics as well as the periphery new, professionally-staffed organizations were created in order to co-ordinate and provide advice, speakers and financial assistance for local party activity throughout the years but especially at general elections. The age of informal influence and the talented amateur was passing, and the age of professionalized politics had arrived.

The growing bureaucratization of politics was one of a number of developments which weakened the role of Britain's traditional political *élite*, the landed aristocracy. As noted above British politics in 1880 was still very much dominated by the old order, but by 1914 a combination of political and economic reversals had brought their political pre-eminence to an end. The agricultural depression, and the fall in rents it occasioned affected most aristocratic families, especially those dependent upon farm rentals and in the Celtic fringe. Legislation to control, tax or eliminate landlord privileges posed a further threat to the value of land as a commodity and landownership as an occupation. The Ground Game Act (1880), the Irish Land Act (1881), the Agricultural Holdings Act (1883), and the Scottish Crofters Act (1886) weakened a landowner's authority in dealing with his or her property. In Ireland widespread agitation rendered even the day-to-day management of estates difficult, and some landlords feared for their lives. As a consequence many Irish landlords took the opportunities offered by the Irish Land Acts of 1896 and 1903, and were effectively 'bought out' by the state. In the rest of the United Kingdom too land sales, whether

---

[44.] C. Seymour, *Electoral Reform in England and Wales* (1929); N. Blewett, 'The Franchise in the United Kingdom, 1885–1918', *Past and Present*, No. 32 (1965).

distressed or otherwise, increased over the early twentieth century as a prelude to the great break-up of the estates in the 1920s. Meanwhile the electoral reforms of 1883 to 1885 forced the aristocracy to confront a new political world. The extension of the franchise posed a problem for aristocratic electoral power in that it introduced a large and potentially hostile force into their once secure electoral fiefdoms. The Redistribution Act of 1885 had almost as big an impact. By abolishing two-member constituencies in the counties, and drawing the boundaries of the new single-member seats roughly according to population rather than to old geographical or estate boundaries, the 1885 reforms destroyed many of the old electoral communities in the counties. This, combined with the effects of the Ballot Act of 1872 and the Corrupt and Illegal Practices Act of 1883, curtailed much of the electoral 'influence' of large landowners. Local government reforms, which saw the introduction of elected county councils in 1888 and parish councils in 1894, removed local authority from the lords lieutenants, magistrates and shrievate. At first the old *élite* performed quite well in gaining election to the new authorities, but after 1900 their presence declined markedly.[45] Similarly the military reforms of the early twentieth century, especially those implemented by the Liberal War Minister R. B. Haldane, reduced the importance of local militias and yeomanry and the role of the aristocracy in another area of county life once seen as its preserve.[46] Finally the 'People's Budget' of 1909, and the constitutional crisis of 1910–11 which it provoked, led to the passage of the Parliament Act which abolished the House of Lords' veto powers and ended the aristocracy's 'watchdog' authority in the constitution. Between 1880 and 1914 the aristocracy was economically, socially and politically in retreat.[47]

The waning of aristocratic authority had general political significance in that it marked the passing of an old order. But it was also of particular importance to the Conservative Party. Throughout the nineteenth century the Conservative Party had above all else been the political arm of the landed interest, drawing its leadership from the aristocracy, its parliamentary cohorts from the squirearchy and retaining a solid electoral base in the English counties. The 1880 general election, however, had demonstrated conclusively that the Conservatives could not live on English counties alone, and that there was a danger of their becoming a permanent minority unless they broadened the basis of their support. The necessity for action was further reinforced by the electoral changes of 1883 to 1885, and the Conservatives made strenuous efforts to attract and organize urban support. Harnessing the rightward drift of urban and suburban middle class *élites* in particular, the Conservatives made an important breakthrough in the general election of 1885, when for the first time they captured a majority of English borough seats. From the late 1880s through to the Edwardian era the Conservatives sustained this appeal to the urban middling classes, thereby consolidating a process which saw them become no longer just the party of the land but the party of property in general.[48] That the Conservative Party, having

45.   A. Adonis, *Making Aristocracy Work* (Oxford, 1993), pp. 54–5.

46.   For these developments see R. H. Williams, *Defending the Empire* (New Haven, 1989), pp. 138–40.

47.   D. Cannadine, *The Decline and Fall of the British Aristocracy* (New Haven, 1990), offers the best summary.

48.   J. Cornford, 'The Transformation of Victorian Conservatism', *Victorian Studies*, VII (1963–4) is the classic study, but see also Frans Coetzee's contribution to this volume and Green, *Crisis of Conservatism*, pp. 101–8.

been dominated by aristocratic grandees for a century, entered the Great War with a Glasgow-born ironmaster at its head was eloquent testimony to a most significant change on the British political right.

Changes were also much in evidence on the left. In the early 1880s a trickle of Whig defections, and dissent in the Liberal parliamentary ranks over a number of imperial and social policy questions, indicated that the coalition of social forces that made up the Gladstonian Liberal Party was in danger of fracturing.[49] Until 1885 the Liberal phalanx held together, but then the social and imperial implications of Gladstone's support for Irish Home Rule sundered the party. Following the defection of the bulk of the Whig aristocracy and a great deal of propertied urban support to the Conservatives in 1886, the Liberals became increasingly dependent on mobilizing working class support. This they achieved only sporadically in the late nineteenth century, but in the Edwardian period the Liberals proved to be a more effective political and electoral force. Blending traditional rallying cries such as the defence of free trade with promises of social reform funded by a radical tax regime the Liberals successfully attracted mass support and, in alliance with the fledgling Labour Party and the Irish Nationalists, pinned the Conservatives in opposition[50]

In the most basic of terms the British political scene in 1914 had some important continuities with the situation 30 years earlier, insofar as the Liberal and Conservative Parties were still the dominant political forces. But the nature of the parties, and of British politics in general, had fundamentally changed. The exigencies of mass politics had seen both parties adopt new forms of political organization, but this was by no means the most important innovation. The issues on which the parties based their appeal to the electorate had also changed – the 'stuff' of British politics in the early twentieth century was very different to that of the 1870s.

In 1883 Joseph Chamberlain had argued that 'the future of politics is social politics',[51] and in many ways he was proved right. To some extent, however, this was a self-fulfilling prophecy. Chamberlain's prediction was based on his assumption that a mass electorate of the kind that existed after 1884 was bound to be a poor electorate, and that it would, therefore, be most interested in material improvement. This assumption was shared by all British politicians, Conservatives as well as Liberals,[52] and it was only reinforced by the social surveys that gained such publicity in the late nineteenth century. Whether or not the masses were interested in social reform leading politicians were convinced that they were, and hence the 'transition to high politics in British social policy' in the late nineteenth and early twentieth century.[53] Both

---

[49.] T. A. Jenkins, *Gladstone, the Whigs and the Liberal Party* (Oxford, 1989); D. Southgate, *The Passing of the Whigs* (1962); D. Hamer, *Liberal Politics in the Age of Gladstone and Rosebery* (Oxford, 1976).

[50.] On the Liberal revival of the early twentieth century see P. Clarke, *Lancashire and the New Liberalism* (Cambridge, 1971); N. Blewett, *The Peers, The Parties and the People* (1972); R. Russell, *Liberal Landslide* (1972). For a study which emphasizes the traditional aspects of the Liberal appeal see G. Bernstein, *Liberalism and Liberal Politics in Edwardian Britain* (1983).

[51.] J. Chamberlain to E. Russell, 22 Jan. 1882, cited in R. Jay, *Joseph Chamberlain* (1975), p. 73.

[52.] See Lord Salisbury's 1883 essay 'Disintegration' in *Lord Salisbury on Politics*, ed. P. Smith (Cambridge, 1974), for an eloquent Conservative statement of this assumption.

[53.] J. Harris, 'The Transition to High Politics in British Social Policy' in *High and Low Politics in Modern Britain*, eds. M. Bentley and J. Stevenson (Oxford, 1984).

Liberals and Conservatives felt constrained to address questions of poverty, unemployment and social reform, and above all to produce recognizably Liberal or Conservative answers.

The incentive for Liberals and Conservatives to think seriously about social issues was made that much greater by the advent of the Labour Party. In 1883 Friedrich Engels had complained that the British working class was content to remain 'the tail of the great Liberal party', but the increasing assertiveness of the trade union movement in the 1880s and 1890s, the founding of the Independent Labour Party in 1893 and, above all, the creation of the Labour Representation Committee in 1900 seemed to indicate that British workers were keen to establish their own movement and their own political voice.

The rise of Labour and the emergence of a distinctive British Socialism had important ramifications for both major parties. As noted above the Conservative Party from the early 1880s was identified as the party of property. With the development of a strong labour movement the already difficult issue of how the party of property and privilege was to survive in an electoral system dominated by propertyless voters was compounded by concerns that a failure to do so could result in the destruction of property rights. Finding an effective means of unifying and defending the propertied classes against possible radical threats was thus central to the Conservative *raison d'etre*. This task was made all the more urgent by the fact that in the first decade of the twentieth century the Liberal Party forged close ideological and electoral links with the nascent Labour Party. The emergence of Labour had helped strengthen the hand of those Liberals who advocated a positive appeal to the mass electorate, with the result that the Liberal Party pursued radical social, fiscal and industrial relations policies with a deliberately class-based appeal.[54] Labour's political impact was thus much greater than the limited electoral success it enjoyed before 1914 might imply.[55] Labour was regarded as a symptom as well as a cause of social and political change, an indication of the new agenda 'demanded' by the mass electorate enfranchised in 1884 and the pressures generated by Britain's mature industrial and urban society.

Labour was regarded by contemporaries as the most apparent symptom of the changing face of British politics, but it was by no means the only one. Until the late 1870s the integrity of the United Kingdom had been taken as a given, but the last quarter of the century saw that certainty eroded. Here the problem was Ireland. With the Irish Nationalists replacing the Liberals as the main electoral force outside Ulster in the 1870s, and with a radical agrarian movement, the Land League, disrupting the day-to-day governance of Ireland in the early 1880s, doubts arose as to whether Ireland could be governed by the rule of law as understood in Westminster.[56] Ireland had been a thorny problem for successive governments since the Act of Union, but the maintenance of the Union had been regarded as a *sine qua non* for 'pacifying' Ireland until the 1880s. However, the growing strength of the Home Rule agitation on the ground, and the willingness of the British Liberal Party to concede Irish

---

[54] Clarke, *Lancashire*; Murray, *People's Budget*.

[55] For a comprehensive survey of Labour's impact see D. M. Tanner, *Political Change and the Labour Party* (Cambridge, 1990).

[56] C. Townshend, *Political Violence In Ireland* (Oxford, 1981).

demands, marked a new departure. The Conservatives' political hegemony of the late nineteenth century precluded concessions on the question of the Union, but that did not mean that the governance of Ireland became any less problematic. Conservative attempts to 'kill Home Rule with kindness' through land reform in the late nineteenth century were predicated on the assumption that land reform would remove the source of Irish grievances and create a socially and politically conservative class of peasant proprietors.[57] Yet the Irish Land Acts of 1896 and 1903, whilst they succeeded in 'buying out' the landlords and transforming much of the Irish tenantry into small owners, did not dispel the Nationalist agitation. Indeed, Irish Nationalism seemed to become more entrenched and radical.

If the Irish question proved intractable for Conservative supporters of the Union the same was true for Liberal proponents of Home Rule, except that for them the great problem was the position of Ulster. Having accepted Irish Nationalism as a legitimate political expression the Liberals confronted the question of what to make of Ulster Unionism. Moreover, as was the case in the south, opinion in Ulster hardened in the late nineteenth and early twentieth century as the Ulster Unionists became increasingly sectarian-minded in their politics.[58] Just as the Conservatives had found it impossible either to conciliate or coerce the Irish Nationalists so the Liberal government in 1912 faced the implacable hostility of Ulster to the third Home Rule Bill. The net result was that by 1914 an irresistible force seemed to face an immovable object, presenting a possible breakdown of political order and a descent into widespread violence. The constitutional and parliamentary procedures, which had long been regarded as the hall-mark of Britain's civilized political conduct, were facing a severe test when the Great War rescued them.

With Ireland there was at least a semblance of familiarity. The Irish question in the late nineteenth early twentieth century was more pressing than ever before, but at least there was the consolation that the problem was confined to Britain's traditional social and political laboratory. The same could not be said of the suffragette movement, which also posed a radical, mainland challenge to the rule of law and constitutional procedure. At first glance the demand for female enfranchisement had the familiar look of a classic mid-Victorian single issue campaign, but its implications were wider and deeper. Female exclusion from the franchise, as noted above, was in many respects simply the coping stone of an arch of social and legal norms and regulations that confined women to the private sphere. In the late nineteenth century a number of legal and extra-legal challenges had been made to the limitations placed on women's participation in the public sphere, most notably in the realms of married women's property, divorce law, education, and the local government franchise.[59] The campaign for the suffrage was in this sense not merely an end in itself, but a means to an end – a way of ensuring that women would have an influence over the legislation that

---

[57.] L. P. Curtis, *Coercion and Conciliation in Ireland* (Princeton, 1963); A. Gailey, 'The Unionist Government's Policy Towards Ireland, 1895–1905' (University of Cambridge Ph.D., 1983).

[58.] A. Jackson, *The Ulster Party* (Oxford, 1989); P. Jalland, *The Liberals and Ireland* (Brighton, 1980).

[59.] See for example P. Hollis, *Ladies Elect* (1987); S. K. Kent, *Sex and the Suffrage in Britain* (1987); M. L. Shanley, *Feminism, Marriage and the Law in Victorian England* (Princeton, 1989); M. Vicinius, *A Widening Sphere* (Bloomington, Indiana, 1977); B. Caine, *Victorian Feminists* (Oxford, 1988).

affected them. As such the suffrage movement posed a challenge not simply to the political disfranchisement of women, but also to the values and assumptions that circumscribed their social, economic and legal status.[60] In short it represented, both in theory and practice, a direct attempt to overturn the idea of separate spheres, and thus threatened to disrupt one more of the old certainties of the Victorian era.

The rich variety of social, economic and political change that characterized late-Victorian and Edwardian Britain cannot be summarized in a single volume of essays, and this collection makes no pretence of doing so. Rather it seeks to follow the advice of Sir John Elliott in his inaugural lecture as Regius Professor of Modern History in Oxford, and cuts into the period from a variety of angles in an effort to open up a cross-sectional view of the types of change underway. Jon Lawrence and Jane Elliott, examining turnouts in borough elections between 1885 and 1910, and suggest new ways of looking at voting behaviour in the period which cast fresh light on the nature and strength of political partisanship under the electoral system introduced in the mid 1880s. Their findings suggest a shifting interplay of national, regional and local influences in shaping the process of political mobilization, and indicate that our understanding of grass-roots party political activity in the late nineteenth and early twentieth century is still incomplete. Frans Coetzee's essay on 'Villa Toryism' provides a complement to Lawrence and Elliott's work through an analysis of the ecology of Conservative support in Croydon over the period. It is now 33 years since James Cornford published his germinal article on 'The Transformation of Victorian Conservatism', and yet historians are still largely in the dark about the processes which enabled the Conservative Party to 'organize' the 'Villa Tories' that Lord Salisbury targeted as a vital potential constituency in the early 1880s. Coetzee's work on Croydon provides us with a window on this key change in Conservative politics, indicating how a hoped-for development at the national level was translated into genuine achievement in a particular locality. If the Conservative Party has, until relatively recently, remained historical *terra incognita* in this period the Liberal and Labour Parties have enjoyed a great deal of coverage. Much of the historiography has been dominated by the electoral fortunes of the two parties, and in particular has addressed the complex dynamics of their political and electoral relationship.[61] The ideological shift of the Liberal Party away from the Gladstonian orthodoxies of state minimalism to the 'New Liberal' interventionism of the Edwardian era has also attracted much attention,[62] and it is this aspect of Liberal thought that Sandra den Otter re-examines in her essay. In particular she addresses the role of idealist thought in helping to shape Liberal discourse on the notion of *community*, and suggests that this paradigm offered an intellectual bridge between old and new Liberal conceptions of relations between the state, civil society and the individual. Her work emphasizes

[60.]   Kent, *Sex and the Suffrage*.

[61.]   See in particular, Clarke, *Lancashire*; R. Mckibbin, H. C. G. Matthew and J. Kay, 'The Franchise Factor in the Rise of the Labour Party', *English Hist. Rev.*, XC (1975); P. Clarke, 'The Electoral Position of the Liberal and Labour Parties, 1910–14', *English Hist Rev.*, XC (1975); M. Hart, 'The Liberals, the War and the Franchise', *English Hist. Rev.*, XCVIII (1983); M. Childs, 'Growing Up With Labour', *Twentieth Century British History*, V (1994); Tanner, *Political Change*.

[62.]   See in particular Clarke, *Liberals and Social Democrats*; S. Collini, *Liberalism and Sociology* (Cambridge, 1979); M. Freeden, *The New Liberalism* (Oxford, 1977).

that it was possible for Liberal thinkers to construct a communitarian social philosophy without departing from essential Liberal tenets. She thus disentangles elements of Liberal social thought from Social Democratic alternatives, and implicitly demands that we look afresh at the legacy of the late-Victorian idealists and their influence over changing concepts of social welfare in the Edwardian and later periods. Duncan Tanner's essay also explores neglected areas of political thought, and similarly disentangles Liberal and Social Democratic ideas but by pulling, as it were, on the other end of the thread. Discussion of the early years of the Labour Party have for the most part concentrated on its institutional and electoral development, and when its ideological frame of reference has been discussed there has been a tendency to emphasize its roots in, and similarities with, radical Liberalism. British socialist thought has thus been characterized (and criticized) as derivative and lacking the intellectual bite of its European counterparts. Tanner, however, shows that, particularly in the realm of political economy, British socialism had a distinctive outlook, and one which was influenced by and it turn influenced currents of continental socialist thought. Whilst Duncan Tanner illustrates that fog in the English Channel did not cut British socialists off from the continent, Margaret O'Callaghan examines the way in which developments on the other side of St George's Channel posed problems for Conservative Unionists. Recent revisionist histories of Ireland have brought home the complexities and factionalism of the Nationalist movement in the late nineteenth and early twentieth century, charting social, regional and ideological divisions between and within the Nationalist forces in Westminster and on the ground in Ireland. O'Callaghan's essay illustrates that defenders of the Union were similarly stratified. Sellars and Yeatman famously argued that it was not that the English did not understand the Irish Question but that the Irish kept changing the question. Margaret O'Callaghan, however, shows that the defenders of the status quo were as capable of deceiving themselves as they were of being deceived by the changing face of Irish Nationalism. Another rearguard action in defence of the status quo is examined by Clare Eustance's discussion of opposition to female enfranchisement. Her work emphasizes that the campaign for the vote posed a challenge to a masculinist conception of politics – the intrusion of women was regarded as just that, an intrusion on a closed, male world. But her work also illustrates that the threat to and ultimate overthrow of *one* masculinist definition of politics did not mean an end to the gendering of political life. Rather she shows how the suffrage campaign led to redefinitions of gender roles which recast rather than replaced notions of male exclusivity. Her essay thus serves as a reminder that transition does not necessarily mean transformation.

Parliamentary Election Results Reconsidered: An Analysis of Borough Elections, 1885–1910

JON LAWRENCE AND JANE ELLIOTT

University of Liverpool   *University of Manchester*

Britain may have come late to the historical analysis of election results, but studies of electoral behaviour now form an integral part of our understanding of the development of the British political system.[1] The critical period between the Third Reform Act and the First World War, when Britain operated a mass, though not fully democratic, franchise, has been studied more extensively than most.[2] In the absence of pollbooks or survey data on 'voter preference', historians have been obliged to focus on the analysis of constituency, rather than individual, voting patterns. Certainly for this period such 'ecological' studies, as they are generally termed, have been more influential than Nuffield-style studies of individual election campaigns.[3] Indeed, the most influential campaign study, Neal Blewett's on the two general elections of 1910, includes a sustained 'ecological' analysis of election results between 1886 and 1906.[4]

Perhaps inevitably historians have disagreed both over the most appropriate basis upon which to undertake such 'ecological' analyses, and on the conclusions that should be drawn from their findings. Most have insisted that, since Westminster politics were determined by constituencies of unequal size, votes should not therefore be aggregated across constituency boundaries.[5] Others, perhaps interested more in electoral behaviour for its own sake, rather than as a window on the fortunes of party, have argued strongly that a genuine ecological analysis can only be undertaken

[1]. See H. Pelling, *Social Geography of British Elections, 1885–1910* (1967), pp. 2–3; J.P.D. Dunbabin, 'British Elections in the Nineteenth and Twentieth Centuries: A Regional Approach', *English Historical Review*, XLV (1980), 265–7; M. Kinnear, *The British Voter: An Atlas and Survey Since 1885* (2nd edn., 1981), pp. 9–10, although Kinnear certainly overstates 'the relative lack of interest in the social background of British politics' since the Second World War.

[2]. See J. Cornford, 'The Transformation of Conservatism in the Late Nineteenth Century', *Victorian Studies*, VII (1963), 35–66; idem., 'Aggregate Election Data and British Party Alignments, 1885–1910', in *Mass Politics: Studies in Political Sociology*, eds. E. Allardt and S. Rokkan (New York, 1970); J. P. D. Dunbabin, 'Parliamentary Elections in Great Britain: A Psephological Note', *English Historical Review*, LXXXI (1966), 82–99; Pelling, *Social Geography*; P. Thompson, *Socialists, Liberals and Labour: The Struggle for London, 1885–1914* (1967); R. Gregory, *The Miners and British Politics, 1906–1914*, (Oxford, 1968); Kinnear, *British Voter*, pp. 13–37, 82–3, 98–102; K. Wald, *Crosses on the Ballot: Patterns of British Voter Alignment Since 1885*, (Princeton, 1983).

[3]. See T. J. Nossiter, 'Recent Work on English Elections, 1832–1935', *Political Studies*, XVIII (1970), 525–8 for a discussion of the division of election studies into three basic approaches: individual-centred, ecological and campaign study.

[4]. See N. Blewett, *The Peers, the Parties and the People: The General Elections of 1910* (1972), pp. 3–42.

[5]. For instance, Cornford, 'Aggregate Election Data', p. 110, and Dunbabin, 'British Elections', p. 243.

on electoral data that have been aggregated into larger 'surrogate units' for which detailed social and economic data are also available.[6] Some historians have concluded that election results between 1885 and 1910 suggest a decisive shift in the pattern of voter allegiance (from religion and personal influence to social class as the principal determinant of voting),[7] whilst others have insisted that patterns remained little altered across the period, and that 'traditional' religious and regional influences remained dominant until 1918.[8] Similarly, some have identified the rise and fall of 'regionalism' between the 1840s and the 1880s, while others have insisted that regionalism has been a more or less constant feature of British politics throughout the nineteenth and twentieth centuries.[9]

Despite these very real differences of approach and interpretation, almost all these analyses share a common intellectual origin in the 'electoral sociology' paradigm developed by pluralist political scientists such as Seymour Lipset and Stein Rokkan in the 1950s and 1960s.[10] Under this influence electoral outcomes tend to be portrayed as the necessary consequence of underlying divisions, or 'cleavages' within society. Political parties play only a passive role in this process – they are simply the political expression of prior social cleavages. The present study grows out of a deep-seated dissatisfaction, part practical and part theoretical, with how this legacy of 'electoral sociology' has distorted the study of election results in Britain since the 1960s.

In practical terms 'electoral sociology' is particularly unsuited to the analysis of late-Victorian and Edwardian election data. Firstly, as we have noted, electoral districts did not correspond to the districts used to publish social and economic data collected through the decennial population census (this remained the case until 1966). Most historians have basically ignored this problem, suggesting, rather unconvincingly, that even if census returns 'do not often directly fit the constituencies, [they] are nevertheless available for closely comparable districts'.[11] In consequence they can only hope to undertake the loosest type of 'ecological' analysis; classifying constituencies according to a simple social schema such as 'upper/middle-class', 'mixed class' and 'working-class' on the basis of data on servant keeping (itself derived from the census), local press reports and miscellaneous official statistics.[12]

In contrast, Kenneth Wald is able to deploy the full armoury of high-level social statistics on his 115 'surrogate units' – but much is lost in the process. Certainly the

6. See Wald, *Crosses on the Ballot*, pp. 82–94; also W. Miller, *Electoral Dynamics in Britain Since 1918* (1977).

7. Blewett, *The Peers*, pp. 377–415; also P. Clarke, 'Electoral Sociology of Modern Britain', *History*, LVII (1972), 31–55.

8. Wald, *Crosses on the Ballot*; also Pelling, *Social Geography*, pp. 5–6 and 414–17.

9. See T. Nossiter, 'Voting Behaviour 1832–1872', *Political Studies*, XVIII (1970), 380–9; Dunbabin, 'British Elections', p. 260.

10. The most important exception is Dunbabin, 'British Elections'. For a classic statement of Lipset and Rokkan's position see S. M. Lipset and S. Rokkan, 'Cleavage Structures, Party Systems and Voter Alignments: An Introduction', in their edited collection *Party Systems and Voter Alignments: Cross-National Perspectives*, (New York, 1967).

11. Pelling, *Social Geography*, p. 2.

12. See *ibid.*, pp. 2 and 22–3; Thompson, *Socialists, Liberals and Labour*, pp. 299–300, and Blewett, *The Peers*, pp. 488–9, which uses a six-point schema: 'Urban: predominantly middle-class'; 'Urban – mixed class'; 'Urban – predominantly working-class'; 'Mixed urban/rural'; 'Rural'; and 'Mining'.

peculiarities of 'place' are lost – something both political historians and political geographers have become increasingly attuned to in recent years.[13] Wald's 115 'surrogate units' aggregate the election results of 537 separate constituencies. If one focuses just on the 204 English borough constituencies analyzed in some detail below, Wald combines the results of 132 of these constituencies into 43 'surrogate units' – the remainder (72 constituencies) were either dropped, or 'merged with county constituencies in the county residual'.[14] This approach ignores the fact that the 1885 Redistribution Act had declined to introduce equal electoral units in deference to the historic claims of small boroughs with strong local traditions (only boroughs with a population under 15,000 were disfranchised).[15] It also takes too little account of the fact that even in these artificial 'surrogate units' the enumerated adult male population and the electorate would in no sense have been identical. Historians may disagree violently over the nature of the pre-First World War franchise, but none has claimed that its exclusions were simply random.[16] Regardless of whether approximately 40 per cent of adult men were excluded primarily on the basis of their social class or their age and marital status, such exclusions make sophisticated forms of ecological analysis very difficult to sustain – especially when one also has to allow for the uneven distribution of perhaps 600,000 plural votes nationwide (or seven per cent of the total electorate).[17]

In recent years there has also been a growing theoretical critique of how 'electoral sociology' has distorted the analysis of electoral behaviour. Political geographers have been understandably keen to reassert the 'politics of place', arguing that the political cultures which shape voting are often highly localized – the result of 'place-based socialization'.[18] Political historians have also increasingly come to recognise that 'localities matter', but their principal contribution to the debate has probably been to question the essentially passive model of politics characteristic of mainstream 'electoral sociology'. Even historians who championed 'electoral sociology' at the height of its influence rarely felt comfortable portraying political parties simply as the passive beneficiaries of social and economic forces beyond their control – at the very least, it was suggested, political parties could respond more or less successfully to such

13. See especially Dunbabin, 'British Politics'; M. Savage, 'Political Alignments in Modern Britain: Do Localities Matter?', *Political Geography Quarterly*, VI (1987); idem., 'Urban History and Social Class: Two Pardigms', *Urban History*, XX (1993); J. Agnew, *Place and Politics: The Geographical Mediation of State and Society* (Boston, Mass., 1987); *The Power of Place: Bringing Together Geographical and Sociological Imaginations*, eds. J. Agnew and J. Duncan (Boston, Mass., 1989); D. Tanner, *Political Change and the Labour Party, 1900–1918* (Cambridge, 1990); J. N. Entrikin, *The Betweenness of Place: Towards a Geography of Modernity* (1991).
14. Wald, *Crosses on the Ballot*, p. 83 – most of our analyses are in fact on the 183 single-member constituencies, but Wald does not break the boroughs down along these lines.
15. Pelling, *Social Geography*, p. 430, notes that smaller constituencies, with under 5,000 electors, were electorally less volatile than the norm throughout the period.
16. N. Blewett, 'The Franchise in the United Kingdom, 1885–1918', *Past and Present*, No. 32 (1965), 27–56; H. C. G. Matthew, R. I. McKibbin and John Kay, 'The Franchise Factor in the Rise of the Labour Party', *English Historical Review*, XCI (1976), 723–52; Tanner, *Political Change*, pp. 99–129; J. Davis, 'Slums and the Vote, 1867–90', *Historical Research*, LXIV 1991, 375–88.
17. Blewett, 'Franchise in the UK', pp. 45–8.
18. *Developments in Electoral Geography*, eds. R. J. Johnston, F. M. Shelley and P. J. Taylor (1990), p. 5; see also R. J. Johnston, *The Geography of English Politics: The 1983 General Election* (1985), and Agnew, *Place and Politics*.

forces of change.[19] In recent years historians have taken this argument much further, insisting both that 'social cleavages' are themselves articulated only through political discourses (including those of the competing political parties), and that the underlying social structure is itself often influenced by the impact of party-driven state policies.[20] Certainly few historians would now subscribe to the pluralist view that political parties are simply an expression of the different interest groups within society – 'representation' is clearly much more problematic than this model implies.

Taken together these various practical and theoretical objections suggest that 'electoral sociology' of the type associated with Lipset and Rokkan has little part to play in the historical understanding of late Victorian and Edwardian election results. On the other hand, it would seem equally unhelpful to conclude that because election results may not be able to offer conclusive explanations of the social bases of politics we should therefore simply abandon them altogether and retreat to the redoubt of 'high politics' or post-modernist cultural history.

There *is* an alternative, though one that demands we make much less grandiose claims for electoral analysis than were once fashionable. We must first preserve the integrity of individual constituencies within our analysis, since, in the absence of mass media (even the national press remained relatively underdeveloped – no more than a third of British households took a national daily as late as 1910), and with general elections fought over three weeks, campaigns remained largely local affairs however much they might be fought on issues of national policy.[21] But having resisted the temptation to aggregate election results, our next step must be to construct hypotheses about electoral behaviour which do not ask questions of the electoral data that they are simply incapable of answering. In essence this means eschewing the sort of grand sociological analyses characteristic of 'electoral sociology', with its reliance on the Lipset/Rokkan model of political 'modernisation', in favour of more limited analyses based on variables such as voter turnout, size of constituency or level of enfranchisement, which, though still subject to some degree of uncertainty, are nonetheless integral to the electoral process itself. To be fair, many of the works already discussed incorporate elements of this approach, but they rarely break free from the hegemony of 'electoral sociology'. The main exception, in this respect, is Dunbabin's discussion of the persistence of regionalism in British elections, but this piece is necessarily confined to a single theme explored over a much longer time span.[22] One might also mention James Cornford's brief discussion of aggregate election data for the period 1885 to 1910, which, whilst it certainly registers the influence of 'electoral sociology', nonetheless confines itself largely to more descriptive analyses. Though incomplete, the paper is highly suggestive, and some of the issues it raises are pursued more fully in the proceeding discussion.[23]

[19.] P. Clarke, *Lancashire and the New Liberalism* (Cambridge, 1971); *idem*, 'Electoral Sociology'.

[20.] See for instance, G. S. Jones, *Languages of Class: Studies in English Working-Class History, 1832–1982* (Cambridge, 1983); R. McKibbin, *Ideologies of Class: Social Relations in Britain, 1880–1950*, (Oxford, 1990). The historical critique of 'electoral sociology' is discussed more fully in *Party, State and Society: Electoral Behaviour in Britain Since 1820*, eds., J. Lawrence and M. Taylor (1997).

[21.] Newspaper circulation calculated from figures in A. J. Lee, *The Origins of the Popular Press, 1855–1914* (1976), pp. 179 and 293; also Pelling, *Social Geography*, p. 10 (though most boroughs polled early in the campaign).

[22.] Dunbabin, 'British Elections'; there are also elements of this approach to Kinnear, *British Voter*, though orthodox 'electoral sociology' often predominates.

[23.] Cornford, 'Aggregate Election Data'.

Table 1: *Average turnout by winning party at English borough elections, 1885–1910 (single-member constituencies)*

	1885	1886	1892	1895	1900	1906	1910J	1910D
Conservative	82.1	74.9	80.4	77.8	72.7	81.7	87.7	81.7
Liberal								
Unionist	–	69.2	73.7	76.0	76.8	77.7	79.4	74.8
Liberal	80.6	73.0	79.5	79.5	78.3	84.5	88.1	81.3
Lib/Lab	70.1	61.3	70.5	71.0	71.8	84.4	88.1	79.8
Labour	–	–	72.5	–	–	82.5	87.1	77.6
Average	81.0	73.6	79.4	77.7	74.2	83.2	87.4	80.8

Note: Includes M.P.s returned as 'independent' representatives of each party
Source: calculated from a database constructed by the authors.

The remainder of this paper will therefore discuss some of the preliminary findings of a project designed to analyze patterns of partisanship at English borough elections between 1885 and 1910.[24] Eventually it is hoped both to extend the geographic scope of the analysis, and to test a wider range of hypotheses about factors which may have influenced partisanship, but here the analysis is confined to three elements. Firstly, patterns of partisanship are analyzed in relation to turnout and levels of male enfranchisement. Secondly, a more focused analysis is undertaken on the relationship between *changes* in the level of enfranchisement and party fortunes. Finally, both the stability of partisanship and the level of turnout are analyzed in relation to size of constituency, and extent of landowner influence.

The historiography of late Victorian and Edwardian popular politics is unusual in the prominence it has accorded to the question of voter turnout. There seems to be a more or less general consensus that Conservative political dominance after 1886 owed a great deal to low turnout on the one hand (especially in 1895 and 1900), and to restricting voter registration on the other.[25] It is suggested that the Conservative Party leadership, still profoundly uncomfortable with the notion of 'democracy', sought to mitigate its dangerous implications by upholding the complex procedures for voter registration and calling elections when voter turnout might be minimized. But do such arguments stand up to a detailed analysis of late Victorian election results?

Certainly the raw figures for voter turnout by winning party across the eight general elections would appear to bear out the traditional argument (see Table 1). In the English boroughs Conservative victories were associated with *higher* turnout in

---

[23.] Cornford, 'Aggregate Election Data'.

[24.] Most analyses deal only with the 183 single-member borough constituencies. Although the old distinction between borough and county seats had become blurred after the Redistribution Act of 1885 thanks to the creation of essentially urban and/or industrial county seats such as Accrington, Gorton and Leigh in Lancashire, or Barnsley and Doncaster in Yorkshire, it had by no means disappeared before the First World War.

[25.] For instance, J. Cornford, 'The Adoption of Mass Organization by the British Conservative Party', in *Cleavages, Ideologies and Party Systems: Contributions to Comparative Political Sociology*, eds, E. Allardt and Y. Litlunen (Helsinki, 1964); idem., 'Transformation of Conservatism'; P. Thompson, 'Liberals, Radicals and Labour in London, 1880–1900', *Past and Present*, No. 27 (1964), 73–101; P. Marsh, *The Discipline of Popular Government: Lord Salisbury's Domestic Statecraft, 1881–1902*, (Hassocks, 1978), and E. H. H. Green, 'Radical Conservatism: The Electoral Genesis of Tariff Reform', *Historical Journal*, XXVIII (1985), 667–92.

Table 2: *Average turnout by winning party at borough elections in the South-East region and the English provinces, 1885–1910 (Liberal and Conservative seats only)*

	1885	1886	1892	1895	1900	1906	1910J	1910D
South-East								
Conservative	77.9	68.4	75.2	71.6	64.8	79.6	85.7	76.1
Liberal	74.2	62.8	72.9	72.6	73.8	79.6	83.8	75.8
English Provinces								
Conservative	85.8	80.3	83.9	83.0	79.5	83.7	89.5	85.7
Liberal	83.2	76.0	82.6	82.0	80.4	87.6	90.3	84.8

Source: as Table 1

the elections of 1885, 1886, 1892 and December 1910, but in 1895, 1906 and especially 1900 turnout was distinctly lower in Conservative won seats. Interestingly, neither variations in the number of seats contested (from 180 out of 183 in 1885, 1906 and January 1910 to just 130 in 1900), nor the inclusion of an unknown number of duplicate entries on some electoral registers, appear to distort these figures significantly. For instance, seats left uncontested in the 'khaki' election of 1900 had seen much the same voter turnout at previous elections as seats contested in that election.[26] Similarly, in 1885 the 60 boroughs known to have included duplicate entries on their electoral registers recorded the same average turnout as the remaining 120 contested boroughs (81 per cent). In other words the widely observed association between low turnout and Conservative victory in the 1890s, and especially in the 'khaki' election of 1900, appears robust enough to merit more detailed investigation.[27]

Following recent suggestions that urban Toryism may have been a more dynamic, genuinely popular force outside the metropolis, we disaggregated our data on turnout and partisanship in order to contrast the South East with the English provinces (Table 2).[28] The results were striking. In the provinces turnout fell only marginally more in seats won by the Conservatives than in those won by the Liberals, even in the key election of 1900. In the South East the pattern was very different: turnout actually rose, albeit marginally, in seats won by the Liberals in 1900, but in Conservative seats it fell sharply. The same pattern can be identified even if one looks solely at London constituencies. Here turnout was down by 5.8 per cent in Conservative-won seats, but by only 1.3 per cent in seats won by the Liberals.[29] Moreover, continuing the comparison between 1885 and 1900, we found that whereas turnout had fallen at a

[26.] The 52 uncontested seats from 1900 had recorded an average turnout of 82.4 per cent when contested in 1885 (one was uncontested in both elections), while seats contested in 1900 had recorded an average turnout of 80.4 per cent.

[27.] See for instance, Cornford, 'Aggregate Election Data', pp. 113–14.

[28.] J. Lawrence, 'Class and Gender in the Making of Urban Toryism, 1880–1914', *English Historical Review*, CVIII (1993), 629–52. Regions based on Pelling, *Social Geography*. The fact that average turnout *rose* in Liberal Unionist seats in 1900 may lend further support to this argument since only one Liberal Unionist was returned for a seat in the South East (Table 1). We have generally analyzed Conservative and Liberal Unionist results separately because they frequently display different characteristics in this period.

[29.] Average turnout within the London county area fell from 70.6 per cent in 1895 to 64.8 per cent in 1900 in Conservative seats, compared with a fall from 70.0 to 68.7 per cent in Liberal seats.

broadly similar rate in seats won by the Liberals at both elections and at seats which had changed hands, those seats already held by the Conservatives in 1885 and won again by them in 1900 registered a sharp fall in voter turnout (Figure 1). The suggestion here is therefore that, whilst low turnout may indeed be associated with Conservative victories in the South East (at least in 1900), it probably does little to *explain* those victories since turnout was falling most sharply in seats already firmly within the Conservative fold.

We turn next to the relationship between partisanship and the extent of male enfranchisement in different constituencies. Here, in the absence of comprehensive data on the percentage of adult males possessing the vote in each constituency, we have had to generate a surrogate statistic which expresses the registered electorate as a percentage of the total male population recorded at the decennial census. No account is therefore taken of variations in the age-structure of the male population, nor of the distorting influence of plural votes (though these would have been concentrated in a small number of seats with major commercial districts such as Liverpool Exchange). In addition it was decided to use the return of electors for 1892 rather than 1891, partly because far fewer returns are *known* to include duplicate returns in the later year, and partly because there is also evidence that local parties may have intensified their registration efforts in readiness for a general election (since 1901 and 1911 follow election years they may register similar influences). Before examining whether levels of enfranchisement in a borough are associated with voting patterns it may be useful to present a summary of the data using Blewett's admittedly rather subjective scheme of social classification (Table 3). Interestingly, this suggests that while differences in the level of male enfranchisement between 'predominantly middle-class' constituencies, and 'mixed class' constituencies were minimal, levels of male enfranchisement were

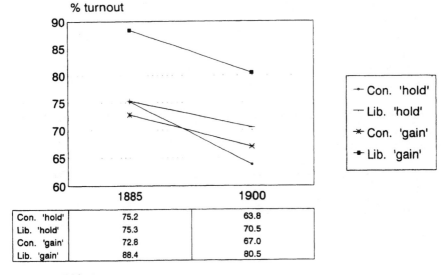

	1885	1900
Con. 'hold'	75.2	63.8
Lib. 'hold'	75.3	70.5
Con. 'gain'	72.8	67.0
Lib. 'gain'	88.4	80.5

Source: as Table 1

Figure 1: *Change in turnout between 1885 and 1900 by party*

Table 3: *Parliamentary electorate as a percentage of resident male population by social characteristics of constituency, 1891–1911*

	1891	1901	1911
Predominantly middle-class	30.8	31.7	35.4
Mixed-class	31.2	31.9	34.8
Predominantly working-class	28.3	29.4	30.9
Average	29.8	30.7	33.2

Note: social classification based on Blewett, *Peers*, pp. 488–94.
Source: *Population Census of England and Wales*, 1891, 1901 and 1911; parliamentary returns relating to electors, 1892, 1901 and 1911.

significantly lower in 'predominantly working-class' constituencies. That said, the absolute differences are not great and may largely be explained by differential birth rates between social groups (i.e. there may have been more males under voting age in more 'working-class' constituencies).[30]

Bearing this in mind, it was decided to include Blewett's social categories in the analysis of the relationship between levels of enfranchisement and partisanship at the general elections of 1892, 1900 and January 1910 (Table 4).[31] However, because the Liberals won so few of Blewett's 'predominantly middle-class' seats (and none at all in 1895), it was decided to merge these with the so-called 'mixed-class' constituencies to form a single category. Once again there is little to suggest that, whatever their private anxieties about democracy may have been, the Conservatives relied in practice upon low levels of enfranchisement for success. Only in 1900 is there any suggestion that the Liberals may have done better in seats with a higher level of enfranchisement, and even then the difference barely reaches the level of significance.[32]

Despite the inconclusive nature of these findings it was decided to pursue the question further by examining whether there was any association between *rising* levels of male enfranchisement within a constituency, and the revival in Liberal Party fortunes either before or after the 1900 election.[33] Using the surrogate figures for male enfranchisement derived from the decennial census, we therefore calculated the percentage change in the level of 'enfranchisement' between 1892 and 1901, and between 1901 and 1911. We then correlated the resulting data against change in the Liberal Party vote in two-party, Liberal-Conservative seats between the elections of 1895 and 1900, and between 1900 and January 1910. In neither case was there any evidence of association – we cannot support the claim that the Liberal revival of the early twentieth century depended upon, or was even associated with, the Liberals'

[30] In addition, Blewett's 'predominantly working-class' group includes 29 London constituencies, many of which recorded unusually low levels of male enfranchisement. Data on age-structure are not available for parliamentary constituencies at this time.
[31] These elections were chosen because our estimates of enfranchisement levels were derived from the decennial census – January 1910 was chosen over December because it was fought on a fresh register.
[32] In a two-way analysis of variance, using 'class' and 'winning party' as two dichotomous factors, as in Table 4, the F ratio for winning party in 1900 was found to be 15.87, with an associated $p = 0.043$.
[33] As suggested by Cornford, 'Aggregate Election Data', pp. 115–16.

Table 4: *Electorate as a percentage of resident male population by winning party at key elections (Liberal and Conservative seats only)*

	Average	Middle–class & Mixed	Predominantly Working-class
1892			
Conservative	29.9 (98)	30.7 (72)	27.5 (26)
Liberal	29.7 (65)	31.9 (24)	28.5 (41)
1900			
Conservative	30.2 (129)	31.4 (76)	28.6 (53)
Liberal	31.5 (32)	33.3 (13)	30.3 (19)
1910(J)			
Conservative	34.3 (86)	35.3 (64)	31.5 (22)
Liberal	32.6 (69)	35.1 (30)	30.7 (39)

Note: as Table 3
Source: as Table 1

ability to get more men on the register in particular boroughs.[34] Interestingly, the analysis did suggest a very strong *negative* correlation between growth in the Liberal vote between 1895 and 1900, and growth in the Liberal vote between 1900 and 1910. This suggests that the 'Liberal revival' prior to 1906 did indeed have a very uneven chronology, and that seats which rallied to the Liberals before 1900 were subsequently much less influenced by the revival in the party's national fortunes.[35]

Finally we will look at two issues traditionally related to the idea of the 'politics of influence': size of electorate and extent of landowner influence. There was, as expected, great variation in the size of electorates among our 183 single-member borough constituencies. In 1885 the electorates ranged from 2,292 (Bury St Edmunds) to 14,991 (Huddersfield). The average (mean) number of electors was 7,860, and the middle 50 percent of all constituencies had between 6,140 and 9,454 electors (an interquartile range of 3,314). By 1910, Durham had become the smallest constituency with 2,601 electors, while the largest was now Wandsworth with 38,523. By then the mean number of electors had grown to 10,980, and the middle 50 per cent of constituencies had between 7,860 and 13,989 electors (an interquartile range of 6,129). The period thus witnessed both a general increase in the size of constituencies, and in the variation between them.

Our analyses have shown some significant associations between size of constituency and party allegiance in 1885, but not in 1910. Although in 1885 the Conservatives tended to do better in smaller seats, by 1910 this effect had declined and was no longer statistically significant. We were also interested in examining voting habits as

---

[34.] The Pearson correlation coefficient between change in the Liberal vote (1895–1900) and growth in the *level* of enfranchisement (1892–1901) was found to be only –0.0148 for the 52 constituencies fought only by Liberal and Conservative candidates at the three elections under consideration. This is so close to 0 that it suggests there is no linear relationship between the two variables. When repeated for the later period the analysis produced a coefficient of 0.0359 – again suggesting no relationship was present.

[35.] The Pearson correlation co-efficient was –0.7308, significant at 0.001.

Table 5: *Average turnout by size of electorate in 1885, 1900 and January 1910*

Size of electorate (quartiles)	1885	1900	1910 (J)
Smallest 25%	85.5	76.1	88.8
Middle 50%	79.5	73.6	87.0
Largest 25%	79.5	73.4	86.7

Source: as Table 1

measured by propensity to vote and stability of party allegiance – did smaller constituencies behave differently, and if so can this be seen as indicative of a persistence of the 'politics of influence'? Looking first at turnout, there is a significant effect in 1885, but not in later elections. In 1885 it was the smallest constituencies which tended to have the highest turnouts. This remained true at the elections of 1900 and January 1910, but the effect was now much weaker (Table 5). As for stability of allegiance, measured in terms of how frequently a constituency changed hands across the eight general elections, there appears to be no general association with size of electorate, nor any evidence that even the ten per cent of constituencies with the smallest electorates were more or less volatile than the average.[36]

Perhaps inevitably our knowledge about the extent of landowner influence within borough constituencies is both incomplete and decidedly subjective. In the following analysis we have made use of a survey of provincial solicitors presented to the parliamentary select committee on town holdings by Charles Harrison in 1887.[37] The replies provide usable information on only 103 of our 183 constituencies, and generally make little distinction between the different constituencies of the large cities. Some replies were too equivocal to classify, but overall 67 constituencies were said to possess one or more major landowners, while 36 were said to possess no significant large landowner. There appears to have been little difference in the partisanship of the two types of constituency.[38] However, the constituencies said to possess major landowners showed a clear trend towards lower voter turnout at every election in our period except one: the 'khaki' election of 1900 (see Table 6). Perhaps at the 1900 election a tendency for some voters to stay away from the polls rather than vote against a powerful landowner was temporarily swamped by general apathy, but this is purely speculative. As for the 'stability' of partisanship in constituencies with large landowners, the evidence is somewhat inconclusive. Again we used changes of

---

[36.]　Seats which never changed hands, or changed hands only once had a mean electorate of 10,257 based on 1900 figures. Seats which changed hands two or three times had a mean electorate of 9,212, but those changing hands on more than three occasions had a mean electorate of 10,570. The 'smallest' 10 per cent of constituencies had on average 2.1 changes of allegiance, the remaining 90 per cent had 2.0 changes on average. Given Pelling's findings on the consistently below average 'swing' recorded by Britain's 34 smallest constituencies, this point may require further investigation, *Social Geography*, p. 430.

[37.]　*Parliamentary Papers*, 1887, XII, 719 (*Report from the Select Committee on Town Holdings*, Appendix 2, 'Papers handed in by Mr Charles Harrison').

[38.]　The mean number of Conservative victories in the eight general elections were 4.0 for 'landowner' seats and 3.6 for 'non-landowner' seats – the difference is not statistically significant.

Table 6: *Average turnout in seats with and without large urban landowners, 1885–1910*

	1885	1886	1892	1895	1900	1906	1910J	1910D
Large landowner?								
Yes	83.4	77.2	81.4	79.5	78.7	83.9	87.7	82.5
No	85.2	79.3	84.6	83.3	79.1	87.1	90.7	85.7

Source: *Parliamentary Papers*, 1887, XIII, 719 (*Report from the Select Committee on Town Holdings*, Appendix 2, 'Papers handed in by Mr Charles Harrison'), and as Table 1

Table 7: *Stability of partisanship in seats with and without large urban landowners, 1885–1910*

Changes in party allegiance	With large Landowner	Without large Landowner
	(No.)%	(No.)%
0 or 1	29 (43.3)	13 (36.1)
2 or 3	30 (44.8)	14 (38.9)
4, 5 or 6	8 (11.9)	9 (25.0)
	67 (100)	36 (100)

Source: as Table 6.

party allegiance as a measure of stability, and found a slight tendency towards greater stability in seats with large landlords (Table 7).

The analyses presented here are derived from a research project which is very much still 'in progress'. The intention has simply been to indicate the lines along which the historical analysis of election data might develop once it finally casts off the legacy of post-war pluralist social science embodied in 'electoral sociology'. Much work remains to be done on the issues raised here, but we feel that even these preliminary findings raise doubts about conventional accounts of Conservative and Liberal electoral fortunes in the late Victorian and Edwardian period. In particular, it seems we will have to revise the old notion that Conservative success between 1886 and 1900 was achieved simply through low voter turnout and keeping the electorate small. Once one shifts the focus away from the jaundiced anti-democratic musings of Conservative grandees to focus on the party's fortunes on the ground, the story becomes a great deal more complicated.

Villa Toryism Reconsidered: Conservatism and Suburban Sensibilities in Late-Victorian Croydon

FRANS COETZEE

George Washington University

For much of the twentieth century it has seemed that, like death and taxes, Conservative governments are an ultimately inescapable feature of English life, and nowhere more strongly entrenched than in suburban constituencies. This article explores suburban Conservatism in its formative stages in the late nineteenth and early twentieth centuries, and, by focusing on the interplay of urban growth, local affairs, and the articulation of political sentiments, seeks to illustrate the inadequacies of the Conservative party's traditional self-image and to suggest some more illuminating approaches to understanding the impact of change on a party priding itself on continuity.

The Conservative party has frequently claimed that it is the 'national' party and has always been so, and that it is a uniquely durable party that justifiably revels in its unbroken tradition. On this reading, the Conservatives win support from all classes and most regions, while their rivals, whether the Liberals in the nineteenth century or Labour in the twentieth, mobilize only sectional interests, primarily from the Celtic fringe. The reaction in 1910 of Leo Maxse, the vitriolic editor of the *National Review*, was typical when he fulminated against a Liberal England 'governed by Scotsmen, kicked by Irishmen, and plundered by Welshmen'.[1] Meanwhile, the fortunes of the various parties of the Left were in constant flux. The Liberals last won a majority of seats in the House of Commons in 1906, Labour its first not until 1945, by which time the once proud Liberal party had been reduced to an isolated fragment of particular interest to subsequent doctoral students probing its decline. This reversal of fortunes stood in sharp contrast to the alleged permanence and stability of the solitary sentinel of experience and tradition, the Conservative party itself.

2

Accordingly, the Conservative party's history has often been bathed in a golden glow, by its political practitioners as well as its publicists. The party's survival thus becomes an occasion for self-congratulation rather than surprise, and its continuity a matter of psychological reassurance. Lord Willoughby de Broke, for example, argued in 1911 that at the core of a lengthy 'Tory Tradition' lay 'instinct rather than intellect'.[2] And a year later, Lord Hugh Cecil pursued much the same course when he contended that the Conservative party was 'of course largely recruited from and dependent on

---

[1] Quoted in A. J. A. Morris, *The Scaremongers* (1984), p. 227.
[2] 'The Tory Tradition' *National Review* Oct. 1911, pp. 201–13.

the natural Conservatism that is found in almost every human mind'.[3] As the collective expression of the individual's innate caution, the Conservative party was attuned to the underlying rythmns of English life, as familiar and assured as the peers who articulated its concerns and populated its cabinets.

But there is something wrong with this picture. Willoughby de Broke, whose memoirs attested to his delight in hunting the fox, was embroiled in 1911 in a struggle against another prey, the cunning leader of his own party, Arthur Balfour, over whether the party should resist Liberal legislation designed to curb the powers of the House of Lords. Willoughby de Broke and his fellow Diehards vowed to fight to the bitter end, even if their resistance split their party and precipitated a constitutional crisis. And Lord Hugh Cecil, despite his undoubted brilliance in a party that sorely lacked it, or his lineage in a party that revered it, had been mercilessly hounded as an unrepentant free trader by tariff reformers determined to enforce the protectionist plank in the party platform. Cecil himself was defeated at Greenwich in 1906 by the intervention of a tariff reform candidate, and his correspondence testifies to the bitter invective he received from (and vented upon) fellow travellers of the Right. In neither case is there much evidence for the equanimity with which Conservatives supposedly contemplated their party's prospects.

In fact, the party's evolution was considerably less tranquil and rather more uncertain than Tory mythology implies. Their indulgence in the glories of the English character notwithstanding, both Willoughby de Broke and Cecil preferred not to dwell on the erratic course of Conservative fortunes during the nineteenth century. In the 1850s the party could not credibly claim to be a national one. Despite its strength in agricultural districts, the party made much less headway in urban areas and demonstrated little promise of being able to win a representative range of constituencies. As England urbanized and industrialized, a party articulating the interests of the countryside might be thought (to choose a sporting metaphor so dear to Willoughby de Broke) to be backing the wrong horse. Yet by 1918 the party incorporated a significant share of the business and professional classes, articulated the interests of a broad range of property owners, and flourished in a wide variety of constituencies, so demonstrating its adaptation to the realities of an urban democracy. This recovery belied both the earlier predictions of its imminent demise (current in the 1850s) and the image subsequently constructed of its uniquely tranquil continuity.

That providential recovery (rather than prudent survival) also undermines the proposition that the Conservative party's success reflected the longstanding innate Conservatism of much of the electorate, for such an interpretation is patently at odds with the erratic course of the party's development. In searching for alternative explanations, historians have tended to look for clearly identifiable seismic shifts, for the dominance of particular issues in enabling the party to transcend its original agrarian base. And so they have stressed the spectre of predatory Socialism, or the threat to imperial unity posed by Irish Home Rule, or the challenge to the allegedly timeworn institutional and moral basis of society associated with religious disestablishment. Whatever measure of truth each of these explanations may possess, they

---

[3.]   *Conservatism* (1912), p. 8.

cannot entirely account for the breadth or chronology of Conservative resurgence. Furthermore, they are too static by implying that the Conservatives prospered primarily as the inert beneficiaries of their opponents' excesses. Seductive as this proposition may be in the light of the party's professedly defensive posture, it ignores the party's internal development, consigns its constituents to historiographical oblivion, and glosses over fundamental questions of context.[4]

It is a mistake, therefore, to restrict oneself to looking only for a single major tremor, for the changing terrain of Conservative politics was, in fact, shaped by a series of smaller, subtler shifts, and it is to these that we must attend. Doing so involves the recognition that Conservative voter loyalties were not just a matter of the percolation of policy from above, but also a function of local organisation, local notables, local concerns and their integration into the institutional role of the party. Historians of Liberalism and Labour have understood this point better, perhaps because of the prominent institutional role of Nonconformist churches and trade unions in progressive politics. But – until quite recently – not so historians of British Conservatism, whose relatively conservative work focused on Westminster and the parliamentary manoeuvres of the leadership; too often the relationship between this world and those of the voters was left unexplored or couched in platitudes similar to those of Willoughby de Broke and Cecil. Although such concerns have their place in the development of the party, if we are to appreciate why voters sustained a resurgence in Conservative fortunes we must also look elsewhere.

In particular, we might look to the local level, especially to the kinds of seats which provided the basis for the new Conservative majorities in the late nineteenth century. Just how much the contours of party support were beginning to change was already visible by 1881, when the pioneering psephologist Alfred Frisby published an article provocatively entitled 'Has Conservatism increased in England since the last Reform Bill?'[5] He went on to argue that it had, and he emphasized that the advance of Conservative sentiment had been especially pronounced in large urban constituencies. Certainly there was a surprising convergence between the location of increasing Conservative voting strength and of demographic growth. When Sidney Low digested the results of the 1891 census, he concluded that the 'greatest advance' in the previous decade had been 'not in the cities themselves, but in the ring of

---

4. Sir R. C. K. Ensor, 'Some Political and Economic Interactions in Late Victorian England', *Transactions of the Royal Historical Society*, 4th ser., XXXI (1949), 17–28 provides a more considered statement of the seismic view. For the argument that the Conservatives were the beneficiaries of Liberal dissension, and that their parliamentary success rested on 'negative hegemony', see J. Cornford's classic article, 'The Transformation of Conservatism in the Late Nineteenth Century', *Victorian Studies*, VII (1963), 35–66; and N. Blewett's equally memorable *The Peers, the Parties, and the People: The General Elections of 1910* (1972). Although the historiography of the Conservative party still lacks regional studies comparable to P. F. Clarke's *Lancashire and the New Liberalism* (Cambridge, 1971) or D. Tanner's comprehensive *Political Change and the Labour party, 1900–1918* (Cambridge, 1990), the literature now includes an outstanding synthesis, E. H. H. Green's *The Crisis of Conservatism* (1995), three helpful volumes in the Longman History of the party, J. Ramsden, *The Age of Balfour and Baldwin, 1902–1940* (1978) and R. Shannon, *The Age of Disraeli, 1868–1881* (1992), *idem, The Age of Salisbury, 1881–1902* (1996), as well as *Conservative Century*, ed. A. Seldon and S. Ball (Oxford, 1994) with its magnificent bibliographic essay. Also relevant here is A. Offer, *Property and Politics 1870–1914* (Cambridge, 1981).

5. *Fortnightly Review*, Dec. 1881, pp. 718–29.

suburbs which spread into the country about them'.[6] Accordingly, he went on to suggest that 'the son and the grandson of the man from the fields will neither be a dweller in the country nor a dweller in the town. He will be a suburb dweller.'[7] It was in this particular rapidly evolving environment that Conservatism flourished, and so the suburbs afford the ideal situation in which to explore the contextual basis of political mobilization. Here could be found, as the acerbic Lord Salisbury noted, 'a great deal of Villa Toryism which requires organisation'.[8] From a different perspective, the Liberal C.F.G. Masterman concurred, describing in a classic account how 'in feverish hordes the suburbs swarm to the polling booth to vote against a truculent proletariat'.[9] With all due respect to E. P. Thompson's poor stockingers, it is the suburbanites who also must be rescued from the condescension of posterity. Usually dismissed as drab, dull, and conformist, the late Victorian and Edwardian suburbs were in the forefront of change, both demographically and politically, a reactionary vanguard.

These changes were most visible in London's suburbs. London's 'life blood' was 'pouring', argued Sidney Low, 'into the long arms of brick and mortar and cheap stucco that are feeling their way out' to Essex, Hertfordshire, and Surrey.[10] Salisbury recalled 'when London was the highest expression of Liberal enthusiasm', and found the subsequent advance of Conservative sentiment most gratifying in the light of his party's earlier lackluster performance in the metropolis. 'We had no chance in those days', the prime minister admitted, 'and anyone who should prophesy that in half a century those London boroughs would be the safest refuge for Conservative statesmen would have been regarded as strictly insane.' Perhaps 'most extraordinary' of all to that pessimistic patrician was 'the great strength of Conservative feeling [that] lies among the vast number of owners of villas of every kind who surround London'.[11] Once again, corroboration from the opposition was to hand; as one Liberal despaired in 1901, 'it may almost be said that the present [Conservative] government owes its predominance to London and the neighboring districts'.[12]

3

Accordingly, it is to the local texture of political life that one might turn, to the owners of villas in their natural habitat, in London's 'neighboring districts'. In particular, the focus here is upon the borough of Croydon, just across the Surrey border to the south of London, familiar to some in our century as the spot to which Neville Chamberlain returned from Munich to announce that he had secured peace with

---

6. 'The Rise of the Suburbs', *Contemporary Review*, Oct. 1891, p. 548. See also H. J. Dyos, *Victorian Suburb* (Leicester, 1961); A. A. Jackson, *Semi-Detached London* (1973), pp. 36–49; D. Olsen, *The Growth of Victorian London* (1976); *The Rise of Suburbia*, ed. F. M. L. Thompson (Leicester, 1982).

7. Low, 'Rise of Suburbs', p. 548.

8. Salisbury to Northcote, 25 June 1882, cited in Cornford, 'Transformation of Conservatism', p. 52.

9. C. F. G. Masterman, *The Condition of England* (1909), p. 71.

10. Low, 'Rise of the Suburbs', p. 550.

11. *National Union Annual Report* (1900), n.p.

12. Greater London R. O., Dickinson MSS. 13/5, 'How London is to be won', memorandum by W. H. Dickinson. According to the figures in Lord Blake's *The Conservative Party from Peel to Thatcher 1885* (1985), p. 112, the party never won fewer than 35 of the 59 London seats after 1885.

honour. When one of its most dedicated antiquarians (himself a municipal councillor as well) sought in 1891 to compile an account of Croydon, he found the town to be 'singularly barren of historical reminiscences', complained that it was 'no easy task' to discuss Croydon's development, and excused his mediocre efforts on the grounds that 'events relating to it have never been of national importance'.[13] We shall return to the implications of this consciously self-effacing definition of Croydon's identity, but the town's political experiences merit attention for at least three reasons. In the first place, with its proximity to London, convenient rail connexions, and dynamic growth (from 20,000 in 1851 to some 130,000 by 1901), Croydon was universally regarded as a prime example of London's suburban development; when Sidney Low conveyed to his readers the prospect of continued suburban expansion, it was here that he looked, predicting that 'not one but a dozen Croydons will form a circle of detached forts around the central stronghold'.[14] Second, as one of the largest single-member constituencies in England, Croydon was an ideal test of either party's capacity to meet the demands of mass politics. Third, once the borough had assumed an independent identity separate from the country of Surrey within whose borders it lay, it consistently returned Conservative M.P.s, at every single election from its first in 1885 through into the interwar period. On the face of it, such monotonous regularity appeared to illustrate the persistence, stability, and durable tradition extolled by Cecil and Willoughby de Broke.

When Croydon's voters finally had the opportunity in 1885 to register a verdict on the town's political sympathies, rather than contributing in a seemingly less distinct way to the election of an M.P. for the county division of East Surrey, few observers were willing to predict with any certainty that its suburban growth necessarily implied a Conservative walkover. Already in the 1860s there had been signs that Croydon's convenient links to London and healthful reputation – its elevation, refreshing breezes, and supposed pure water – made it attractive as 'a dormitory for the merchant princes of London'.[15] But it was less clear that local Conservatives were poised to reap electoral rewards from this situation. In 1868, for example, when the Croydon District Committee met to bewail East Surrey's preference for Liberal M.P.s, its efforts to promote a Conservative candidate betrayed all the signs of haste and waste. The committee did not assemble until after the election had been called, and then hurriedly rented rooms at a local hotel and hired a solicitor (as agent) to compensate for the more permanent organizational presence that had been lacking.[16] In this particular

[13] J. O. Pelton, *Relics of Old Croydon* (Croydon, 1891), p. 3.

[14] 'Rise of the Suburbs', p. 551.

[15] *Croydon Chronicle*, 9 June 1860. J. M. Thorne observed that 'monotonous streets and lines of villas are fast encircling the town, the neighborhood of which being pleasant and picturesque, and within easy reach of the city, is a favorite residence for men of business, who may be seen flocking to the morning trains in surprising numbers': *Environs of London* (1876), p. 128. Croydon was also extolled as 'a town where a really large proportion of the residents take an interest in sanitary matters.': *Report of Dr. George Buchanan to the Medical Department of the Local Government Board* (Apr. 1876), p. 5. For recent work on the borough, see J. N. Morris, 'A Disappearing Crowd? Collective Action in late Nineteenth-Century Croydon,' *Southern History*, XI (1989), 90–113; and his subsequent book, *Religion and Urban Change: Croydon, 1840–1914* (Woodbridge, 1992).

[16] Croydon Reference Library, Election ephemera, leaflet of Croydon District Conservative Committee, misc. election boxes.

instance, the Conservative candidate was defeated, but the more general point is the lack of a strong Conservative tradition in Croydon even after its suburban growth had begun.

Even by the mid-1880s, by which time Croydon's spectacular expansion (to a population of some 80,000) had qualified it both for incorporation and redistribution as a borough, there were still unresolved questions about its probable political allegiance. In 1885 the Conservatives initially feared – with some reason – that they might lose the seat. The newly founded local Conservative Club admitted that 'there might be more difficulty in returning a Conservative member for the Borough than for the County Division' (which had recently begun to return Tory members).[17] While the Liberals were rapidly in the field with a strong candidate, J. Spencer Balfour, who had served as the town's first mayor upon its incorporation in 1883, the Conservatives appeared unable to persuade a bold spirit to venture into such uncharted waters. It was not until several weeks before the actual polling that the sitting M.P. for East Surrey, William Grantham, finally consented in the face of pressure from Salisbury to stand for Croydon, despite reportedly having spurned previous local offers in an 'abusive and boastful manner'.[18] Grantham preferred to contest a Sussex seat, to which 'hereditary and social ties' drew him, or one in Surrey, to which his earnest service surely entitled him.[19] Reluctantly, however, he conceded[20]

> as a matter of public duty . . . to accept the risk and fight the Borough of Croydon. It is numerically the largest and is the most important political division in the county and if it is not fought in the next election as I am told it would not be if I refused, that result must have a very damaging effect on the numerous new constituencies that now surround it.

In the contest that followed, the loquacious Liberal Nonconformist, J. Spencer Balfour, sought to reconcile the rival factions of moderate Liberalism and Radicalism within the borough and to mute his commitment to disestablishment by tactfully (and tactically) demurring over its immediate implementation. Nonetheless, the somewhat coarse and rather self-important Grantham, a barrister by training, proved a determined and effective advocate for local Conservatives. Although both men had parliamentary experience (Balfour for Tamworth, Grantham for East Surrey), the campaign focused less upon the impact either man might make at Westminster than the suitability of either to embody a sense of what Croydon represented. Balfour claimed that 'he did not base his candidature on local grounds, [but] he pointed out that he had resided in Croydon for sixteen years, during twelve years of which he had taken a more or less active part in public work'.[21] Fellow Liberals extolled the first mayor's local service and philanthropic contributions, and emphasized that 'in

---

[17] *Croydon Guardian*, 14 Feb. 1885; *Croydon Advertiser*, 28 Feb. 1885.
[18] *Croydon Advertiser*, 7 Mar. 1885.
[19] Salisbury MSS. (the Marquess of Salisbury, Hatfield House, Hertfordshire), Class E, Grantham to Salisbury, 24 Mar. 1885, In a letter the previous day, Grantham had attributed a good deal of Tory success southeast of London to his own efforts, referring to the Conservative M.P.s elected there as his 'political children': Grantham to Salisbury, 23 Mar. 1885.
[20] Salisbury MSS., Class E, Grantham to Salisbury, 24 Mar. 1885.
[21] *Croydon Advertiser*, 14 Mar. 1885.

more senses than one it might be said that Mr Balfour lived in the heart of Croydon'.[22] The local Liberal paper threw its weight behind this argument, stressing:[23]

> It will be a great calamity if we are represented by a non-resident and almost a stranger. Mr Grantham is scarcely known to the people of Croydon. He has never resided among us, except when he dwelt at South Norwood, and then but little was seen of him and less was known of him. Since that he has not lived amongst us, and has scarcely mixed amongst us in local public life. Mr Balfour, on the other hand, has been at the head of almost all local movements, and has been actively concerned and engaged in all. His return to Parliament would promote the health of the town, the wealth of the town, and the dignity of the town.

Croydon's Conservatives responded by reiterating familiar party themes of imperial unity and established religion as elements of a precious national heritage that was embraced by many, yet scorned by godless Little Englanders whose nefarious designs could only be scotched by a Tory administration. Grantham's canvassers attempted to capitalize upon this distinction and marginalize local Radicals by trolling for 'true Liberal' votes. But his most persistent theme was to recast the sectional/national couplet within a distinctively Croydonian frame of reference. The Conservatives countered Balfour's claim of superior localist credentials by contending that:[24]

> it by no means follows that because a man has aptitude for local administration, that therefore he will make as good a figure in imperial affairs. . . . Minds capable of designing a streetlamp and of formulating a bye-law for the compulsory opening of windows is [sic] not necessarily of that calibre to which we would confidently entrust the vital interests of this great Empire. Yet if Croydon returns Mr Balfour she will be sending her quota to swell that phalanx of 'vestryism' to which thoughtful men are dreading to commit the complexities of British policy.

Perhaps recognizing that Grantham exhibited neither penetrating vision nor 'that calibre,' local Tories amplified 'vestryism' during the 1885 campaign to designate the inability of mayor Balfour (and, by extension, most local Liberals) to grasp what representing Croydon's interests really meant. In effect, the parliamentary election became something of a referendum on the impact of incorporation two years earlier, the mayor's prominent advocacy of that measure, and the more general direction of change within the borough. The Conservatives assailed Balfour for having given evidence against a railway bill that, if enacted, might have provided greater employment for local workmen, a sensitive issue when an uncertain economic climate nourished

---

[22]   A. Ashcroft, *ibid.*, 21 Mar. 1885.

[23]   *Ibid.*, 7 Nov. 1885. In a sense, of course, this sounds like the familiar strategy of nursing a constituency. Sir Edward Clarke (who introduced the pro-incorporation case in Croydon, recalled that in Southwark he 'lectured on various subjects at parochial schoolrooms, joined Conservative clubs and spoke at their smoking concerts; subscribed to athletic clubs and presided at their dinners; and was always seen and very often heard at public functions in the borough': *The Story of My Life* (1918), p. 149–150. In Balfour's case, such an emphasis was explicitly invoked to counter charges that he had violated not just the local interests, but the prevailing tenor of the borough.

[24]   *Croydon Guardian*, 14 Feb. 1885; *Croydon Advertiser*, 14, 21 Nov. 1885. Grantham had claimed that there was a greater similarity between his Conservatism and Liberalism than between Balfour's Liberalism and Radicalism: *Croydon Guardian*, 11 Apr. 1885.

agitation for fair trade. Balfour responded that 'some of the best walks and footpaths around Croydon had been destroyed by railways', and, seeking to preempt his critics, he claimed to have been preserving the borough's 'charm of its country surroundings' in the face of complaints that 'Croydon was becoming like Peckham'.[25]

Liberals also absorbed criticism for having supported an expensive programme of urban renovation, including the widening of some central streets within Croydon, at ratepayers' expense, to improve access for local business.[26] Hence one of the principal fractures in Croydon which found political expression in the parliamentary elections had little to do with the weighty issues debated at Westminster; rather it reflected a divide in this suburbanizing community between the commuting sector, itself criticized for not spending money or employing labour locally, and the original economic nucleus of the town, before its suburban boom. The former group provided the backbone of local Conservatism, the latter the core of Croydon Liberalism, but the two groups habitually divided on issues that ostensibly were free from the taint of partisan politics – the question of incorporation, of municipal responsibility for moderately priced housing, of the provision of cheap public transport (by tramway) directly through the whole of the borough.

These divisions had emerged with particular clarity during hearings in 1881 over the issue of incorporation. Balfour and other proponents of the reform argued that Croydon's rapid growth had simply overwhelmed its archaic parochial system of administration, and that bodies such as the Local Board of Health could not cope adequately with the demands of urban development. Moreover, they argued, the property-weighted franchise of the older system made it both unresponsive and unrepresentative, and so both failings needed to be corrected together. Petitions indicated that a majority of those who signed them favored incorporation, but that those who opposed it represented, on average, double the per-capita rateable value of those who supported the measure.[27]

Opponents of incorporation, among whose numbers were ranged many of the town's prominent Conservatives, seized immediately on the likelihood of increased municipal expenditure, and disparaged the petitions by questioning 'how far they were to be taken as representing the feeling of the parish and how far they represented the feelings of those best qualified to form an opinion'.[28] But they also justified their opposition by submitting a more intriguing definition of what Croydon would lose by incorporation. Sir Frederick Philbrick, Q.C., led the onslaught, suggesting to the enquiry that: 'They had heard some people talk of it [Croydon] as a town, but never was there a greater misnomer. There were, it was true, a large number of houses and shops nestling round the High-Street, which might be termed the centre', Philbrick admitted, 'but [outlying] South Norwood and Selsdon had also their central High-streets and their resident population – (laughter) – and there was a vast amount of farm land and open spaces.' Accordingly, he continued:[29]

[25] *Croydon Advertiser*, 14 Mar. 1885.
[26] See R. C. W. Cox, 'The Old Centre of Croydon: Victorian Decay and Redevelopment' in *Perspectives in English Urban History*, ed. A. Everitt (1973), pp. 184–212.
[27] C. M. Elborough, *Croydon a Borough. Reprint of the Report of Enquiry* (Croydon, 1883); Morris, *Religion and Urban Change*, pp. 147–55.
[28] Elborough, *Croydon*, p. 57.
[29] *Ibid.*, pp. 57–8.

a certain class of houses were [sic] here built with a nice amount of garden in which persons having daily business in London lived with their families, and with such an extension of the populace there arose, of course, a demand for shops and business establishments to supply the wants of those who made Croydon their place of residence, their business being in London. The tradesmen were, therefore, to a great extent, dependent upon Londoners who made Croydon their place of residence. He ventured, therefore, to say that there was no reason for granting a charter of incorporation to so strictly suburban a population as that which extended over the district of Croydon. . . . The population of Croydon was undoubtedly one which had great elements of respectability and wealth, but to say that Croydon had a local population which entitled it to come forward and say they wanted a charter of incorporation was, he thought, to attribute to its class of residents an intention which they did not themselves entertain, and which if carried out, would be to them a most serious objection to the district as a place of residence. It seemed to him that the introduction of party and local politics through the establishment of a town council would prove a curse to the place, and would be a great objection in the eyes of those persons who came to Croydon to make it a place of quiet residence, and free from the cares of business and public life.

Philbrick's vision, much of which might have been lifted wholesale from a suburban builder's advertisement, furnished a number of themes which the Conservatives could profitably employ over the succeeding years. The inclination toward quietism, the recuperative rather than commercial nature of Croydon which permitted the undisturbed enjoyment of a peaceful life, could be contrasted with Liberal interventionism, especially the 'coercive moral reform' of militant Nonconformity.[30] Preserving the dominance of the commuting sector was the surest way to avoid diluting the 'quality' of its inhabitants, even if propagating this view entailed fictionalizing Croydon's development – denying its status as a town and insisting that its economic functions solely followed from, rather than partially preceded, the influx of commuting residents. Conjuring the spectre of narrow-minded partisanship intruding upon the once judicious local administration in 1883 prefigured the accusations of 'vestryism' levelled in 1885.

During that latter campaign, Croydon's Conservatives mobilized voters to defend the suburban vision. Balfour proved vulnerable to charges that he had neglected the commuters (by stifling railway construction) and diminished the town's residential attractiveness (by promoting tramways, and so, presumably, encouraging excessive social mixing, and by procuring the institution of a daily workman's train to London, and so enabling Croydon residents somewhat down the social scale to commute as well).[31] The suburban vision co-existed, somewhat uneasily, with a robust populist Conservatism, to which Grantham applied himself effectively by promoting 'Beer and Bible Toryism' and contrasting that with the Liberal ascetic repudiation of traditional pleasures and inept management of imperial affairs. As a result, when

---

[30] The term is Jon Lawrence's, in his excellent article, 'Class and Gender in the Making of Urban Toryism, 1880–1914', *English Historical Review*, CVIII (1993), 629–52.
[31] The emphasis on Balfour's character was not altogether misplaced, for he was involved in spectacular fraud in connexion with the Liberator Building Society.

political sympathies were demonstrated at the ballot box, they were in part the incidental expression of periodic exposure to party propaganda, but also a reflection of the more regular cultivation of loyalties between elections, in a variety of settings and through a variety of informal mechanisms.

In the general election of 1885 the Conservative, Grantham, was returned with 56 per cent of the poll and a majority of nearly 1,200 (from some 9,800 votes). Most analysts accepted that, in line with the national trend, the local Irish vote (estimated at anywhere from 200 to 600) had gone to Grantham on this occasion but that the Conservatives could not count upon such support in the future. Few observers were willing to predict an extended Conservative ascendancy; the Liberals' adoption of Balfour had polarized opinion more than would have been likely with a less visible or controversial candidate. About the 'snobs', namely 'those people who live in villas and are called gentlemen in common parlance', there was little question. They were, the local Liberal paper sneered, 'chiefly Conservative and therefore not likely to trouble to attend public meetings or to think about the political questions now before the public'.[32]

Within two months, in January 1886, Grantham resigned to accept a judicial appointment, and Croydon was plunged into another election with fresh candidates on both sides. Fought on the now stale 1885 register, the Conservative vote dropped by some 270, and although the Liberal vote rose by some 150 (the Irish?), the Conservatives held the seat. In retrospect, the most significant aspect of the campaign was the initial confusion among local Tories over whom to adopt. Premature reports indicated that local party boss Thomas Edridge would carry the party's standard, to the consternation of Central Office, which considered him of insufficient weight and persuaded Croydon's Conservative Association to accept Sidney Herbert instead. Edridge withdrew gracefully, alluding to the undesirable strain a campaign would place upon his wife's delicate health, but the enforced substitution of candidates still rankled among some party activists.[33] The sting was then partly assuaged by a knighthood for Sir Thomas a year later.

When Croydon's voters next went to the polls, in 1892, Sidney Herbert was reelected with nearly 58 per cent of the poll and a handsome majority of 1,700. 'Croydon has embedded herself in Toryism', admitted local Liberals, who characterized the town as 'a pocket borough of the Carlton Club' and predicted that 'it will not be very easy in times to come to secure a Liberal candidate for this constituency'.[34] The Liberal Association decried the fact that Croydon had been reduced to a nursery for Liberal candidates who hastened to depart as soon as more promising vacancies occurred elsewhere.

[32] *Croydon Advertiser*, 17 Oct. 1885; 2 Jan., 6 Feb. 1886. Croydon's Conservative Working Men's Club honored its victorious M.P.s with torchlight processions, led by banner-bearers and a brass brand. Following were carriages decorated as Australia (with cattle driver and gold-digger), India (Bengal Lancer), and the United Kingdom (emblazoned with 'united we stand, divided we fall'), succeeded by a banner of Beaconsfield, a carriage from the Primrose League, and finally Mephistopheles, 'intended with more or less success to represent the first Radical'.
[33] *Croydon Guardian*, 18 Jan. 1886.
[34] *Croydon Advertiser*, 9 July 1892.

4

The contrast appears all too stark: a handful of dispirited, apathetic Liberals trounced by a succession of triumphant Conservatives returned to Westminster by battalions of Tory voters turned out with monotonous regularity. The pattern established in 1885 simply repeated itself without significant change. Or so the story seems to go. But the borough's electoral geography and political sympathies were more fluid and complex than the broad strokes of 'Villa Toryism' might lead one to suppose. In Croydon, as elsewhere, geographic elevation was a good guide to social elevation as well. Villa residents could be found clustered on the higher ground to the north and east of the town centre, especially toward Upper Norwood. The lower lying areas to the south and west expanded rapidly from the 1870s, partly in response to London's insatiable appetite for clerks, but also in view of the local boom in the building trades and the gradual diversification of the local economy (including the development of breweries, bleachworks, a boot and shoe factory, and the railyards). These differences in class siting manifested themselves in various ways, most noticeably perhaps, at the morgue and the polling booth. The death rate in the Upper Norwood ward in 1901 stood at 9.8 per thousand, compared to a figure of 14.8 in the populous West ward where, as a Labour activist put it, families struggled 'bravely, but in vain, against evil and unspeakable conditions'.[35]

Unfortunately, since it was forbidden to release parliamentary electoral results for subdivisions within a constituency, one has to rely on subjective data to correlate social geography and political preference. Upper Norwood was consistently cited for its prominent display of Tory colours and its high turnout achieved by mid-morning on polling days (which was interpreted as evidence of middle-class commuters voting before making their way into London). Less consistency, in party colours or polling times, was attributed to the other wards, and the Liberals were even judged to produce a respectable showing in the East and South wards, the former residential but of 'lower quality' than Upper Norwood, the latter a mixed ward of 'all classes of property'.[36]

Yet how secure were the foundations upon which Croydon's reputation for Villa Toryism had been built? In the first place, it was clear that villa residents, even if their sympathies could be taken for granted, were insufficient to sustain Conservative majorities. Moreover, although the party had benefited from the outright hostility of many Anglican Churchmen to Liberal policies, the 1902 religious census undertaken by the *Daily News* indicated that members of the Church of England now constituted a minority of the local church-going population (some 45 per cent).[37] And there was the question of whether the image of Croydon the local party had constructed could continue to resonate with voters as the borough's residential exclusiveness (always

---

[35] Croydon Reference Library, misc. election boxes, 'Pricking the Bubbles', address by Labour candidates Mardell and Young, Nov. 1902

[36] *Croydon Guardian*, 1 Sept. 1900; *Croydon Citizen*, 4 Nov. 1905.

[37] See, e.g., one Anglican vicar's sermon reminding 'all Church people' that in the event of an election they should put the question of 'Church Defence first . . . in their thoughts and their prayers [and presumably their votes]': *Croydon Advertiser*, 13 July 1895; R. Mudie Smith, *The Religious Life of London* (1904), p. 385.

more imagined than real) further declined and its municipal tranquility (also more
celebrated than experienced) ended.

Croydon's Conservatives had prided themselves on a combination of superior
organisation and the ability of their adopted candidate to embody Croydon's interests.
Although the local machine was reasonably well run, the borough's growing reputation
as a reliable Conservative seat and the periodic inability of the Liberals to contest it
induced a degree of apathy and inefficiency. Complaints began to surface after 1900
regarding the sparse attendance at meetings, the periodic neglect of canvassing, and
the diminution in donations and subscriptions. Within three years this dissent was
quite visible, prompted by a sense that Croydon's wishes were being ignored, both
by Central Office (as in the Edridge fiasco) and its sitting member. One voter, just
'a trifle disgusted', claimed that Croydon's M.P. (C.T. Ritchie) had not visited his
ward in eight years, another speculated that Ritchie seemed 'to have forgotten that
such a place as Croydon exists', a third bitterly remarked that Ritchie restricted himself
to perfunctory appearances at semi-private banquets or Primrose League functions,
while a fourth explicitly predicted that the Tories would lose the seat unless the
situation was rectified.[38]

Indeed, in late 1903 and 1904 Croydon Conservatism was all too publicly fractured
in response to Ritchie's persistent, prominent advocacy of free trade and his repudiation
of Joseph Chamberlain's call for tariff reform. Ritchie, the Chancellor of the Exchequer
and so a lightning rod for disputes over fiscal policy, eventually left the Cabinet and
agreed in July 1904 not to stand for re-election for Croydon. His concession of the
seat is customarily attributed to the intensive pressure applied by the Tariff Reform
League, which threatened to form a rival local Unionist Association and run a protectionist candidate, but Ritchie's position would have been less exposed if he had not
already lost the confidence of many local Conservatives.[39] But from a local perspective,
it was hard to see how matters improved with the adoption of Ritchie's successor, H.
O. Arnold-Forster. Arnold-Forster was also prominent, and of sufficient flexibility on
tariffs to court little trouble on that score, but some Croydon Conservatives suspected
that 'a vanishing majority in West Belfast [his previous seat] had more to do than
anything with Mr Arnold-Forster's sudden affection for Croydon'.[40] It was an ominous
sign that the Tory battalions might not turn out in their accustomed force.

The second and more decisive blow to the suburban sensibilities of Croydon's
Conservatives stemmed from the emergence of organised labour on the local scene.
The initial vision of Croydon's 'quality' ignored the concerns, even the very presence,
of working people. By the turn of the century, however, Croydon's spectacular

---

[38] Croydon Conservative Association, minute book, 8 Oct. 1896, 25 Jan. 1900; *Croydon Guardian*,
23 May 1903; *Croydon Advertiser*, 12 Sept. 1903.

[39] *Croydon Guardian*, 10 Oct. 1903, 5 Dec. 1903, 30 July 1904; *Norwood News*, 6 Feb. 1904; *Croydon
Times*, 3 Feb. 1904; Northumberland R.O., Ridley MSS., ZRI 25/99, 'Work Accomplished by the
League in Croydon and typical of the work undertaken in every Free Trade Unionist's constituency',
undated memorandum compiled by Edward Goulding's Organisation Committee of the Tariff Reform
League. The decision by the association to withdraw its support for Ritchie was a stormy one, more like
the confrontation of Kilkenny cats than of turtle doves (as some local Conservatives had implied): *Croydon
Times*, 6 Feb. 1904. As a result, the association's chairman (Edridge), treasurer, and a number of other
officials resigned their positions, though not their membership.

growth, periodic economic distress, and division of the municipal electorate into wards all facilitated the 'politicisation' of municipal affairs. A Croydon Labour Council had been founded in 1890 to promote the candidature of working men for the Croydon Borough Council, and two years later it secured the election for the populous West ward of the local secretary of the Bricklayers' Society. The Croydon Labour Council continued to intervene in municipal elections with increasing success, and 1905 its candidates won three of the 12 contested seats. Croydon's propertied classes, of whatever political hue, villified the first Labour councillors for advocating 'crude experiments in Socialism at the cost of the ratepayers' and responded by forming ratepayers' alliances at ward level to ward off the threat.[41] Sir Frederick Edridge, who followed in his father's partisan footsteps after the latter's death in 1892, wasted little time in leading local Conservatives into the fray to preserve the Council Chamber from the taint of politics. As early as 1901 he was emphasising to the Primrose League 'the unadvisedness of too many Labour candidates' and urging league members – unofficially, of course – 'to use their influence in support of the candidate they thought worthy'.[42] Local Liberals, too, were prominent in mobilizing the ratepayers' vote, prompting the Croydon Labour Council to observe that 'a Liberal is all for progress in the abstract, but bring it into the sphere of the practical and the concrete and he is with the Tories, hand-in-glove with those whom at election times he is never tired of denouncing as the enemies of progress! Where was he when the facts of overcrowding were brought to light?'[43]

The next two parliamentary elections demonstrated the acrimonious impact of local political alignments and the importance of appreciating that stress when addressing the hold of villa Toryism. Arnold-Forster failed to excite much enthusiasm and efforts to turn out the vote among Croydon's Unionists were still complicated by the divisiveness of tariff reform (a number of prominent local Liberal Unionists began to appear on Liberal platforms).[44] The local Liberal association had made significant progress in reinvigorating its organization and expanding its membership but, in part from the bitter legacy of the ratepayers' alliances, it was unable to marshall all of the borough's progressive forces under a single banner. With assistance from the L.R.C., a Labour candidate, Sidney Stranks, entered the fray; he might not have done so had

[40] *Croydon Advertiser*, 13 Jan. 1906. Arnold-Forster's wife, speaking to a local habitation of the Primrose League, admitted that she and her husband were strangers in the borough, and warned them that her husband was a 'busy man', *Primrose League Gazette*, Jan. 1905.

[41] *Daily Telegraph*, 21 Dec. 1905.

[42] Croydon Reference Library, Primrose League, Grantham Habitation minutes, 7 Oct. 1901. The Conservative association's secretary, however, was directed to respond to enquiries by emphasising that it had never advocated contesting municipal elections on party lines: Croydon Conservative Association, minutes, 3 Oct. 1893. A decade later, the association's executive committee agreed in a confidential meeting that there was widespread feeling in favour of partisan intervention, but decided that there was too little time before the next round of council elections to openly adopt individual candidates: Croydon Conservative Association minutes, 6 Oct. 1903.

[43] *Croydon Citizen*, 6 Jan. 1906.

[44] Howard Houlder was one prominent local Unionist to appear on Liberal platforms: *Croydon Citizen*, 6 Jan. 1906; B. L., Add. MSS. 50340, f. 141, Arnold-Forster diaries, 29 Nov. 1904; 50351, ff. 100–1, 18 Oct. 1905; 50353, ff. 52–4 11 Dec. 1905. Arnold-Forster castigated his new constituents (in the privacy of his diary) as 'jelly-fish', and bemoaned 'how unreasonable that . . . I should be compelled to go through this utterly meaningless and irrelevant process of teaparties, twiddle twaddle and boredom to everyone concerned'.

he not been emboldened by the results of the municipal elections. In fact, after considerable debate, the Croydon Labour Council rejected John Burns's suggestion that Labour stand aside in Croydon if the Liberals would reciprocate in Deptford.[45]

In the ensuing general election, in January 1906, the Unionist was returned to Westminster, but with a mere 41 per cent of the vote in the three-cornered contest. The Liberal was nosed out, 8,211 votes to 7,573, while Labour polled 4,007. Embittered Liberals, deprived by this split of the triumph they had anticipated, responded by circulating tales of 'Tory gold', whereby the Conservative Central Office allegedly subsidized the Labour candidate to split the Labour vote.[46] They also sought to shore up the ratepayers' alliances to gain a measure of revenge by defeating Labour's municipal candidates in November 1906; when they did so, it was, as one Liberal gloated, 'a lesson taught'.[47]

It is in this context that one can best approach the famous Croydon by-election of March 1909. The campaign was fought in the midst of the 1909 naval scare, and the Conservative candidate's impressive victory (57 per cent of the poll and a margin of nearly 4,000 votes) was widely interpreted as evidence of the popularity of defense and imperial issues among villa and lower middle-class voters alike. But this interpretation cannot explain why the Conservative margin slipped to 4 per cent in January 1910 when the naval issue was again prominent, and it makes less sense to regard this by-election as a conscious verdict on national questions than as the logical culmination of local trends.[48]

Once again, it was a three-cornered contest, though Labour was later in the field, and with a weaker candidate, than in 1906. He gained a mere quarter of the votes accorded his predecessor (886), and struggled against frequent calls for Labour voters to abstain or, on just this occasion, to vote Conservative, and so administer a lesson of their own to duplicitous Liberals. Accordingly the Tory majority was artificially inflated: it was judged against a base year (1906) when Conservative apathy and dissension had depressed their turnout; and it was exaggerated by the diminution in the progressive vote prompted by recrimination over municipal politics. Turnout tended to be lowest in the working-class wards of West Croydon and South Norwood, suggesting the importance of abstentions, but even in solidly Conservative polling districts the Tory faithful did not vote in the dreadnought-intoxicated droves associated with navalist mythology.[49]

[45] P. Poirer, *The Advent of the British Labour Party* (New York, 1958), p. 266 n. 59; *Croydon Advertiser*, 25 June 1904; Transport House, London, Labour Representation Committee MSS. 16/373, William Hancock to J. R. MacDonald, 7 July 1904; Labour Party MS. GC 3/72, A. Gore to J. R. MacDonald, 10 Apr. 1906.

[46] *Croydon Citizen*, 3 Feb. 1906. The figure most commonly cited, £35, was, as the paper indignantly noted, not only fallacious, but an insult. The total campaign expenses for Stranks amounted to some £137.

[47] *Croydon Advertiser*, 3 Nov. 1906; *Croydon Citizen*, 10 Nov. 1906.

[48] G. J. Marcus, 'The Naval Crisis of 1909 and the Croydon By-election', *Journal of the Royal United Services Institution*, CIII (1958), 500–14. For a fuller critical account see F. Coetzee, *For Party or Country: Nationalism and the Dilemmas of Popular Conservatism in Edwardian England* (New York, 1990), pp. 109–10.

[49] *Morning Post*, 17 Mar. 1909; *Croydon Advertiser*, 20 Mar. 1909, 3 Apr. 1909; *Croydon Times*, 17 Mar. 1909. The local Labour paper, the *Croydon Citizen*, had recently suspended publication, illustrating Labour's local difficulties. Tariff reform also figured prominently in the campaign, for the Tory candidate, Hermon-Hodge, was a stalwart protectionist who played up the threat to the local building trades of imported Scandanavian materials.

When in January 1910 there was finally a straight two-party fight, and Croydon's Liberals succeeded in mobilizing an unprecedented number of voters, the Conservatives barely held the seat, by some 900 votes in a poll of 23,550 (the highest turnout yet recorded, over 86 per cent). The Conservatives duplicated that feat in December 1910 and so preserved their record of having returned only Unionist M.P.s. But if their hegemony had gone unbroken, it had not gone unchallenged, and recognition of that point serves as a fruitful point of departure to consider the impact of suburban Conservatism.

5

Croydon's experience alerts us to the much more dynamic nature of the formation of political loyalties. Too often, when electoral historians have thought about the course of change they have focused on structural developments, especially the extension of the franchise, and unwittingly implied that the intervening periods between the peaks of reform, such as that from 1885 to 1914, were more stable. In Croydon during that period, in absolute numbers the electorate more than doubled, but given the turnover of population (characteristic of the suburbs, as some inhabitants leap-frogged to avoid residential proximity to less affluent social strata), the magnitude of change was greater still. After 20 years, only three of 20 original members of the local Conservative association still served. In 1904 that organisation estimated that no more than a ninth of its subscribers had been members a decade earlier.[50] *The Times* estimated in 1907 that some 2,000 Croydon voters had been dropped from the previous year's register, and that some 3,500 new voters had been added.[51] So despite the presumptions of permanence and stability, Conservative majorities were not simply reproduced from election to election, but reconstituted from a continually shifting pool of voters.

Such extensive turnover complicated efforts both to organize the electorate and to minimize tensions between longer term stable residents and the newer residents pouring in. The Conservative party's local agent methodically and successfully pressed his party's claims before the revising barrister each autumn in an attempt to ensure that most of the voters added to the register were prospective Conservatives, and that a majority of those stricken from it were likely Liberals.[52] Perhaps the most effective

[50] *Morning Post*, 8 Jan. 1904.

[51] *The Times*, 19 Mar. 1909.

[52] Though the annual reports of the Croydon Conservative Association played up the agent's skill in registration, in many cases he was simply repeating a claim sustained the previous year, so one cannot necessarily presume a cumulative improvement. Moreover, in some cases, whether inadvertently or over-zealously, Conservative agents struck sympathetic voters from the register: *Croydon Guardian*, 5 Sept. 1885. The association itself was judged to be 'in good order' by the National Union in 1885, and it placed second in a national competition sponsored through the Union by Sir William Bull in 1913. The local Conservative Workingmen's Club suffered initially from financial difficulties, but these were soon rectified by the installation of a billiards table, and the club was lauded for its assistance in 1909. Not so the neighbouring West Croydon and Selhurst Club, whose sociable members were reminded that 'a candidate is not returned by drinking success to him at the bar': Churchill College, Cambridge, Lord Randolph Churchill MSS., RCHL iii/337, W. H. Rowe, *Summary of Reports on the Affiliated Associations visited by Commissioners from the National Union* (June 1885), p. 17; *Croydon Guardian*, 1 Mar. 1913; *Conservative Clubs Gazette*, Feb. 1904, p. 21; May 1909, p. 81.

vehicle for promoting Conservative interests in the borough lay outside the formal party organisation, however. The Primrose League was frequently scorned as little more than an outlet for the pretensions of middle-class snobbery, with its elaborate medieval hierarchy of membership classifications, its garden parties where members could mingle with their social superiors, and its recourse to jugglers, ventriloquists, mimes, and other purveyors of entertainment. But the snobbish and faintly ridiculous proved irresistible in Croydon, where the League eventually enrolled some 5,000 members.[53]

The League's success pointed to a flourishing grass-roots politics which consciously sought to incorporate the respectable, constitutional community. The Primrose League began at the beginning by enrolling children and nursing them on the basic elements of Conservative politics. So-called 'Primrose Buds' in Croydon were challenged to demonstrate 'the advantages of European supremacy in China' or to 'show that we have an individual liberty beyond that enjoyed in any other European country'. Admittedly these efforts lacked something in sophistication; when pressed to compare the reigns of Queens Elizabeth and Victoria, one child explained, 'Elizabeth chopped off Mary's head. Victoria did not chop off anybody's head.' She then volunteered, 'in Elizabeth's reign they had very few sweets. Now they have lots of them.'[54]

For the adults, though, the Primrose League afforded an important outlet in two respects. First, it provided an army of unpaid, volunteer campaign workers whose contribution was essential when, after 1883, electoral laws imposed strict limits on campaign spending. In 1910, for example, Croydon's Primrose Leaguers checked and re-checked an electoral register of some 30,000 voters, and canvassed over 100 miles of suburban streets, leading the appreciative party agent to liken their efficiency to that of the German General Staff.[55] Second, a majority of the League's members were women, and the most active local habitation was entirely female. In the meetings and committee minutes one finds an almost ritualistic disavowal of any intention to encroach upon the prerogatives of men, but in practice female Primrose Leaguers were exceptionally active, whether in the campaign to secure womens' parliamentary suffrage, to enfranchise female ratepayers for the municipal franchise, and to articulate an agenda rooted in fidelity and dutiful custody of the nation's precious heritage.

Those efforts, often couched in platitudes from the past, might also point a way forward, to link localist concerns and national images. Despite the emphasis in much of the historiography of this period upon the primacy of national issues, the trajectory

---

[53] *Croydon Guardian*, 8 Apr. 1913. See also M. Pugh, *The Tories and the People, 1880–1935* (Oxford, 1985).

[54] *Primrose League Gazette*, Nov. 1898, p. 12; Dec. 1900, pp. 18–19.

[55] *Ibid.*, Jan. 1912, p. 3; Croydon Ref. Lib., Primrose League, Grantham Habitation, minutes, 14 Jan. 1909; *The Tory*, Sept. 1902, pp. 126–7. Primrose Dames were instructed in the procedures of effective canvassing and the provisions of electoral law in a local Conservative Club. It might be imagined that the discrepancy between the party's slim majorities in the 1910 elections and its marked success in municipal contests owed something to support from female ratepayers, though most observers believed that most eligible female ratepayers did not vote. See, e.g., *Croydon Express*, 7 Oct. 1911, which estimated that of some 600–700 female voters on the West ward's municipal rolls, only 30–40 had actually polled. According to *Ward's Croydon Directory* (1910), the parliamentary register for the ward numbered 5,118, the municipal one, 5,588.

of Croydon Conservatism suggests that local factors had by no means been superseded. Certainly the experience of municipal politics directly affected parliamentary elections by providing (or provoking) different local factions to assess or demonstrate their effective strength.[56] Indirectly, the prevalence of the 'unprogressive alliance', the various ratepayers' organizations, predisposed some Liberals to regard working men as their opponents and Conservative voters as their allies in local affairs, and it seems fanciful to suppose that such views could be entirely discounted in national elections. Few local Liberals or Tories bothered to dispute one Liberal's admission that such alliances were 'a step toward an amalgamation of forces with the view of wiping out the Labour Party'.[57]

The mobilization of Croydon Conservatism also owed something to a belief that the borough's size and character entitled it to due consideration from its M.P.s. and the party leadership. Roy Foster has demonstrated that a good deal of Tory Democracy in the 1880s amounted to self-promotion by the self-absorbed provincial party bosses, and this theme resonated in Croydon to the Tories' benefit in 1885, and to their detriment in 1906.[58] Croydon's Conservatives, like many of their urban counterparts, were not reluctant to press their claims upon their superiors, and even the ritualistic expressions of support to the prime minister were often framed to elicit some token of recognition and gratitude in return. Little wonder that Salisbury wryly noted that his epitaph should read 'Died of writing inane letters to empty-headed Conservative associations.'[59]

More broadly, though, Croydon Conservatism also drew upon a suburban sensibility.[60] In the 1880s this sense of place was specifically residential and sustained by a selective interpretation of the sorts of deleterious influences whose absence in Croydon ensured that people of quality might lead an undisturbed life there. During that same decade, the newly incorporated borough's council, for all the dispute preceeding its establishment, provided a theatre of power, its legitimating rituals displaying the grave, dignified local notables such as Edridge in a favourable light. So

[56] On municipal elections, see D. Tanner, 'Elections, Statistics, and the Rise of the Labour Party, 1906–1931', *Historical Journal*, XXXIV (1991), 893–908, and his authoritative discussion of the franchise, *Political Change*, pp. 99–129.
[57] *Croydon Advertiser*, 3 Feb. 1906; *Croydon Guardian*, 28 Feb. 1903. The degree to which enfranchised ratepayers were receptive to Conservative arguments is suggested by D. Jarvis, 'British Conservatism and Class Politics in the 1920s', *English Historical Review*, CXI (1996), 66–7.
[58] 'Tory Democracy and Political Elitism: Provincial Conservatism and Parliamentary Tories in the early 1880s', in *Parliament and Community: Historical Studies XIV*, eds. A. Cosgrove and J.I. McGuire (Belfast, 1983), pp. 147–75.
[59] Quoted in E.J. Feuchtwanger, *Disraeli, Democracy and the Tory Party* (Oxford, 1968), p. 211. For typical intrusions from Croydon upon the prime minister's schedule, Salisbury MSS. Class M, Edridge to Salisbury, 13 Feb. 1884; Salisbury MSS. Class E, S. Herbert to Salisbury, 28 July 1886.
[60] Other helpful studies of the suburban experience include J. Archer, 'Ideology and Aspiration: Individualism, the Middle Class, and the Genesis of the Anglo-American Suburb', *Journal of Urban History*, XIV (1988), 214–53; R. Fishman, *Bourgeois Utopias: The Rise and Fall of Suburbia* (New York, 1987); M. Marsh, *Suburban Lives* (New Brunswick, 1990); K.T. Jackson, *Crabgrass Frontier: The Suburbanization of the United States* (New York, 1985). For the relationship of place and politics, K.R. Cox, 'Suburbia and Voting Behavior in the London Metropolitan Area', *Annals of the Association of American Geographers*, LVIII (1968), 111–127; R.J. Johnston, 'Places and Votes: The Role of Location in the Creation of Political Attitudes', *Urban Geography*, VII (1986), 103–17; M. Savage, 'Understanding Political Alignments in Contemporary Britain: Do Localities Matter?', *Political Geography Quarterly*, VI (1987), 53–76.

partial a vision grew increasingly difficult to sustain, especially as Croydon simultaneously remained a suburb yet evolved into something quite different from the classic
definition which it once – in aspiration at least – had resembled. As *The Times* noted
in 1909, 'until quite recently a residential district of a rather superior class, the borough
of late years has attracted a general, or, as they say locally, a "mixed population". It
is now, broadly speaking, the home of the middle and better-paid artisan classes.' [61]
The *Morning Post* concurred, reporting that 'Croydon is a very mixed constituency
and every year as it becomes more suburban and more populous presents greater
difficulties from the organizer's point of view.'[62]

Seemingly swamped by new residents, assailed by some councillors in municipal
government, and manifestly unable to secure the impressive majorities or uncontested
returns of a generation before, Croydon's Conservatives began, in the decade before
the Great War, to adopt a different political tone. Gone was the emphasis on the
unique attributes of the local community, and on its insularity from the shocks of
the outside world extolled by J. O. Pelton in 1891; in its place came an initially
diffuse stress on how Croydon could more directly be aligned with what was best
within the nation, how it could embody and identify with the nation's most respectable
and patriotic elements.[63]

The shift in emphasis from the commuter to the ratepayer reinforces the notion
that Villa Toryism was more of a process than a once-and-for-all fact.[64] In Salisbury's
usage it implied the significance of class, the increasing willingness of middle-class
propertied interests to cast their lot with the Conservatives. Croydon's observers,
whatever their sympathies, were unanimous in assigning villadom to the Tories, and
it is probable that, given some degree of residential stability, these villa voters were
a crucial ingredient in the majorities the Conservatives were continually reconstitut-
ing.[65] Yet Villa Toryism is as evocative of place as of class, and it leads one to
reconsider the impact of suburban development. The notion that Croydon Conservatism was sustained by a homogeneous middle-class suburban presence was dubious
enough in the 1880s and even more fanciful thereafter. Equally untenable is the idea

---

[61]   *The Times*, 19 Mar. 1909.

[62]   *Morning Post*, 20 Mar. 1909.

[63]   For an account of this process elsewhere in suburban London, see T. Jeffery, 'The Suburban Nation:
Politics and Class in Lewisham', in *Metropolis London: Histories and Representations since 1800*, ed. D.
Feldman and G.S. Jones, (1989), pp. 189–216. Ironically, in Croydon aspects of the renewed vision of
the suburb in the nation resembled a reformulated vestryism.

[64]   Green, *Crisis of Conservatism*, p. 117.

[65]   One is tempted to characterize the basis of Conservative success in Croydon as snobbery and jobbery.
An American visitor from Cleveland described the borough as one where 'London clerks play gentlemen
on seven dollars a week', and claimed that 'it is estimated that of every five of the male population, one
is a rich or well-to-do-man, two are working men and two are snobs': *Croydon Advertiser*, 14 Jan. 1911,
reprinting an extract from the *Cleveland Press*. Even the most elementary quantitative analysis of these
figures would predict a Conservative majority. For an account of the political consequences of status-anxiety,
see R. Price, 'Society, Status and Jingoism: The Social Roots of Lower Middle-Class Patriotism, 1870–1900'
in *The Lower Middle Class in Britain, 1870–1914*, ed. G. Crossick, (1977), pp. 89–112. It was estimated,
though, as early as 1903 that 61 per cent of local inhabitants were working-class. On the challenges of
characterizing constituencies, P. Thompson, *Socialists, Liberals and Labour: The Struggle for London,
1885–1914* (1967), pp. 299–300, and Blewett, *Peers*, p. 488, are useful, as is H. Pelling, *Social Geography
of British Elections, 1885–1910* (1967).

that it reflected an enervating conformity and continuity. Rather, Croydon was the site of migration not only of affluent former Londoners, but of rural migrants as well, and for the local Conservatives to cull their fair share of votes from this mix required something more than the grateful affirmation of policies percolating down from Westminster.[66] Masterman memorably likened the mobilization of the suburbs to being suddenly butted by a sheep, but in Croydon and other suburbs the task of keeping the Conservative flock together could strain the patience and ingenuity of any shepherd.[67]

[66] See also Thompson, *Suburbia*, p. 16.
[67] Masterman, *Condition of England*, p. 74.

The Development of British Socialism, 1900–1918

DUNCAN TANNER

University of Wales, Bangor

Historians of European labour and socialist movements often contrast the moderation of British Labour politics with the radicalism of sophisticated Continental socialist parties.[1] The 'Labourism' evident in Britain was apparently induced by a series of unique characteristics: by the protective and conservative aims of trade unions, whose votes, ethos and values dominated Labour politics;[2] by the Liberal origins of many Labour leaders;[3] by the naïve and vacant ethical socialism espoused by much of the party;[4] by a matrix of social and cultural constructions which limited horizons and aims[5] and by the integration of British labour into the nation state.[6] For many, Labour had few ideas and little ideology of its own before 1914. It continued to act as a trade union pressure group into the 1920s,[7] absorbing much from Liberalism when it began to develop new ideas in the 1930s.[8] By contrast, European socialist parties were more receptive to Marxist ideas, more prone to theoretical analysis, more likely to act in accordance with the aims and objectives of the Socialist International.

A doubly heretical counter-argument has been developing over recent years. Marxism was evidently weaker in Britain, that is incontestable. And the political inclinations of many leading Labour figures in Britain were evidently rooted in a mix of experiences and outlooks, rather than in Marxism alone. However, the suggestion that Labour's early leadership were Victorian Liberals, and that Labour's only distinctive ideological feature was the contribution made by trade unionism, is being actively

[1.] This has been a general assumption, although the seminal statements were political and polemical rather than academic P. Anderson, 'Origins of the Present Crisis', *New Left Review*, XXIII (1964); T. Nairn, 'The English Working Class', *ibid.*, XXIV (1964). Academic examples of this 'exceptionalist' literature are usefully reviewed in S. Berger, *The British Labour Party and the German Social Democrats 1900–1931* (Oxford 1994), pp. 11–16.

[2.] Some of the best examples are J. Saville, 'The Ideology of Labourism', in R. Benewick *et al*, *Knowledge and Belief in Politics* (1973), and R. I. McKibbin, *The Evolution of the Labour Party, 1910–24* (Oxford 1974).

[3.] E.g. D. Martin, 'Ideology and Composition', in *The First Labour Party, 1906–14*, ed. K. D. Brown, (1985).

[4.] L. Panitch, 'Ideology and Integration: The Case of the British Labour Party', *Political studies*, XIX 1971; S. Pierson, *British Socialists: The Journey from Fantasy to Politics* (1979), pp. 345–50; G. Foote, *The Labour Party's Political Thought. A History* (1986), p. 37.

[5.] R. I. McKibbin, 'Why Was There no Marxism in Britain', *English Historical Review*, XCIX (1984); G. Stedman Jones, 'Working-Class Culture and Working-Class Politics in London, 1870–1900: Notes on the Remaking of a Working Class', reprinted in his *Languages of Class* (Cambridge, 1983).

[6.] M. Van der Linden, 'The National Integration of European Working Classes, 1871–1914', *International Review of Social History*, XXXIII (1988); J. Schwarzmantal, *Socialism and the Idea of the Nation* (1991), pp. 88–96.

[7.] As in McKibbin, *Evolution*, pp. 224–7, and R. Skidelsky, *Politicians and the Slump* (1967).

[8.] See esp. M. Freeden, *Liberalism Divided* (Oxford 1986); D. Blaazer, *The Popular Front and the Progressive Tradition. Socialists, Liberals and the Quest for Unity, 1884–1939* (Cambridge, 1992).

challenged. Such views understate the contribution of radical intellectual strands and experiences – including an awareness of socialist arguments of varying kinds[9] – to Labour's development. Moreover from the 1890s onwards Labour figures had to explain a series of new problems, and present remedies and proposals which suggested a way forward. In the process, party leaders developed more sophisticated policy aims than has hitherto been recognised (the first heresy).[10] Although these 'political visions' drew on indigenous socialist and radical trends, it is increasingly argued that they were also broadly consistent with aspects of socialist ideological and political developments outside Britain (the second heresy).

Numerous European socialist parties had a strong Marxist tradition and many did not wish this emphasis to change. But these elements were being attacked or challenged. European revisionists drew on and co-existed with indigenous radical but non-Marxist traditions, but also learnt directly from British ideas and events.[11] Forms of democratic socialism developed by British Labour leaders parallelled the more well-known democratic socialist debates within Europe.[12] The core similarities between these democratic socialist tendencies in Britain and Continental Europe have been overshadowed, in part because of the tactical emphases and disagreements which seemed to divide British from Continental reformers at the time.[13] Moreover, until recently little attention was paid to the further changes within Continental socialism in the 1920s, changes which highlight not the ideological *differences* between Britain and Europe but the similar pathways of development. Whilst some parallel studies of democratic socialist policy orientations across the period 1910–31 reveal differences of emphasis between Labour and the equivalent European parties,[14] like other studies they show

9. For Marxism and British Labour intellectuals, see the work of Mark Bevir, esp. 'The British Social Democratic Federation, 1880–1885. From O'Brienism to Marxism', *Internat. Rev. of Social History*, XXXVII (1992), and his 'The Marxism of George Bernard Shaw, 1883–1898', *History of Political Thought*, XIII (1992). For the 'plebeian radical' tradition, *Currents of Radicalism*, eds. E. F. Biagini and A. J. Reid (Cambridge 1991), pp. 1–19.

10. For various aspects of this reappraisal, P. Thane, 'Labour and Local Politics: Radicalism, Democracy and Social Reform, 1880–1914', and D. M. Tanner, 'Ideological Debate in Edwardian Labour Politics: Radicalism, Revisionism and Socialism', both in Biagini and Reid (eds.), *Currents of Radicalism*; D. M. Tanner, 'Travail, Salaires et Chômage: L'Économie Politique du Labour à L'Époque Édouardienne, 1900–14', in *Aux Sources du Chômage*, eds. M. Mansfield, R. Salais and N. Whiteside (Paris, 1994); and 'The Labour Party and 1918', unpublished conference paper, Warwick, 1994. For more recent contributions, N. Thompson, *Political Economy and the Labour Party* (1996); F Trentmann, 'The Strange Death of Free Trade: The Erosion of "Liberal Consensus" in Great Britain, c. 1903–1932' , in *Citizenship and Community. Liberals, Radicals and Collective Identities in the British Isles, 1865–1931*, ed. E. F. Biagini (Cambridge, 1996); and his 'Wealth Versus Welfare: The British Left between Free Trade and National Political Economy before World War I', *Historical Research*, LXX (1997).

11. F. Andreucci, 'The Diffusion of Marxism in Italy During the Late Nineteenth Century', in *Culture, Ideology and Politics*, eds. R. Samuel and G. Stedman Jones (1983), pp. 214–7; R. Fletcher, *Revisionism and Empire* (1984) for indigenous radicalism in Germany. For the British influence on Bernstein, e.g. R. Fletcher, 'Bernstein in Britain: Revisionism and Foreign Affairs', *International History Review*, I (1979); and his 'British Radicalism and German Revisionism: The Case of Eduard Bernstein', *ibid.*, IV (1982).

12. Tanner, 'Radicalism, Revisionism and Socialism', pp. 274–9.

13. For 'reformist' debates outside Germany and France, e.g. J. Polasky, *The Democratic Socialism of Emile Vandervelde* (1995), Chapter 8; T. Tilton, *The Political Theory of Swedish Social Democracy* (Oxford 1991), Chapter 2; J. E. Miller, *From Elite to Mass Politics. Italian Socialism in the Giolittian era, 1900–1915* (1990).

14. J. N. Horne, *Labour at War. France and Britain, 1914–18* (Oxford 1991); S. Pederson, *Family, Dependence, and the Origins of the Welfare State. Britain and France, 1914–45* (Cambridge 1993).

socialist parties addressing the same problems and travelling in broadly the same direction.[15]

It is often suggested that these changes were a consequence of socialists diluting or deserting their ideals. Yet socialist concerns with particular issues could be a natural consequence of a democratic socialist outlook which was neither Liberalism masquerading as a new ideology nor a pragmatic response to political circumstances.[16] Problems may be common across parties and some 'solutions' at least partially shared; but the mix of ingredients can produce orientations with a subtly different focus. The changing ideological outlooks of Labour politicians from the 1890s onwards are studied here as examples of how individuals adapted an ideology to new circumstances, giving programmatic structure to ideological imperatives and the debates of socialist intellectuals in the process. The result was a distinct orientation which was more than radical Liberalism.

Party leaders, and their relationship with contemporary ideological and intellectual debates, form the basis of this study because such people often had vigorously ideological aims and a significant political impact. They shaped what democratic socialism meant in practice. In Edwardian Britain (when all parties were adapting to new problems and to new social and economic perceptions) the boundaries of political debate were even more fluid than usual. The political visions developed by Labour politicians in this period emerged from a silent but mutually reinforcing dialogue between their ideological orientations on the one hand and their understanding of the immediate context and the means necessary to realise their aims on the other. They drew on parallel intellectual debates which were taking place across the political spectrum and across Europe and on direct knowledge of circumstances in other countries. The democratic socialism of Labour leaders did not emerge by absorbing Liberalism (or by absorbing what historians generally understand as 'Fabianism')[17] but through and in conjunction with an understanding of concrete economic realities and living social problems.

This study examines attempts made by Labour leaders to negotiate change and create practical forms of democratic socialisms. It highlights both the complex processes through which the ideological orientations of politicians are developed and the significance of the resulting outlooks. These orientations were not a rupture with the concerns of the late nineteenth century, but evolved from some of its intellectuals' principal concerns. The article charts the emergence of two related but significantly different forms of democratic socialism, which encompassed particular approaches to political economy and the role of the state. It examines a process of ideological reevaluation which informed policy orientations for decades to come.

15. See esp. Berger, *Labour Party and the German Social Democrats*; H. James, *The German Slump. Politics and Economics, 1924–36* (Oxford 1986), Chapter 9.
16. For examples of sophisticated, progressive and neglected forms of contemporary democratic socialism, Tilton, *Swedish Social Democracy*; A. G. Meyer, *The Feminism and Socialism of Lily Braun* (Bloomington, 1985).
17. Some of the more dismissive notions of Fabian thought are now rightly being challenged. See e.g. I. Britain, *Fabianism and Culture. A Study of British Socialism and the Arts, 1884–1918* (Cambridge, 1982); and M. Bevir, 'Fabianism, Permeation and Independent Labour', *Historical Journal*, XXXIX (1996).

2

The socialism of leading Labour figures in the Edwardian period is generally seen as emotional and rhetorical, lacking the Marxist edge so common in mainland Europe. Many leading British figures certainly rejected Marx's belief in class struggle as a force for social progress (although they recognised its existence). They wrote and knew less about Marxism than Continental socialist leaders (although they knew more that the European Socialist rank and file, who read rather less Marx than was once thought). None the less, Marxist ideas were more influential in Britain than many have recognised. It was not just a handful of Labour intellectuals and the future Labour representatives of south Wales and Clydeside who were actively studying Marx at this time.[18] Some socialist assumptions were absorbed into the outlooks and ideology of politicians such as Margaret Macmillan, Fred Jowett, George Lansbury and George Barnes, who were centrally involved in debates over policy. Even if they did not understand or accept every aspect of Marxist theory, they approved the tone and broad sympathies of some Marxist arguments.[19] Their instincts and preconceptions were founded in a climate where socialist ideas were part of the intellectual discourse. Philip Snowden, hardly known for his radical views by the 1920s, was critical of Marx's views and style. Like many ethical socialists he rejected Marx's ideas on class conflict. However, he still found it necessary to summarise Marx's views and to conclude thus in 1913:[20]

> From the foregoing very brief and inadequate survey of the theories and teachings of Marx, it will be seen how valuable and interesting are the contributions which he made to the scientific study of the Social Problem.

Labour leaders were even better informed about the views of continental Revisionists. Eduard Bernstein lived in Britain for many years, and returned later to undertake lecture tours. MacDonald, Hardie and others knew him well.[21] Bernstein visited MacDonald's home and his views appeared in socialist publications and series through MacDonald's interventions. Like other British socialists, MacDonald also praised Jaurès, and wrote an introduction to his *Studies in Socialism*.[22] MacDonald's major venture into publishing – the *Socialist Review* – was meant to create a Revisionist intellectual school in Britain. It was sufficiently successful for Snowden to be described as a revisionist and MacDonald's critics to tar the whole party with the same brush.[23] Those who defended Labour's 'Revisionism' did so cautiously, but without denying the label. Rather they distanced themselves from the notion that 'revisionism' meant socialism was being diluted, often preferring the more radical form of democratic

---

[18.] *The ILP on Clydeside*, eds. A. McKinlay and R. J. Morris (Manchester, 1991), pp. 74, 103, 105; R. Lewis, *Leaders and Teachers: Adult Education and the Challenge of Labour in South Wales, 1906–40* (Cardiff, 1993).

[19.] Tanner, 'Radicalism, Revisionism and Socialism', pp. 280–1; C. Steedman, *Childhood, Culture and Class in Britain. Margaret McMillan, 1860–1931* (1990), pp. 160, 177–9.

[20.] P. Snowden, *Socialism and Syndicalism* (1913), p. 72.

[21.] For Hardie, Berger, *Labour Party and the German Social Democrats*, pp. 209–10. By 'revisionists' I do not mean only those who consciously attempted to 'revise' Marxist theory in a democratic socialist direction, but all socialists who were redefining or revising socialism along similar lines.

[22.] Tanner, 'Radicalism, Revisionism and Socialism', pp. 274–6.

[23.] *Ibid.*, pp. 280–1.

socialism developed by Jaurès to the more ideologically sophisticated, but strategically moderate, policy of Bernstein.

In his book *Modern Socialism* (1903) the Fabian socialist R. C. K. Ensor placed British socialism emphatically within a European context. The press, he noted, depicted a bifurcation of socialism into two schools – 'one "Marxist" or "revolutionary" the other variously called "Possibilist", "Opportunist", "Revisionist", "Fabian", "Ministerial", "Reformist" – the last term being the most exact and comprehensive'. Some, he continued, liked to portray reformists as 'really mere Liberals, men who have found socialism worthless, and gone back on it without having the courage to say so'. But this, he contended, was quite false. 'The difference between the two schools, although profoundly interesting, is not so bald and elementary . . . reformists have not abandoned socialism . . . In principle they remain very close to Marx.'[24] For Ensor, Bernstein was a less important guide than Jaurès. The former, writing from within a Marxist framework, corrected abstract Marxist theory. But much of his approach had already been introduced into German socialism by other less controversial figures. Jaurès had developed a more effective statement of ethical intent without exacerbating party divisions. Other British socialists emphasised the similarity between Britain and Germany without reference to the political theorists. In two full page articles on 'Revisionism in Germany', Keir Hardie emphasised the growing similarity between British and German socialism. Trade unionism, he argued, had modified Germany's socialist party; socialism was modifying Britain's trade union based party. With due allowance for national differences, there was greater tactical and ideological similarity than ever before.[25]

Many British socialists were also well informed about the practical details of socialist politics in other countries. Socialist and trade union newspapers in Britain reported on electoral trends and political events in Europe and Australasia, where British socialist figures were also frequent visitors.[26] Detailed knowledge of legislative reforms in Australia was an important but neglected influence on socialist perceptions in Britain. The Australian experiments with state wages boards were noted on a number of occasions.[27] Socialists did not just visit other European countries on fraternal delegations. They visited to examine and discuss practical matters – elections and their organisation, the relative merits of free trade and tariffs, the strategy of socialist parties. They were keen to demonstrate that British policy was consistent not simply with what European socialists *thought*, but with what they did. As E. P. Wake, a socialist organiser, put it when defending Labour's moderate policy in Parliament against its radical critics:[28]

[24.] R. C. K. Ensor, *Modern Socialism* (1903), pp. xxxiii–xxxvi.

[25.] *Labour Leader*, 14 Oct., 21 Oct. 1910.

[26.] Socialists who made extended visits to Australia and New Zealand included Tom Mann, Ben Tillett and E. G. Hartley. For the inter-change of contacts with Germany, Berger, *Labour Party and the German Social Democrats*, pp. 208–16, 220, 225–9.

[27.] E.g. W. P. Reeves, *State Experiments in Australia and New Zealand* (1902), noted by Ensor in *Modern Socialism*, p. xxv. See also references below, n. 60.

[28.] *Manchester Weekly Citizen*, 27 Jan. 1912. See also 'The Review Outlook', *Socialist Review*, Feb. 1911, p. 407.

a study of the evolution of the German movement will show clearly that the ILP in its alliance with the Labour party is following the true Marxian tradition as to method, and that the impossibilism of that British section finds no counterpart in the present methods of our German comrades. Liebnecht quickly renounced the impossibilist idea of using the Reichstag as a platform of protest from which to give dramatic displays to satisfy the hunger of frothy revolutionaries.

British socialists did not derive most of their detailed ideas nor their emotional commitment to socialism from the ideas and practices of European socialists. They placed less emphasis on their relationship to Marx than those working within parties where such an approach was tactically necessary. However, broadly speaking British socialists were addressing the same problems and proceeding on similar lines to European democratic socialists. They drew on and learnt from their experiences. British ethical socialists – despite having their own intellectual traditions and a tendency to evaluate matters in a religious or ethical language – saw themselves as part of a broader socialist movement.

3

The ethical critique of capitalism which Labour developed and adopted has received considerable attention. Rather less attention has been directed at the parallel attempts of Labour intellectuals (and European socialists) to critically evaluate the political economy of capitalism, and to provide a basis for alternative policies. This section addresses the attempts made to turn broad ideological orientations into a more solid understanding of capitalism, which had implications for how that system might be reformed.

Within British labour circles there was broad agreement on the causes and social consequences of the poverty which capitalism produced. An unorganised capitalist system produced irregular and low wages. An economy dependent largely on manual labour, rather than skill, meant that older workers lost their premium and were 'washed up at forty'. Capitalism needed, and created, a constant pool of unskilled and cheap labour, which was regularly augmented because cyclical conditions meant even the skilled suffered regular bouts of unemployment. However, democratic socialist intellectuals were well aware that changes were taking place within the nature of capitalism. They developed an understanding of these changes which built on and augmented the analysis prevalent in the 1880s. The main writers here were Fabians. Sidney Webb contributed through *Industrial Democracy* (1897) and *Problems of Modern Industry* (1898), as did William Clarke in *Fabian essays* and elsewhere, but many other Fabians were also involved.[29] Their solutions focussed on the role which the state might play in creating a less chaotic system.

As is well known, Fabians attacked Marx's labour theory of value and denounced

---

[29]. J. Tomlinson, 'From National Efficiency to New Social Order. Labour's Industrial Policy, 1900–1918', unpublished conference paper, Business History Unit, L.S.E., Apr. 1992. See also Thompson, *Political Economy and the Labour Party*, Chapter 2, largely discussing Fabian political economy, and more policy-minded contributions from Fabians, e.g. W. Stephan Sanders, *The Case for a Minimum Wage* (1906).

contemporary Marxists and their simplistic theories.[30] Although they recognised the
deficiencies of capitalism as a means of creating and distributing sufficient wealth to
sustain a respectable lifestyle, they considered it could be turned in a progressive
direction through the directing hand of the state. Capitalism, they argued, was changing.
The scale of industrial production was increasing; capital was becoming more concentrated. Competition, the basis of capitalism, was being reduced through the development
of trusts, combinations and price-fixing cartels. To some extent, Fabians argued, this
was a good thing. Excess competition meant employers cut costs to maximise their
share of the market. This produced sweated labour and low-wage economies. Combinations meant larger scale production and economies of scale. They facilitated the
introduction of new technology and eliminated wasteful duplication. Fabians believed
all large industrial organisations (not simply monopolies) exploited the consumer. They
considered all such organisations should be taken over by the state and the 'rent' used
by the community. The economic benefits of large scale production and reduced
competition would then be utilised for the public good. In a manner reminiscent of
Marx, Fabians saw the phase of reduced competition as a stage in the progress of
capitalism towards a new economic system.[31] The role of trusts within this changing
capitalist economy was popularised by the Fabian writer H. W. Macrosty in a series
of much-cited books and pamphlets published between 1899 and 1907.[32]

Other socialists shared this concern with the changing nature of contemporary
capitalism, even if they did not share Fabian optimism about the potential for reform.
American socialists had been disseminating critical information on the impact of
American trusts and combines since the early 1890s.[33] Cartels were also a marked
feature of the German economy and German socialists were equally active in discussing
their implications. Bernstein argued that they would bring economic stability to
capitalism by restricting price fluctuations. This was partially denied by Rudolph
Hilferding, the foremost Marxist authority on political economy between the wars,
who became the S.P.D.'s main financial advisor in the 1920s. Hilferding argued that
trusts were having a major impact on the nature of capitalism. In *Finance Capital*
(1910) he argued that such organisations were falling under the control of a few large
financial institutions. Once this process was complete, he continued, the state could
take control of the financial institutions and through these influence production itself.
Capitalism could evolve into socialism, and socialisation could occur, through the
expropriation of finance capital. Trusts were a stage on the road towards a more
efficient and eventually a socially owned economy. Despite Hilferding's Marxist past,
the refined version of his analysis presented to the S.P.D. in the 1920s was used to
justify policies which were scarcely more radical than Labour's.[34]

---

30. Thompson, *Political Economy and the Labour Party*, is now the most concise and helpful discussion
of these changes.

31. *Ibid.*, p. 21 for ways in which Fabians distinguished themselves from Marxists in this respect. For a
fuller discussion see M. Bevir, 'Fabianism and the Theory of Rent', *History of Political Thought*, X (1989).

32. H. W. Macrosty, *The Growth of Monopoly in English Industry* 1899; *Trusts and the State* (1901);
State Control of Trusts (1905); *The Trust Movement in British Industry* (1907).

33. E.g. H. Gaylord Wilshire, *Free Trade Versus Protection* New York, 1892 and *The Problem of the
Trust* (Los Angeles, 1900).

34. For Hilferding's discussion of 'organised capitalism', H. James, 'Rudolf Hilferding and the Application
of the Political Economy of the Third International', *Hist. Jour.*, XXIV (1981). MacDonald met Hilferding
in 1919: P.R.O. (J. R. MacDonald papers) 30/69/1163, J. Walton Newbold to MacDonald, 24 Aug. 1919.

4

Labour politicians had to turn these ideological aims and intellectual views on political economy into a practical socialist approach and a broad political vision. Historians generally assume that nothing of this kind took place. It is not difficult to see why. In addition to the Liberal backgrounds of many early leaders, significant influences on the ethos of the party – including many trade unions M.P.s. – were often unconcerned with abstract ideals or questions of broader policy. More immediate matters, such as the condemnation of unemployment and the need to expand organisation and electoral support, dominated party thinking. Labour's initial response to increased unemployment, for example, was support for the provision of unemployment relief, rather than an alternative policy.[35] The 'Right to Work' bills which Labour or its back bench Liberal allies introduced into Parliament were propagandist ventures, calling on government to provide work or maintenance for the unemployed.[36] The campaign for a national minimum wage of 30 shillings per week, initiated in 1911 and followed in 1913–14 by the I.L.P./Fabian Society 'War against poverty' crusade, was supported with speeches short on economic depth and high on emotional hostility to unemployment and poverty.[37] The demands made by some trade unions from the 1890s onwards for an eight hour day and a 48 hour week, supported by minimum wages and other changes were sometime based on more sophisticated outlooks than was once allowed. But they were portrayed (sometimes justly, sometimes unfairly) as narrow and sectional policies, with little broader thinking behind them. The suggestion that Labour was a defensive and protective electoral machine thus has some substance.

However, a broader policy outlook did begin to emerge, especially after 1910. Labour and socialist leaders wrote passionately of poverty and its adverse consequences, but this did not preclude reflective thought on how to tackle such matters at the roots.[38] Unemployment, low wages and poverty aroused Labour hostility not because they existed, but because of the deprivation of opportunity, hope and dignity which so frequently resulted. There was a considerable, but largely unstudied, Labour debate over the way to achieve real and permanent changes in the economy which would address the underlying causes of poverty and lay the basis for a broader reform programme. Incorporated into this debate was a concern with the values and culture which any such change in the economic and social system might stimulate. Labour politicians displayed a more substantial long-term vision, and a more analytical approach, than is generally attributed to the party at this stage in its development. Leading Labour figures blended their moral and socialist orientations with a conception of political economy which had clear socialist overtones.

British Labour leaders knew and accepted socialist views on the changing nature

[35] Labour Party, *Annual Report* (1905), pp. 61–8.

[36] K. D. Brown, *Labour and Unemployment* (Newton Abbot, 1971), Chapters 3–4.

[37] E.g. W. Crooks, *The Minimum Wage* (1911); *Labour Leader*, 19 May–21 July 1911. For the campaign more generally, papers of the standing committee of the I.L.P. and Fabian society, I.L.P. archives (British Library of Political and Economic Science, London School of Economics) and Labour Party campaign files LP/CAM/14/1 (Museum of Labour History, Manchester, Labour Party Archives).

[38] See esp. the series of articles by prominent I.L.P. and Fabian figures, 'Why I Became a Socialist', *Labour Leader*, beginning 12 May 1912.

of capitalism. Several made critical comments on trusts and their impact. Lansbury wrote in the mid 1890s that 'The improvements in machinery . . . the formation of trusts and syndicates, the competition of foreign powers . . . will displace more and more labour'.[39] Hyndman asked the American socialist Gaylord Wilshire for further information about the subject in 1902, while Hardie wrote in Wilshire's journal 'like hell and the grave (Trusts) can never be satisfactory . . . either the nation must own the trusts or the trusts will own the nation'.[40] However, it was not just the more radical British socialists who embraced this issue. MacDonald and Snowden also wrote a good deal about trusts. The importance of their views can hardly be over-stated. They were at the heart of Labour policy for 30 years. Both have been (mis) construed as Victorian Liberals, when both developed related, but significantly different, demo-cratic socialist outlooks. In particular, they were well aware of the changing nature of capitalism, of the impact which trusts and cartels had played in limiting competition, and of the potential which state-regulated trusts had for encouraging investment and growth. This became central to their economic outlook and to their attempts at defining a practical socialist policy for the Labour Party.[41]

Both MacDonald and Snowden built on the intellectuals' views and socialist analysis outlined earlier. They made direct and indirect reference to Fabian texts. However, their initial observations on these matters were made in articles and speeches written between 1901 and 1904, largely in response to the fiscal debate prompted by the Tories' tariff campaign and the reference which this made to the economic success of Germany and the U.S.A.[42] MacDonald argued that British firms would be unable to compete with larger German and American companies unless they replicated some of their attributes. He argued that trusts had considerable potential as a means of regulating the economy. Unregulated competition would lead to an escalation of small firms in Britain. Most would produce cheap goods through the exploitation of labour and by paying sweatshop wages. Unemployment and poverty would be the inevitable consequence. Excessive competition drove prices ever downwards, creating wasteful and pointless bankruptcies. The search for markets meant money was frittered away on advertising and other non-productive activities. Trusts could reduce this wastefulness in Britain (as they had elsewhere) by reducing competition. For Mac-Donald the key aim was increased industrial efficiency. He accepted the idea that firms needed to be larger and more technologically advanced. After 1918 these ideas developed into support for 'rationalisation', the concentration of resources in larger and more profitable units of production.[43] Unlike many Tories, however, MacDonald

---

[39] J. Schneer, *George Lansbury* (Manchester, 1990), p. 26.

[40] *The Challenge*, 15 July 1902, 4 May 1901.

[41] This analysis differs in some respects from that offered by Trentmann and Thompson in recent pieces which also focus on MacDonald and Snowden, although all are consistently 'revisionist' when compared to most older accounts.

[42] See e.g. J. R. MacDonald, 'The Electorate and the Tariff Problem', *New Liberal Review*, Nov. 1903, and his *The Zollverein and British Industry* (1903); P. Snowden, *The Chamberlain Bubble. Facts about the Zollverein and an Alternative Policy* (1903). These were contributions to a broader political and economic debate on these issues. See e.g. *Spectator*, 27 June 1903; L. C. Money, *British Trade and the Zollverein Issue* (1902); A. C. Pigou, *The Riddle of the Tariff* (1903).

[43] For this, A. Thorpe, 'The Industrial Meaning of Gradualism: The Labour Party and Industry from 1900 to 1931', unpublished conference paper, L.S.E., Apr. 1992; D. M. Tanner, 'The Labour Party, Social Ownership and Clause 4', *Contemporary British History* (forthcoming).

did not accept that only a combination of trusts with tariffs would allow companies to both restructure production and maintain employment and wages. He made this clear in a little known series of articles on the position in Germany, first published in the *Daily News* in 1909.[44] Tariffs combined with trusts, he argued, produced monopolies. Tariffs allowed undemocratic governments in Germany to support the interests of the employing class over the interests of the public. MacDonald's consequent support for democratising the British state resulted from his concern that the British government could otherwise engage in similarly sectional policies. Here he reflected a longstanding labour and radical tradition, rather than a classically Liberal desire to protect and support the individual and the consumer.[45]

MacDonald argued that trusts were likely to fall into the hands not of 'captains of industry', not of producers, but of a 'new breed' – the financial magnate. In such circumstances, he continued, the government would 'be forced to control and manage . . . beginning with monopolies, Trusts and prime necessities for communal life'.[46] The formation of trusts was part of a process of economic change leading to social ownership and to socialism. Socialism, he wrote 'is the law of the economy moulding industrial forms, creating the Trust from competitive industry and extending the economy of the Trust until it is merged into the greater economy of socialism'. The formation of trusts he later wrote, 'marks the end of one phase of the function of capitalism in society and the beginning of a new one'.[47] These were hardly 'Liberal' words.

Like MacDonald, Philip Snowden also emphasised the part which trusts were playing in creating a new economic climate. Their existence was an important element in his support for social ownership. Snowden argued that the 'poverty problem' could not be solved 'without a revolution of our economic system'. In a detailed account of 'the evils of competition', he wrote that 'competition causes enormous waste of labour and of capital'. Like MacDonald, he noted that vast amounts of money had to be spent by individual companies on persuading people to buy their product. He too commented on the huge number of companies forced into bankruptcy by cut-throat competition. He noted that the economic benefits of technical changes were frittered away or taken by a single company, not utilised by the whole community.[48]

Like MacDonald, Snowden also recognised that trusts were minimising competition. He listed areas of British industry where trusts had been instituted, and noted the potential ability of trusts to eliminate much wasteful or destructive competition. Again like MacDonald he argued that trusts were part of a process of economic evolution which would culminate in socialism:[49]

the Trust like competition is doing necessary work. Competition has served the purpose of weeding out the incompetent and ill-equipped capitalists. The Trust is

[44.] Republished as *Tariff-Ridden Germany* (1910).

[45.] Thane, 'Radicalism, Democracy and Social Reform', p. 266.

[46.] J. R. MacDonald, *Socialism* (1907), cited in *Ramsay MacDonald's Political Writings*, ed. B. Barker (1972), pp. 150–1.

[47.] *Ibid.*, p. 52, and MacDonald's *Socialism: Critical and Constructive* (1921), *ibid.* p. 191.

[48.] Snowden, *Socialism and Syndicalism*, pp. 42, 86–91.

[49.] *Ibid.*, pp. 106–7.

concentrating industry and is evolving Capitalism to that stage where the public ownership and control of the great industries will be possible. Competition – the Trust – and then Socialism.

Snowden too placed his views in a socialist perspective.

5

The programmatic implications of these perceptions were altered and revealed by the engagement of Labour leaders in the debate over fiscal policy, state collectivism and social reform which developed in response to the Tory proposals on tariff reform. This debate revealed how politics had changed. The centre ground of the Liberal party had shifted, as the radical Liberal J. A. Hobson himself recognised, and its economic views had altered.[50] Cobdenite economics had already been reformulated by Jevons, Marshall and Pigou. The restriction of international competition and of free trade by trusts had been recognised by Liberal financial experts such as F. W. Hirst. J. A. Hobson took the process of adapting Liberal political economy even further – further than most Liberals were willing to tolerate – but like Hirst he too identified the role which trusts were playing.[51]

Conservative economists were equally attentive to these changes.[52] In Britain (as in Germany) the political economy of free trade was being challenged by an emphasis on national economics, although in Britain's case it was the nation as the hub of an integrated empire which dominated discussion. Professional economists such as Hewins and Ashley (from the L.S.E. and Birmingham respectively) developed ideas on the potential role of trusts and tariffs in the creation of a more productive economy. Drawing (like MacDonald) on the experience of the German Zollverein, they made considerable reference to the productive power of a reformulated economy in which competition was limited and regulated. They denied that free trade could create an internationally competitive British economy. They saw the limitation of competition through cartels, trusts and protection as a means to develop a sounder national (i.e. imperial) economy within a world of economic super-giants. They wanted to enhance the power of producers, even if this meant attacking free trade and the financiers who lived off those who created the nation's wealth. These ideas were popularised and developed on the political stage through the Tariff Reform League and by politicians like Leo Amery (as in his book *The Economic Fallacies of Free Trade*). It was not just in the Labour Party that politicians espoused policies which reflected a real vision of the way forward, based in part at least on their conception of political economy.

Both MacDonald and Snowden participated in and responded to this debate. They knew Hobson and Hobson's work,[53] as they knew and respected Ashley. MacDonald

50. J. A. Hobson, *The Crisis of Liberalism* (1909), pp. 133–8.
51. A. Howe, 'Towards the "Hungry Forties": Free Trade in Britain, c. 1880–1906', in Biagini (ed.), *Citizenship and Community*; Trentmann, 'The Strange Death of Free Trade', p. 223. For Hobson and trusts, *The Evolution of Modern Capitalism* (1894). Hobson's views were much-influenced by the position in the U.S.A. and by the Fabians.
52. For more on the following, E. H. H. Green, *The Crisis of Conservatism* (1995), Chapters 5–6.
53. Textual observations and their reviews of Hobson's books show this clearly.

had met Ashley during the late 1890s. He was impressed by his arguments.[54] Snowden was delighted to receive Ashley's favourable comments on his book *Socialism and Syndicalism*.[55] But neither Snowden nor MacDonald simply adopted the economists' views. Hobson was far more skeptical about trusts than MacDonald, fearing that they would elevate the producer over the consumer by holding the latter to ransom. MacDonald was not inattentive to this concern (unlike some Fabian socialists)[56] but he did not concur with Hobson's emphasis. Neither did he accept Ashley's support for tariffs and his limited conception of the state's role in regulating trusts. None the less, the collectivist programmes which radical Tories and radical Liberals advocated – and the legislation which the Liberal government produced – presented a practical challenge to Labour politicians. Their programmes were clear and populistic statements of how Liberals and Conservatives could reform capitalism in a manner which would produce real benefits for the poor and the unemployed. Labour politicians had to show what reforms *their* principles and perceptions – *their* conception of collectivism – could sustain if they wished to compete. Fabian *intellectuals* certainly began to develop more detailed ideas on forms of state action and finance, producing papers on nationalisation and on other aspects of state involvement.[57] But Labour *politicians* were almost silent on such matters. Rather, they revealed their conception of the state's constructive role in future development through discussion and advocacy of the party's most distinctive policy, the national minimum wage. Although no Labour figure developed a complete picture of the way this would function, nor of the of economic and social reforms which would accompany it, the speeches and statements of MacDonald and Snowden on this issue reveal both the varying nature, and the limitations, of the Labour leaders' conception of socialism.

6

Labour's commitment to a national minimum wage began in the 1880s and 1890s.[58] However, it was made more explicit when the Liberals developed proposals for limited minimum wage rates in sweated industries, mines and agriculture and when some Tories began to argue that protected (and successful) industries could sustain both minimum wage rates and more regular employment. The cross-party intellectual debate which ensued considered both the aims and the consequences of such legislation. This is significant because whilst there was an evident link between Labour's proposals in this field and the Fabian and other arguments in favour of such a policy, MacDonald developed a slightly different approach, based in part on his understanding of the practical difficulties of implementing minimum wage legislation. The Liberals' Trades

[54]. For Ashley and MacDonald, A. Ashley, *William James Ashley* (1932), p. 75. See also P.R.O., 30/69/1155, W. J. Ashley to MacDonald, 7 Mar. 1911.

[55]. Letter, Snowden to Ashley, 24 June 1913, bound into Snowden's *Socialism and Syndicalism*.

[56]. Tanner, 'Travail, Salaires et Chômage', pp. 347–9.

[57]. Fabian 'plans' for nationalizing the railways and mines were based on the model of the Post Office. See A. M. McBriar, *Fabian Socialism and English Politics, 1884–1918* (Cambridge, 1962), pp. 107, 114–5.

[58]. See labour representations made to the Royal Commission on Labour, noted in C. Tsuzuki, *Tom Mann, 1856–1941* (Oxford, 1991), pp. 90–2, and more generally, N. N. Feltes, 'Misery or the Production of Misery: Defining Sweated Labour in 1890', *Social History* XVII (1992), 441–52

Board legislation had been examined by R. H. Tawney (amongst others).[59] MacDonald
also had 'much correspondence on this subject' with Ashley in 1908, and he drew
negative conclusions from examining the Australian system of compulsory arbitration
and minimum wages.[60] An examination of MacDonald's views on such practical
issues suggests his political inclinations were less clearly a part of a Fabian tradition
than his writings on political economy might suggest.

For MacDonald and other Labour figures an effective minimum wage was impossible without a fundamental reconstruction of the economy. He was unhappy
about a national scheme which took no cognizance of regional and other variations.
Like others in Labour politics, he was concerned at the impact which this would
have on employment.[61] Low pay could not be outlawed by the state; legislative
action might indeed be counter-productive. Rather than relying on state legislation
to effect change, he wanted large companies and the trade unions in them to establish
minimum wage agreements. The state should make such agreements binding on all
firms in that industry or area. This would drive out inefficient employers who could
not pay the minimum, and concentrate production in larger and more efficient units
(of the kind which MacDonald supported when discussing the potential value of
trusts). There would be benefits for the efficiency and quality of production and an
improvement in the economic capacity of the country; companies could thus provide
well-paid employment.[62]

As with the creation of trusts, such changes could rebound upon the consumer
and might also be resisted by employers. Compared to Liberals, MacDonald paid
little attention to this, preferring to emphasise the benefits of creating a sounder
economy by semi-voluntary, state-backed, policies. Compared to Fabians, he proffered
a more restricted role for the state. The impression from MacDonald's speeches and
articles is that for him public ownership of the larger companies to be created by
trusts was a more distant, less desirable and more restricted prospect, with employer-led
minimum wages an end in their own right in most competitive industries. He took
a more cautious view of the state and preferred individual over state action where
this was possible. His views on political economy were not a value-free response to
practical problems nor a reflection of Liberal (or Fabian) economic orthodoxy. They
were a construction which encompassed a set of social values and assumptions.

As noted earlier, MacDonald was concerned that an unchecked state could act
against the interests of the people and in favour of an economic *élite*. Part of his
response to this problem was constitutional. He advocated the democratisation of the

[59.] For the general background, S. Blackburn, 'Ideology and Social Policy: The Origins of the Trade
Boards Act', *Historical Jour.*, XXXIV (1991).
[60.] Ashley, *W. J. Ashley*, p. 135. On the Australian system, I.L.P., *Conference Report* (1907), pp. 23–5.
[61.] I.L.P., *Conference Report* (1904), p. 29. For similar doubts from Labour economic 'experts', Nuffield
College, Oxford, Fabian Society MS., A 9/1, f. 112–3, H. B. Lees-Smith to E. Pease, 15 Sept. 1905; P.
Wicksteed, 'The Distinction Between Earnings and Income, and Between a Minimum Wage and a Decent
Maintenance: A Challenge', in *The Living Wage*, ed. P. Snowden (1912). Some on the left shared parts
of this view, although not the conclusion. See e.g. I.L.P., *Conference Reports* (1907), pp. 62–3 (McLachlan);
ibid., (1912), pp. 90–1 (Keir Hardie). For some of the complexities of the minimum wage debate, Tanner,
'Travail, Salaires et Chômage', pp. 349–50.
[62.] See *Labour Leader*, 9 June 1911, 12 Sept. 1911; and Liverpool University Library, J. Bruce Glasier
diary, 6 Sept. 1912.

state to ensure that executive authority was not abused. The extension of formal democracy through franchise extension, local government reform, devolution and alterations to the machinery of government would check the power of the executive. Yet further 'democratic' changes of the kind proposed by New Liberals and radical socialists – the referendum, proportional representation, the introduction of a consensual committee system into national government – were resisted.[63] The explanation of this adds substantially to any appreciation of MacDonald's ideology and values. Moreover, MacDonald was by no means untypical, and his views draw attention to an important and continuing strand within British democratic socialism.

To some extent the opposition to further democratisation reflected practical considerations. The referendum, for example, was thought to be a conservative device. The Swiss experience and the conservative political views of the referendum's principal supporters in Britain were often noted.[64] Proportional representation also presented practical and political dangers to electoral and other party interests. Yet MacDonald's opposition to such democratic devices also had an ideological edge. The referendum, he argued, was 'the grave of an active democracy'.[65] It would put power into the hands of the press and of those who framed the question. The involvement of the citizen in decision-making should be real and informed. The spurious involvement of the citizen in state decision-making which the referendum created was no answer. Government had a duty to weigh up the totality of a problem and make decisions – citizens should be encouraged to do exactly the same. A democratic state was one 'where the democracy does the thinking as well as the electing'.[66]

This concern to create a participatory citizen democracy also underpinned Mac-Donald's thinking on social reform. Here MacDonald built on intellectual discussions in which a 'Fabian' concern with efficiency was not the only force at work. For example, Labour intellectuals such as R. H. Tawney were concerned that youth unemployment and the existence of 'dead end' jobs should be tackled not just for economic reasons but so that social alienation was nipped in the bud. The answer was employment legislation and improved education, within a framework of economic changes which would reduce the number of unskilled jobs. The underlying problems which confined these people to a life of insecurity, and hence limited their commitment to the state and its aims, would thus be tackled.[67] Legislation which simply tried to abolish problems was deemed insufficient. MacDonald and others like him were concerned that all social legislation should contribute to an institutional framework in which the 'right' attitudes were reinforced. Social reforms should be part of a wider restructuring of the relationship between men and society. Central aims were the cultivation of self-respect and social responsibility. The state's responsibility for 'ad-

[63]. Tanner, 'Radicalism, Revisionism and Socialism', pp. 285–7.
[64]. *Labour Leader*, 6 Mar. 1908; L. Barrow and I. Bullock, *Democratic Ideas and the British Labour Movement, 1880–1914* (Cambridge, 1996), p. 174.
[65]. 'The Review Outlook', *Socialist Review*, Jan. 1911, p. 329.
[66]. Thane, 'Radicalism, Democracy and Social Reform', p. 265. For later examples of this emphasis, e.g. S. Fielding *et al*, *'England Arise!'. The Labour Party and Popular Politics in 1940s Britain* (Manchester, 1995), Chapters 3–4.
[67]. H. Hendrick, *Images of Youth. Age, Class and the Male Youth Problem, 1880–1920* (Oxford, 1990), Chapter 2.

vancing human character' should be taken seriously.[68] State welfare was a poor replacement for fuller employment and better pay as a means of attacking poverty and promoting independence. In the longer term, the worker in receipt of benefit would 'accept the industrial conditions under which he is at present existing'. Dependency would encourage acceptance and apathy.[69] Welfare reforms were not a substitute for work. When introduced they should be part of a social system which allowed people independence, self-respect, and dignity.[70] Like many ethical socialists, MacDonald still believed that real change meant changing people and their attitudes. In 1920 he wrote that the state was turning itself into the guardian of public morality by taking a leading role in welfare and other social matters. It could not fill this role with any degree of success, or with favourable consequences for individuals or society as a whole.[71] His pre-war comments had anticipated this account in a number of significant respects.

MacDonald (and other, similar, labour leaders) were not hostile to welfare policies, especially by the time the Liberals were introducing them. State maintenance payments were an essential safety-net designed to 'keep body and soul together'. But the form of the safety-net was significant. Employment on publicly useful projects at a fair rate of pay was preferable so that personal pride would not be diminished. The obligation was on the local authority to provide relief work and on government to encourage economic growth and change.[72] In a similar manner, MacDonald opposed non-contributory national insurance contributions on the basis that this would destroy the individual's sense of dignity and increase the role and power of the state.

MacDonald's views were not the consequence of a Victorian hostility to welfare. In the longer term, MacDonald felt Labour policies would ensure that the stigma attached to receipt of state benefits by those in need would be removed. Many Labour moderates supported the abolition of the Poor Law, and received the Webbs's *Minority Report* with enthusiasm for exactly this reason. Welfare benefits, financed wholly or partially by the state, should be a right, provided as part of a relationship of equals. In order to obtain this right, to achieve the position whereby the receipt of welfare should bear no stigma, the *right* to welfare had to be matched by the *duty* to participate, to be an 'ethical' citizen.[73] In 1906, for example, Arthur Henderson moved a bill providing for the feeding of necessitous school children. If parents could provide, but did not, Henderson argued, the law should step in and recover the cost or even punish the parents. There should be obligations to act, as well as an entitlement to receive.[74] At the request of some trade unions (and despite the opposition of some socialists) Labour's unemployment measures of 1908 drew a distinction between those

---

[68.]   Thane, 'Radicalism, Democracy and Social Reform', p. 267.

[69.]   J. R. MacDonald, *Socialism* (1907), pp. 119–20; *Labour Leader*, 9 June 1911.

[70.]   For Labour hostility to welfare payments because of their association with charity, e.g. Labour Party, *Annual Report* (1908), p. 27.

[71.]   J. R. MacDonald, *Parliament and Democracy* (1920), pp. 68–72.

[72.]   D. Marquand, *Ramsay MacDonald* (1977), pp. 138–9; J. Harris, *Unemployment and Politics. A Study in English Social Policy, 1886–1914* (Oxford, paperback edn., 1984), pp. 242–3; Thane, 'Radicalism, Democracy and Social Reform', p. 267.

[73.]   J. R. MacDonald, 'The People in Power', in *Ethical Democracy: Essays in Social Dynamics*, ed. S. Coit (1900).

[74.]   Cited in D. Read, *Documents from Edwardian England* (1973), p. 227.

who deserved benefit, and those who refused work and therefore deserved no benefit.[75] For MacDonald and others, people should be obliged to act in the interest of the whole, to participate, to work when work was available. Welfare payments would hold no stigma if they were part of a responsible system, in which the recipients were responsible citizens who discharged their social duties. The function of social policy was not simply to enhance incomes, but also to foster and develop social attitudes.

Of course, many of MacDonald's concerns and views were shared by intellectuals from different political traditions. The desire to integrate citizens into the state reflected a deep moral concern with the disintegration of community and the decline of individual commitment, a concern which was prevalent amongst intellectuals of vastly differing ideological outlooks. However, MacDonald did not simply adopt the Fabian or New Liberal view on the state's role in welfare (or the economy). As he and other Labour figures responded to the welfare agenda set by the Liberals, they revealed their roots in a rather different and more moralistic labour tradition, and combined this with a view of capitalism and its future which created a particular form of democratic socialism.

7

The version of democratic socialism developed by MacDonald was actively criticised by other contemporary British socialists. One Fabian writer dismissed MacDonald views as 'a jumble of influences – Spencer, Ferri, Jaurès, Geddes, Galton and the rest'.[76] Snowden regarded MacDonald's emphasis on participation and individual effort over state guarantees of minimum standards as 'unadulterated sixty year old individualism'.[77] Despite sharing many of MacDonald's moral assumptions, he and others attacked MacDonald's limited conception of the state's role in creating guaranteed minimum wages and welfare entitlements.[78] Fabians remained dissatisfied with the party leader's attitude to their schemes, although their own discussions on the state's future role were not without limitations.[79] At the same time, many on the left felt that MacDonald (and the Fabians) paid too *little* attention to the potentially undemocratic nature of the state structures which they wished to create. Collectivism could serve the interests of the wealthy and create a 'servile state'. In particular, and building on syndicalist and guild socialist ideas, they challenged both MacDonald's and the Fabians' views on the malleability of the system, arguing for more participation in the management of industry by workers and a greater role for co-operative organisations of consumers.[80] Left critics (in Britain as in Germany) argued that

---

[75.] Labour Party, *Annual Report* (1908), pp. 85, 90, and *Labour Leader*, 30 June 1911, special conference on national insurance.

[76.] *Fabian News*, Mar. 1910.

[77.] *Labour Leader*, 16 June 1911.

[78.] See esp. Snowden, *The Living Wage*.

[79.] Fabian arguments on minimum wages were outlined in e.g. R.C.K. Ensor, 'The Practical Case for a Legal Minimum Wage', *The Nineteenth Century* (1912); S. Webb, *How the Government Can Prevent Unemployment* (1912), and *The Economic Theory of the Minimum Wage* (1912). For Fabian naïveté on broader aspects of the state's role, Tanner, 'Labour, Social Ownership and Clause 4'.

[80.] Thompson, *Political Economy and the Labour Party*, Chapter 3, and Barrow and Bullock, *Democratic Ideas and the Labour Movement*, Chapter 12.

'Revisionists' (like MacDonald and Bernstein) had absorbed too much from Liberalism.[81]

Such politically-charged observations tell us a good deal about the tensions which existed within Labour politics. But they tell us little about the ideological derivation of MacDonald's views and even less about why and how the nature and content of Edwardian debate was changing. Liberal and Tory advocates of change along collectivist lines faced accusations from party traditionalists that they were absorbing not 'Liberalism' but 'socialism'.[82] Similarly, socialists who supported MacDonald labelled their assailants on the left 'anarchists', impractical dreamers or libertarian individualists. Such claims were political abuse not intellectual analysis.

To argue that Labour figures were absorbing Liberalism (or that bourgeois politicians were absorbing socialism) places the ideological turmoil of Edwardian Britain in an unhelpful and one-dimensional context and creates a misleading impression of the dynamics of change. Across the political parties, ideological orientations were shifting in response to a common spur – the transformation of social and economic conditions and the parallel transformation of popular politics. Practical but ideologically committed politicians of all persuasions – politicians who wanted to turn ideological orientations and desires into real changes which advanced their broader aims – found themselves facing similar problems and similar pressures. Their solutions displayed similar core concerns – a concern with the competing roles of the state and producers on the one hand and the individual and consumers on the other, and a willingness to expand and alter the operating methods of their party in order to create an effective political machine. They produced not pragmatism and consensus but different – and deeply ideological – visions of how their parties should proceed along more collectivist lines.

The existence of some common content is hardly evidence of a common ideological aim. Critics of the collectivist direction taken by Labour, Liberals and Tories launched counter-offensives which themselves contained common elements. They shared a concern that politicians with principles were being replaced by demagogues and manipulators.[83] Intellectuals from the left and right argued that the 'servile state' would destroy real liberty and individuality (and the party's traditional values). Radical socialists in Britain as in Europe raised some similar points to libertarian writers like Belloc and Chesterton, whose views they knew and respected.[84] Yet this was not because they shared a common ideology. Rather they too were adapting to circum-

[81] E.g. on MacDonald, Liverpool Univ. Lib., J Bruce Glasier diary, 7 Jan. 1912. For Bernstein, E. Belfort Bax, *Neue Zeit*, 21 Dec. 1897, reply by Bernstein, 19 Jan. 1898; Bebel to Bernstein, 16 Oct. 1898, and reply, 20 Oct. 1898, all in *Marxism and Social Democracy: The Revisionist Debate, 1896–98*, eds. H. Tudor and J. M. Tudor (1988), pp. 144, 171–2, 319–28.

[82] R. D. Holt diary, 19 July 1914, in *Odyssey of an Edwardian Liberal*, ed. D. J. Dutton (Gloucester, 1989), p. 31; and the views of Robert Cecil, cited in D. Dutton, *His Majesty's Loyal Opposition. The Unionist Party in Opposition, 1905–1915* (Liverpool, 1992), p. 87.

[83] For the contemporary intellectual treatment of this problem, see e.g. G. Quagliariello, *Politics without Parties. Moisei Ostrogorski and the Debate on Political Parties on the Eve of the Twentieth Century* (Aldershot, 1996); P. Pombeni, 'Starting in Reason, Ending in Passion. Bryce, Lowell, Ostrogorski and the Problem of Democracy', *Historical Jour.*, XXXVII (1994); R Michels, *Political Parties. A Sociological Study of the Oligarchical Tendencies of Modern Democracy* (1915). For similar if less articulate responses within the political parties, D. M. Tanner, 'Aristocrats, Industrialists and Professionals: The Characteristics of the British Political Elite and the Professionalisation of Politics Before 1914', Ecoles Français de Rome, *Les Familles Politiques en Europe Occidentale au XIXe Siècle* (forthcoming).

[84] Barrow and Bullock, *Democratic Ideas and the Labour Movement*, pp. 260–6; and for European interest, C. Levy, conclusion to *Socialism and the Intelligentsia*, ed. C. Levy (1987), p. 280.

stances, addressing new issues in the light of existing perceptions, and finding areas of contact with others of different ideological orientations. Critics of the 'new politics' of Edwardian Britain offered alternative forms of socialism (or liberalism, or conservatism) to the forms of socialism, liberalism and conservatism offered by the New Liberals, the MacDonaldite Labour Party and the radical right. They were not the guardians of ideological and political purity, resisting those who wished to absorb ideas from other ideologies, but part of a contested political and ideological process, in which parties adapted to a changing world.

The British Labour Party (like the British Liberal and Tory Parties) adapted to new pressures and circumstances more rapidly and fully than most parties in continental Europe, at least before 1914.[85] Within European socialist parties, entrenched Marxist traditions inhibited change along democratic socialist lines, and encouraged comparatively moderate policies to be wrapped in a Marxist rhetoric. The weaker democratic framework of European countries also partially undermined the rationale for adopting an analysis which emphasised the possibilities of reform through capturing the state machinery. None the less, there were signs that a reconsideration of practice and ideology was taking place in many continental countries even before 1914. This was often a result of internal changes, but a host of European socialists – and not just Bernstein – had lived in or visited Britain and examined British practices and political traditions.[86] Not all changed their views as a result, but the introduction of democratic systems, the failure of Communism in the early 1920s, and the formation of socialist parties which excluded Communists after 1920, created structures more closely related to those in Britain. Amongst those with 'ethical' socialist views, these events encouraged further reformulations of ideology and strategy along lines already evident in Britain.[87] The productivist vision of a modern economy being developed in Germany and France across this period was similar in some respects to that advanced by intellectuals in Britain (even if the balance of constituent elements was different). Across Europe, socialists' belief in the state's potential role in economic affairs was enhanced by the experience of war.[88] Rationalization, planning and the socialization of the economy – logical extensions of the attitudes discussed before 1914 – were debated everywhere and formed the basis of economic plans in most European socialist parties in the 1920s and 1930s. Of course the emphasis varied; those advocating a role for the state could do so from quite different ideological angles.[89] Democratic socialist politicians

[85.] For a discussion of pan-European trends in socialist politics before 1939, D. M. Tanner, 'Socialist Parties and Policies, 1890–1945', in *Blackwell Companion to Modern History*, ed. M. Pugh (forthcoming); S. Berger, 'European Labour Movements and the European Working Class in Comparative Perspective', in *The Force of Labour. The Western European Labour Movement and the Working Class in the Twentieth Century*, eds. S. Berger and D. Broughton (Oxford, 1995).

[86.] Including German reformists Lily Braun and Lothar Erdman and the influential Flemish writer Hendrik de Man.

[87.] P. Dodge, *Beyond Marxism: The Faith and Works of Hendrik de Man* (The Hague, 1966); F. Stern, 'Ernst Reuter: The Making of a Democratic Socialist', in his *Dreams and Delusions. National Socialism in the Drama of the German Past* (New York, 1989), Chapter 3.

[88.] Horne, *Labour at War*, Chapter 5, and pp. 344–9; M. Rebérioux and P. Fridenson, 'Albert Thomas Pivot du Réformisme Français', *Le Mouvement Social*, LXXXVII (1974). More generally, D. S. White, 'Reconsidering European Socialism in the 1920s', *Journal of Contemporary History*, XVI (1981).

[89.] For 'corporatist' conceptions of state control and economic plans, see E. Hanssen, 'Depression Decade Crisis: Social Democracy and *Planisme* in Belgium and the Netherlands', *Journal of Contemporary History*, XVI (1981). However, such plans could also be supported by those with apparently different conceptions of the state's role, including Leon Blum and G. D. H. Cole.

involved in constructing a new way forward could create differing 'political visions'.
The French and Belgium socialist leaders, Blum and Vandervelde, constructed a
socialism which was more 'traditional' than MacDonald's; the Swedish leader Per
Albin Hansson constructed a form of socialism which embraced new ideas more
freely.[90] But the same issues continued to be debated across Europe, because there
were core problems, core aims, and core similarities in the parties' ideological
orientations – and because parties continued to learn from each others' views and
experiences.[91] If differences remained, contemporaries were convinced that the gap
was narrowing.[92] Once wartime changes stripped away some of the obstacles, the
apparently large gap between Britain and continental Europe was substantially reduced.

This paper is part of a broader conceptual and historical challenge to still common
notions of both Edwardian politics and of the Edwardian Labour Party. It argues that
the motor of ideological change in Edwardian Britain was not the absorption of ideas
from a particular source (be it Liberalism or socialism) but a desire to debate and
adapt to collectivism and mass politics, to create a new synthesis which adapted a
party's own ideology to meet key issues of the day. It thus shows how the concerns
of politicians in the late nineteenth century were adapted, rather than abandoned, in
debates which fashioned the post-war political outlooks of party leaders. It is argued
that the priorities and orientations of such people can best be gleaned by examining
both their abstract writings *and* their views on the contemporary policy debate. The
article thus reinforces approaches to intellectual history and to the study of policy
which integrate the politicians into their intellectual environments, rather than portraying them as ideological ciphers or as the mouthpiece of policy experts.[93]

As an example of this, the article suggests a rather different view of Edwardian Labour
politics than that evident in many texts. It suggests that between the 1890s and 1914
British socialism went through a series of changes, some of which were parallelled
within European socialist parties. Similar problems demanded similar solutions from
politicians anxious to turn ideological orientations into practical means of achieving
change. In particular, socialist hopes came to rest on a picture of political economy in
which the state would play an important part in achieving real improvements in living
standards and social attitudes. The 'political visions' developed by key Labour politicians
in Britain were not based on ideas absorbed from Liberals or from Fabians (nor, for that
matter, from continental Europe). Party figures *developed* competing versions of a
democratic socialism in which competing views on the role of the state was a key theme.
British Labour leaders faced the future not with an open mind, but with outlooks based
on the morals, economics and ideological orientations of the late nineteenth century,
which they struggled to mould into a practical policy for a changing world.

[90.] J. Jackson, *The Popular Front in France. Defending Democracy, 1934–38* (Cambridge, 1988), pp.
57–8; Polasky, *Emile Vandervelde*, pp. 259–64; Tilton, *Swedish Social Democracy*, Chapter 6.

[91.] Cole, for example, co-authored a pamphlet with De Man, translated his work and studied the
evolution of Swedish socialism. Cole's own work was studied in a number of countries when the socialization
of the economy was under discussion, as was the Webbs' (Tilton, *Swedish Social Democracy*, pp. 86–102;
Dodge, *Beyond Marxism*, p. 137, n. 1; Horne, *Labour at War*, pp. 287, 346–7).

[92.] E. Wertheimer, *Portrait of the Labour Party* (1929), p. 95.

[93.] E.g. J. Harris, 'Political Thought and the Welfare State, 1870–1940: An Intellectual Framework
for British Social Policy', *Past and Present*, No. 135 (1992).

'Thinking in Communities': Late Nineteenth-Century Liberals, Idealists and the Retrieval of Community

SANDRA DEN OTTER

Queen's University, Kingston, Ontario

At a meeting of the Rainbow Circle at the Rainbow Tavern in 1895, the Liberal politician and writer Herbert Samuel proposed a transition from the liberalism of Adam Smith and Bentham to a social philosophy whose 'root idea must be the unity of society – complex in its economic, cooperative, ethical and emotional ties'.[1] The theme of unity which Samuel highlighted was a common refrain at the end of the nineteenth century. The apparent decline of custom, the expansion of a consumer society, and the increased scepticism of moral and religious foundations were also variously held to account for the apparent weakening of the social tissue. Periodic economic depressions, rapid urbanization, the plight of the London casual labour market, and the magnitude of urban poverty moved many, from William Morris to the Positivists, to favour a 'restoration' of community. Observing that 'many of the old bonds of our society, the ties of loyalty that formerly united the different classes to each other, are becoming loosened', the idealist Edward Caird concluded that it was essential to keep alive 'the consciousness of those ethical bonds which unite us to our fellow citizens and lift us above the weaknesses and uncertainty of our individual lives'.[2] The desire to cultivate those points of connexion which recovered the collective was a characteristic idea of *fin de siécle* political culture, prompting Sidney Webb to observe: 'In short, the opening of the twentieth century finds us all to the dismay of the old fashioned individualist, "thinking in communities".'[3]

Community, in fact, became a central pre-occupation for late nineteenth century liberals, and an examination of this attachment provides a useful way of interpreting liberal thought and practice. This evocation of community was of course not peculiarly liberal: community was not the preserve of any single party or ideological label. Nor was 'community' a new concept. None the less, closer scrutiny of how liberals interpreted this theme addresses the much debated problem of weighing continuity against the innovations of the nineteenth century.[4] The appeal to community had

---

[1.] *Minutes of the Rainbow Circle*, ed. M. Freeden (1989), p. 28, 6 Nov, 1895.

[2.] E. Caird, 'The Nation as an Ethical Idea', *Lay Sermons* (Glasgow, 1907), p. 118.

[3.] S. Webb, 'Twentieth Century Politics', in *The Basis and Policy of Socialism* (1908), p. 78.

[4.] See P. Clarke, *Liberals and Social Democrats* (Cambridge, 1978); S. Collini, *Liberalism and Sociology* (Cambridge, 1979); M. Freeden, *The New Liberalism* (Oxford, 1978); R. Bellamy, 'T. H. Green and the Morality of Victorian Liberalism' in *Victorian Liberalism*, ed. R. Bellamy (1989); A. Vincent, 'Classical Liberalism and its Crisis of Identity', *History of Political Thought*, XI (1990); on political culture more generally see R. Price, 'Historiography, Narrative and the Nineteenth Century', *Journal of British Studies*, XXXV (1996), 220–256; J. Vernon, *Politics and the People: A Study in English Political Culture, 1815–1867* (Cambridge, 1993); and J. Parry, *The Rise and Fall of Liberal Government in Victorian Britain* (New Haven, Conn., 1994).

singular implications for liberals, for the incorporation of communitarian perspectives required adjustments to principles which had been judged fundamental by liberals throughout the century. At the same time, the liberal pursuit of community was circumscribed by a concern to preserve these principles in some form. Late nineteenth century liberals were constantly balancing often apparently contradictory commitments as they responded to changing social and political imperatives. The question is not whether the result was invariably logical or coherent – it was often neither – but how developments within liberal culture, broadly defined, were dictated by desire to find a rendering of liberalism that persuasively enhanced communitarian ends. The tensions generated by this juggling of political goods not only shaped discussions of such concepts as individual rights or the common good, but it also permeated debate around public policy.

This is an inquiry into how the philosophical idealists framed 'community' and the forms it subsequently took in liberal political culture. Idealism provides a useful and illuminating entry into this discussion. While the idealist treatment of community was one of many influences upon liberal discourse at the end of the century, it exerted a particularly potent authority. Built up around T. H. Green, F. H. Bradley, Edward Caird and a circle of earnest younger scholars, idealists challenged the bulwarks of mid century liberalism, not least individualism, utilitarianism, and the defence of a minimal state.[5] They argued powerfully for a moral state which would facilitate the development of character and enhance the common good. Idealism dominated Oxford philosophical discussion in the 1870s and 1880s, but much of its authority lay outside the University. As R. G. Collingwood recalled: 'The School of Green sent out into public life a stream of ex-pupils who carried with them the conviction that philosophy and in particular the philosophy they had learnt at Oxford was an important thing and their vocation was to put this into practice.'[6] Although it is difficult to trace precisely the circuitry fusing thought and practice, Liberals like H. H. Asquith, Alfred Milner, Charles Gore, Scott Holland, Herbert Samuel, and R. B. Haldane were all persuaded by idealism to varying degrees. Asquith, an undergraduate at Balliol College, Oxford – the centre of philosophical idealism – remembered the impact of the 'ardent Liberal' T. H. Green: 'For myself, though I owe more than I can say to Green's gymnastics, both intellectual and moral, I never "worshipped at the Temple's inner shrine".'[7] Haldane, on the other hand, combined his political vocation with more overt philosophical inquiry.[8] Idealism permeated political culture through the inter-locking progressive circles of the metropolis: 'The teaching of men like Thomas Hill

5.   Among those younger idealists were B. Bosanquet, R. B. Haldane, Henry Jones, J. S. Mackenzie, David George Ritchie, and William Wallace, See D. Boucher and A. Vincent, *A Radical Hegelian: Sir Henry Jones* (Cardiff, 1994); S. M. den Otter, *British Idealism and Social Explanation* (Oxford, 1996); P. J. Nicholson, *The Political Philosophy of the British Idealists* (Cambridge, 1990); M. Richter, *The Politics of Conscience* (1964); and A. Vincent and R. Plant, *Philosophy, Politics and Citizenship: The Life and Thought of the British Idealists* (Oxford, 1984).
6.   R. G. Collingwood, *An Autobiography* (Oxford, 1939), p. 16.
7.   H. H. Asquith, *Memories and Reflections* (2 vols., 1928), I, 19.
8.   Haldane described the impact of this idealist ethos on his own work: 'its essence led me to the belief in the possibility of finding rational principles underlying all forms of experience, and to a strong sense of the endeavour to find such principles as a first duty in every department in public life'. *An Autobiography* (1929), p. 374.

Green was penetrating deeply, and that turned on much more than *laissez-faire*. There was earnestness about State intervention to be seen everywhere.'[9]

While philosophical idealism did not dictate any particular political affiliation, most idealists supported the Liberal Party, and indeed were active in its more radical wing, until the end of the First World War when many turned to the Labour Party.[10] Bosanquet, for example, characterized himself as a strong or advanced Liberal, aligning himself with radical Liberals on such issues as support for Home Rule and trade unionism, and opposition to the South African War; but in his antagonism to old age pensions or other family welfare initiatives, he identified much more closely with the older guard within the party. In the company of Haldane, he turned to the Labour Party around 1919.[11] Liberalism will be used here to refer to the many shades of thought and practice within the Liberal Party and more broadly in late nineteenth century political culture, for late Victorian liberalism absorbed an eclectic range of commitments.

Many idealist positions were not new, but referred back to older, pre-utilitarian forms of political argument. The importance given to the collective good, an active state, citizenship and the repudiation of individualism which, in different ways, had characterised Whig rejoinders to utilitarianism resonated in new ways, via idealism, in the late nineteenth century liberal pursuit of community.

1. The Individual and the Moral Community

The starting point for idealists was, in common with most late nineteenth century theorists, a form of social organicism. Reacting against the atomism of Bentham, Mill and Spencer – which they tended to represent in a rather overly stylised manner – the idealists looked back to Plato, and even more authoritatively, to Aristotle, and to the Hegelian discussion of *sittlichkeit*. Idealists like Green, Caird, Bosanquet, Wallace and others who produced commentaries on and translations of Greek and German philosophers were instrumental in transmitting the communitarian accounts of these authors to a wide audience particularly concerned to uncover such themes. According to idealist variants of social organicism, society itself conferred meaning on the individual. As Green argued, 'without society, no persons'.[12] Similarly the idealist political theorist and sometime Fabian D. G. Ritchie maintained that 'the individual apart from all relations of a community, is a negation'.[13] The individual was the creation of society; the individual, extracted from a larger community, 'is a mere abstraction – a logical ghost, a metaphysical spectre'.[14] Any political theory which imagines that the individual was unencumbered and autonomous failed to recognise that the individual 'implies in every fibre relations of community'.[15]

[9.] *Ibid.*, p. 229.

[10.] This is not to suggest that idealism did not have an impact on Conservatives; see E. H. H. Green, *The Crisis of Conservatism: Politics, Economics and the Ideology of the Conservative Party, 1880–1914* (1994), pp. 179–80; W. Cunningham, *Politics and Economics* (1885), Chapter 4.

[11.] See B. Bosanquet, 'Practice and Research', *Charity Organisation Review*, XLII (1917), 148; H. Bosanquet, *Bernard Bosanquet: A Short Account of his Life* (1924), pp. 97–8.

[12.] T. H. Green, *Prolegomena to Ethics* (Oxford, 1883), sect. 288.

[13.] D. G. Ritchie, *Principles of State Interference* (1891, 4th edn., 1902), p. 11.

[14.] *Ibid.* See also B. Bosanquet, 'Symposium: Do Finite Beings Possess a Substantive or an Adjectival Mode of Being?' *Proceedings of the Aristotelian Society*, XVIII (1917–1918), 479–506.

[15.] F. H. Bradley, *Ethical Studies* (1st edn., 1876), p. 155.

The idealists did not confine their case for the inescapably organic identity of individuals to an exploration of the human impulse to cohere in 'society'. Community, they argued, was also essential for 'the genesis of the moral self'.[16] Individuals seek a self-satisfaction which is only found in a common good and which is attainable within society alone. Rather than highlighting the need to protect the individual from the incursions of an interventionist state or from the stultifying pressures of social conformity, idealists regarded society as indispensable to the development of character. Consequently, Bosanquet criticized Mill's idea of individuality, and in particular his distinction between other-regarding and self-regarding acts, on the grounds that it was neither possible, nor desirable, 'to treat the central life of the individual as something to be carefully fenced round against the impact of social forces'.[17] Social forces provide the ethical frame for the construction of a common good.

Although idealism stressed the individual's ties to the community, it saw no contradiction in simultaneously endorsing the value of autonomous character. The sanctity of the individual was defended by late nineteenth century liberals who employed communitarian arguments, but there were considerable differences in interpretation. Indeed, difficulties in describing the proper spheres of the individual and society underwrote the general endorsement of social organicism. Bosanquet's account of the individual and contemporary reactions to it reveal some of the peculiarities generated by the desire to strike this balance, for Bosanquet advanced the strongest account of the organic nature of society. Rather than beginning with the premise of 'the natural separateness' of individuals which he read in earlier liberals, he maintained that individuals in a society form a common self which expresses a will that is different than the will of its individual members. This collective self has a personality; it has its own will and its own duties and responsibilities. To some, this account seemed to endanger such liberal orthodoxies as the uniqueness of the individual and the capacity for self-determination. A fellow idealist, Henry Jones, believed that Bosanquet had pressed the organic analogy much too far – little was left of the independence of individuals.[18] Similarly, A. D. Lindsay maintained that the differences between society and person were much more critical than the similarities which Bosanquet traced.[19] By 1914, Bosanquet's account had attracted widespread censure.

Bosanquet regarded society as possessing real personhood and in consequence placed great weight on community. Nevertheless, the self-standing, self-actualizing individual occupied an important position in Bosanquet's world. For much of his life, Bosanquet was closely affiliated with the Charity Organization Society and in that capacity advanced its creed of personal independence and self-reliance in a most

[16.] S. Alexander, review of B. Bosanquet, *Psychology of the Moral Self, International Journal of Ethics*, VIII, (1898), 254; See H. Jones, *Working Faith of the Social Reformer*, (1910), p. 114.

[17.] B. Bosanquet, *Philosophical Theory of the State* (1899; 4th edn., 1930), p. 56.

[18.] See H. Jones to Miss E. M. Mahler, Mar. 1913, in *The Life and Letters of Sir Henry Jones* (1924), 235. See A. Seth Pringle-Pattison, *Hegelianism and Personality* (Edinburgh, 1887) for an earlier criticism of T. H. Green's description of the individual.

[19.] A. D. Lindsay, 'Symposium: Bosanquet's Theory of the General Will', *Proceedings of the Aristotelian Society*, supp. VIII (1928), 37.

practical fashion.[20] His support for the C.O.S. ideal of the self-maintaining character was not, he argued, at odds with his philosophical conviction that the individual was thoroughly formed and shaped by society. In fact, he regarded the C.O.S. as 'to a large extent an attempt to apply the philosophy of T. H. Green to current problems'.[21] 'My own position', Bosanquet averred, 'is not one which any careful thinker could call Individualist.'[22] He saw the individual as deeply embedded in a network of institutions, associations and communities and yet called to act autonomously, rationally and independently. This was akin to the view of the citizen which Gladstone so strikingly expounded in the Midlothian campaigns. Bosanquet's concomitant endorsement of the C.O.S. vision of individual character and his influential reading of social organicism accentuated more widely held tensions underlying late Victorian 'individualism'. While Bosanquet was opposed to many of those measures of state intervention which progressive liberals advocated, such as old age pensions, an emphasis on the importance of individual character did not necessarily entail opposition to state intervention. In fact, those, like L. T. Hobhouse and G. D. H. Cole, who raised alarms about Bosanquet's abandonment of individual will and personality were persuasive proponents of increased state intervention. It should also be stressed that even those who most vehemently opposed Bosanquet's rendering found the task of balancing individual and collective goods troublesome and difficult. While the New Liberal theorist Hobhouse maintained that society moved towards a state of greater and greater integration, characterized by increased harmony and co-operation, he consistently maintained that this movement did not compromise the distinctness of individuals caught up in the evolutionary process; he energetically attacked any diminution of the individual. Anxious that society was 'liable to yield to the crude instincts of naked self-assertion which it scarcely covers and with difficulty holds in', Hobhouse none the less worried that too strong a assertion of the collective, like Bosanquet's, would overwhelm the individual.[23]

The difficulties of balancing individual and communal interests which followed from attempts to make community central was also highlighted in the contemporary debate about rights. The idealists challenged the language of individual natural rights, for as Caird stated: 'The rights of the individual are exactly those which society gives him, no more and no less'.[24] Ritchie, who made an extensive study of natural rights doctrines, agreed that the individual has rights only as a member of a society, for 'all rights – legal, moral or metaphorical – rest upon membership of a society'.[25] In addition to emphasizing that all rights are conferred by social membership and therefore cannot be regarded as 'natural', the idealists shifted emphasis from rights to duties. Accordingly, Jones argued that rights ought to be considered essential to a liberal

[20.] *Nineteenth Annual Report of the Charity Organization Society* (1906). Bosanquet joined the Chelsea branch of the C.O.S. in 1881. In 1890 he became a member of the Administrative Council; he acted as chairman of the Council in 1896, 1897, 1916 and as vice-chairman from 1901–1915.

[21.] B. and H. Bosanquet, 'Charity Organisation: A Reply', *Contemporary Review*, LXXI (1897), 112–13.

[22.] B. Bosanquet, 'Aspects of the Social Problem: A Reply', *International Journal of Ethics*, VII (1897), 227.

[23.] L. T. Hobhouse, *The World in Conflict* (1915), p. 28.

[24.] E. Caird, *The Moral Function of the State* (1887), p. 9.

[25.] D. G. Ritchie, 'Discussion: The Rights of Animals', *International Journal of Ethics* X (1900), 388.

society, but only if they coincided with the duty to serve the wider good of society.[26] This approach was not peculiar to the idealists. Gladstone spoke of the duties of land ownership, rather than the rights to land. Morley attacked Chamberlain's use of natural rights language in the Radical Programme, regarding Chamberlain's invocation of Natural Rights with 'as much surprise and dismay as if I were this afternoon to meet a Deinotherium shambling down Parliament Street'.[27] The idealist discussion of rights was not restricted to a critique of natural rights theories on the grounds that they were inescapably atomistic – idealists argued further for a transformation in our understanding of right as entitlement. Rights rather ought to be regarded as conferring the power to contribute to the good of community.[28] So here too community is regarded as thoroughly moral. Membership in community confers rights which are powers enabling one to act morally by contributing to a common good. This interpretation of rights as duties enabled idealists to counter the potentially divisive force of a defence of individual rights, for it emphasized a collective good rather than individual goods which might be conflictual.

None the less, liberal critics of the idealists cautioned that the emphasis on community ought not to lead to an abandonment of individual rights, however their divisive properties. As the keepers of British liberal traditions, both Hobson and Hobhouse criticized what they perceived to be an idealist dismissal of rights.[29] Ritchie's sociological treatment of rights led Hobson to regret his 'abandonment of the individual' and to warn that 'a certain conspiracy has arisen to lay exclusive stress on duties, and to shove "rights" in the background, or even to ignore their claims altogether'.[30] On the other hand, Hobson himself incorporated communitarian perspectives in his own account of rights which caused him to pay much more attention to rights held by society than individual rights. In fact, he faulted Bosanquet, not for disregarding individual rights, but in some cases for emphasizing them too much and accordingly, for having too meagre a commitment to social rights. Employing a principle which was axiomatic in idealist and New Liberal circles that property was required for self-realization or the development of character, Hobson argued that Bosanquet erred in restricting the merits of property ownership to the individual. Rather, 'society also needs to realize herself by means of her property'. Social property would raise money for municipal improvements, or for old age pensions and so seek to build up 'a growing commonality which shall correspond with, and react upon, the rising individuality of its constituent members'.[31] Hobson used the idealist communitarian reading of rights and the principle of self-realization to justify limited land nationalization. Unlike Green, Bosanquet and Caird who were reluctant to call for dramatic intervention in the distribution of wealth, Ritchie, like

[26.] Jones, *The Working Faith of the Social Reformer*, p. 114.

[27.] J. Morley cited in C. A. Hamer, *Morley* (Oxford, 1968), p. 155.

[28.] See T. H. Green, *Lectures on the Principles of Political Obligation* in *The Works of T. H. Green*, ed. R. L. Nettleship (2nd edn., 3 vols., Oxford, 1890), II, sect. 47, 99, 211–232.

[29.] J. A. Hobson, *The Social Problem* (1901), p. 94; *idem*, 'Rights of Property', *Free Review* I (1893), 130–49; M. Freeden, 'Hobson's Evolving Conceptions of Human Nature', *Reappraising Hobson*, ed., M. Freeden (1900), pp. 62–3.

[30.] Hobson, *The Social Problem*, pp. 4, 91.

[31.] *Ibid.*, p. 152.

Hobson, extended his communitarian position to endorse a radical redistribution of land.[32]

In describing the individual as deeply embedded in community, owing personality, moral development, and the possession of rights to society, idealists advanced a potent communitarian vision. But even as they pushed liberalism into new places, they recalled older discussions about similar dilemmas. The idealist notion that through community the individual reaches self-realization looks back to the idea that character is forged through a consideration of a collective good, and that every individual has a distinct and different role to play in the creation of this public interest, which late eighteenth century Whigs had expounded.[33] Although the idealists gave a distinctive metaphysical expression to the idea that individuals are formed by society, they were also enlivening and strengthening earlier liberal attempts to balance freedom of the individual with a consideration of the common good. Their treatment of the cultivation of character is reminiscent of Mill's view of the virtues of active citizenship, though the idealists argued much less ambiguously that character is built through community. But tracing the continuities between earlier shades of communitarian argument ought not obscure what was distinctive about late nineteenth-century interest in community or how particular issues shaped this interest. Debate in the 1880s and early 1890s about the causes of urban poverty, for example, highlighted with especial clarity the importance of adjudicating the relative responsibilities of the individual, the community and the state.

2. Re-casting Utilitarianism

Central to the re-casting of liberalism at the end of the century was a re-interpretation of Benthamite utilitarianism. By the 1880s, many social theorists had become sceptical of a classical or early nineteenth-century utilitarian account of the balance between individual and social interest. Liberal critics as diverse as Bosanquet and Hobhouse questioned its atomistic premises, which were encapsulated in the view of society as the sum or aggregate of its parts, and in the interpretation of public interest as the sum of many private interests. Secondly, they were sceptical of utilitarian assurances that the individual self-interest which motivated all action would ultimately coincide with a collective good. Herbert Spencer had re-stated this assurance in evolutionary terms when he maintained that, as societies evolved, individuals would no longer be motivated by private interest. Rather 'just that kind of individuality will be acquired which finds in the most highly organised community the fittest sphere of its manifestation . . . the ultimate man will be one whose private requirements coincide with public ones'.[34] But other late nineteenth-century figures increasingly abandoned individual interest as the starting point for a discussion of the public good. Impressed by the fragility of the social tissue, Ritchie warned that a utilitarian account which hoped that private interest would accumulate into public interest threatened to

---

32. See D. G. Ritchie, *Darwin and Hegel*, (1893), p. 192.

33. See J. W. Burrow, *Whigs and Liberals* (Oxford, 1988), p. 119. On the continuity of Whiggism, see also B. Fontana, *Rethinking the Politics of Commercial Society* (Cambridge, 1985); S. Collini, D. Winch and J. W. Burrow, *That Noble Science of Politics* (Cambridge, 1983), pp. 110–26; and P. Mandler, *Aristocratic Government in the Age of Reform* (Oxford, 1990).

34. H. Spencer, *Social Statics* (1851), p. 483.

degenerate into a 'chaos of conflicting individual impulses, instincts, desires and interests'.[35] The idealists desired to knot private good more firmly into the common good. Green for one tended to describe the private and collective good as one and the same, a non-conflictual and non-competitive goal. Some stressed the importance of educating individuals into a greater sense of the collective;[36] others argued that by evolutionary processes, societies were ineluctably moving in that direction. The concern to balance individual and public interest was of course a much older pre-occupation; however, by the end of the nineteenth century liberal theorists had more clearly enumerated what was entailed by public interest and were more concerned to defend it. Thirdly, late nineteenth-century figures questioned whether happiness rather than embetterment ought to be the chief end of individual and collective action. As Herbert Samuel enjoined: 'Now a day we have gone back from Bentham to Aristotle & say that the State exists to promote the best life of its members rather than their happiness, if by "happiness" we mean their pleasure as judged at that moment by themselves.'[37] The idealists had with particular energy attacked those hedonistic assumptions about the individual which underlay earlier utilitarianism. Green waged a campaign against hedonist psychology in favour of a more transcendental measure of good than pleasure.[38] But it must be noted that the idealists were reacting against tired stalking horses, for by the 1870s and 1880s, the utilitarianism which had provoked Green's critical energies had been moderated. Such writers as W. K. Clifford, Leslie Stephen and G. H. Lewes had re-placed the pursuit of pleasure with a pursuit of the well being of society and, with reference to J. S. Mill, were evolving a less simplistic account of public interest.

Rather than abandoning utilitarian argument, idealist critics commonly re-cast utilitarianism to fit a more communitarian mould. 'The premature abandonment of the utilitarian setting by many thinkers, through pique arising from the narrow and degrading interpretation', Hobson noted, 'has not been justified'. He observed that even those 'like the late Professor Green, who are stoutest in repudiating Utilitarianism, invariably return to that terminology to express their final judgement on a concrete moral issue'.[39] This was certainly true of Ritchie who devoted considerable energy to updating utilitarianism in keeping with contemporary social evolutionary accounts. Utility, he maintained, ought to be measured in reference to a common good. This common good was not a fixed but a relative standard. Societies esteem particular values because these values facilitate evolution towards a moral society which leads its citizens to develop to their highest potential. This was a utilitarianism fused on to an idealist notion of self-realization. Ritchie concluded: 'The doctrine of Natural Selection applied to society has given a new force and a new meaning to the Utilitarian theory while correcting its errors and its narrowness.'[40] But this notion of utility

---

35.   D. G. Ritchie, *Natural Rights* (1895), p. 87.
36.   Hobson defended the need to 'educate the social nature of the individual as to lead him to identify himself more closely with the welfare of others'. *The Social Problem*, p. 173.
37.   Freeden (ed.), *Minutes of the Rainbow Circle*, p. 88, 1 May 1901.
38.   T. H. Green, 'Popular Philosophy in its Relation to Life', in *The Works of T. H. Green*, III, 97–125; *Prolegomena to Ethics*, ed. A. C. Bradley 1st edn., Oxford, 1890), Book IV, sub section III and IV.
39.   Hobson, *The Social Problem*, pp. 4, 5.
40.   Ritchie, *Principles of State Interference*, 108. See also D. G. Ritchie, *Philosophical Studies* (1905), p. 116.

reflected, not only a reforming energy, but an abiding concern to augment social coherence.

The durability of the language of utility ought not to surprise us. Utilitarianism had been such a formidable vehicle for political change throughout the century and late nineteenth-century writers were anxious to harness this critical force. The target of their criticisms was not so much the vested interests which earlier utilitarians had assaulted but those threats to social cohesion which a rampant individualism posed. In so doing, idealists drew out communitarian sentiments which earlier proponents of utilitarianism had not so clearly defined. Community had become a desirable political good and was no longer regarded as inimical to progress.

3. *The General Will*

The late nineteenth-century desire to anchor the bonds of sentiment which connect individuals in a community was also expressed in a revival of appeals to a general will. Given its troubled history and its potentially intricate theory, the general will was an unlikely fashion. Yet it was very much in the air in the 1890s. This more popular engagement took several forms: social psychologists like Graham Wallas, Gustav Le Bon and others argued for the reality of a group or collective mind, whereas progressive politicians and liberal theorists discussed ' "the general will" as a spiritual reality, organic in character and operative through the State as through other organs of cooperation'.[41] The 1890s saw a revival in interest in Rousseau's account of the general will, prompting H. S. Maine to lament the 'new Rousseauism . . . which made every form of government, except Democracy, illegitimate'.[42] From a different vantage point, T. H. Huxley complained of Rousseau's 'vicious method of *a priori* political speculation' which was 'not only in full vigour but . . . is exerting an influence upon the political action of our contemporaries which is extremely dangerous'.[43] The first new English translation of *The Social Contract* (1895) published in almost 100 years rapidly ran to four editions.[44]

The revival of interest in Rousseau and the general will more broadly owed much to the idealists' retrieval of community. While the idealists found much of interest in Rousseau – primarily his treatment of the general will as a thoughtful explanation of the close bonds that tied individual to individual[45] – they also expressed the objections which Rousseau drew more generally from his late nineteenth-century audience. They were critical of aspects of Rousseau's use of the general will: they disagreed with his insistence that only small immediate communities could articulate a general will; that the general will could not be expressed in representative assemblies; and that the legislator could personify the general will.[46] To the idealists, Rousseau had ultimately failed to safeguard community against the demands of individualism.

[41.]   J. A. Hobson, *Confessions of an Economic Heretic* (1938), p. 54.

[42.]   H. S. Maine, *Popular Government* (1895), pp. vii, 75. When John Morley published his account of Rousseau in 1873 he scathingly reviewed Rousseau's treatment of the will: *Rousseau* (1873).

[43.]   T. H. Huxley, 'Natural Rights and Political Rights', *Collected Essays* (9 vols., 1890), I, 338.

[44.]   See H. J. Tozer, *Rousseau's Social Contract* (1895; 4th edn., 1905).

[45.]   T. H. Green regarded 'the element of permanent value in Rousseau' to be 'his conception of the state as representing the "general will" '. *Lectures on the Principles of Political Obligation*, sect. 78.

[46.]   See Bosanquet, *Philosophical Theory of the State*, Chapter 5.

This was because he was inclined 'to treat the social bond in all its forms as something secondary and artificial' and had maintained 'the natural independence of the individual in site of the social union'.[47]

The idealists tended, as did other late Victorian commentators, to regard the general will as lodged in representative governments. In this vein, Ritchie argued that general will was nothing more than the 'ultimate force of public opinion' which holds governments accountable.[48] Similarly, Hobson demanded that governments ought to maintain close contact with its citizens so that its policies might legitimately be described as 'substantially correct interpretations of the general will'.[49] In keeping with the moral force of much of idealist argument, the general will as expressed in representative government was regarded as an ennobling, virtuous test of political conduct. The general will was 'a community of ethical aims with each other'.[50] This notion of a general will sprang from a deeply organicist reading of the relationship between the individual and society. It was predicated on the view that society is much more than the sum of its parts and that its wholeness was a new product. Other liberals echoed the idealists in describing the general will as a moral force, 'urging individuals to the fulfillment of a purpose which is but slightly theirs' which embodies 'some wider purpose of the still larger organic whole'.[51] This language parallels Whig beliefs that political representation forged a balance of interests.

While the general will was invoked to extol the merits of parliamentary reforms and often of an extension of the franchise, it was clear that by the general will the idealists did not mean the wishes of an aggregate but rather a collective interest. Not surprisingly then while it was almost a commonplace to identify the formation of 'a collective will of the community' as essential to the maintenance of democratic society,[52] this did not lead inevitably to a defence of universal suffrage. Opposition to women's suffrage, for example, continued even as progressive liberals invoked the principle of representative government expressing a general will.[53] When Herbert Samuel distilled the essence of late Victorian Liberalism, he represented those Liberals who believed that 'fitness in a class is an absolute condition of enfranchisement; and lacking that fitness, the English woman can no more establish a natural claim to the franchise than the English child or the Indian man'.[54] The movement towards the woman's vote must be gradual; it must await an expansion in women's activities and participation in public affairs. Opinion was of course divided among Liberal ranks, but Samuel was himself opposed to unrestricted female suffrage – though not to women's election to the Commons – until after the First World War.[55]

[47.] E. Caird, *Essays on Literature and Philosophy* 2 vols., (Glasgow, 1892), I, 124, 128.

[48.] D. G. Ritchie, 'On the Conception of Sovereignty' in *Darwin and Hegel* (1893), p. 254.

[49.] J. A. Hobson, *Work and Wealth* (1914), p. 359.

[50.] H. W. Hetherington, review of Hobhouse, *The Metaphysical Theory of the State, Hibbert Journal*, XVII (1918–19), 330.

[51.] Hobson, *Work and Wealth*, p. 352.

[52.] J. Bryce, *The Hindrances to Good Citizenship*, (New Haven, Conn., 1909), p. 6.

[53.] See Hansard, *Parl. Debs.*, 4th ser. III, 1506–13, H. H. Asquith, 27 April 1892.

[54.] H. Samuel, *Liberalism* (1902), p. 251.

[55.] See Minutes of Samuel's paper on the Democratic Franchise, 7 Oct. 1896 in Freeden, (ed.), *Minutes of the Rainbow Circle*, p. 39; see B. Wasserstein, *Herbert Samuel: A Political Life* (Oxford: 1992), p. 232.

Late nineteenth-century references to a general will did more than update older Whig notions of representation. For the idealists, the general will was not contained only in the political process but in a plethora of social institutions. Idealists believed that the general will was expressed in social institutions like the family, trade union or Church and, to varying degrees, in the state. If the state could claim a special status to embody the general will as some like Bosanquet claimed it did, this was because, compared to these institutions with partial membership, the state could encapsulate the whole of society. Caird opined that the 'state, however some of its organs may become inefficient, is always in the last resort, the outward expression of the national spirit'.[56]

Once again it was Bosanquet's treatment of the general will which solidified concern about the authoritarian implications of associating the state so closely with the general will. While it was clear that Green could not countenance the subordination of individual to a general will, Bosanquet's position seemed rather more murky. Criticism of Bosanquet's treatment of the general will in *Philosophical Theory of the State* grew dramatically, for Hobhouse saw it as extolling 'that Hegelian exaltation of the state . . . deeply interwoven with the most sinister developments in the history of Europe'.[57] Critics challenged Bosanquet's identification of the real will with the state on the grounds that such an identification robbed the individual of independence from the state, that it regarded the nation state and not an international federation as the ultimate expression of a general will and that it sanctioned a dangerous acquiescence to state initiatives.[58]

But to insist that the idealist appeal to a general will was a design to increase state power misinterprets their more central concern to entrench connection among individuals. The general will was not only contained in the state but in institutions and associations more generally. This was in fact a prevalent form of communitarianism, expressed, for example, in Gladstone's view of the importance of the many religious, professional, philanthropic, and educational associations, trade unions and friendly societies.[59] But in suggesting that the state, as the largest and most comprehensive of all these associations most fully articulated a general will, the idealists raised concerns that the distinction between society and the state which was so vitally important to the preservation of liberty might become blurred. Hobhouse, for example, insisted that the state was not community.[60] He was reluctant to use the term 'general will' at all, because of its associations with despotic rule, and referred instead to a social mind or will which was not necessarily shared by everyone in a political community.[61] While the general will had some utility for those seeking alternatives to an atomistic

[56.] Caird, *The Moral Function of the State*, p. 10.

[57.] L. T. Hobhouse, *The Metaphysical Theory of the State* (1918), p. 23. For a discussion of Hobhouse's critique see S. Collini, 'Hobhouse, Bosanquet and the State', *Past and Present*, No. 72 (1976), 86–90; M. Freeden, *Liberalism Divided* (Oxford, 1986), pp. 33–9.

[58.] See Hobhouse, *The Metaphysical Theory of the State*, lecture 3; G. D. H. Cole, *Social Theory* (1920), pp. 92, 93, 116; J. A. Hobson, 'The Morality of Nations', *Crisis of Liberalism* (1909), p. 250; C. Deslisle Burns, B. Russell and G. D. H. Cole, 'Symposium: The Nature of the State in View of its External Relations', *Proceedings of the Aristotelian Society*, XVI (1915–16), 290–325.

[59.] See *The Diaries of W. E. Gladstone*, ed. H. C. G. Matthew, (14 vols., Oxford, 1968–94).

[60.] L. T. Hobhouse, *Social Development* (1966), p. 50.

[61.] L. T. Hobhouse, *Social Evolution and Political Theory* (New York, 1911), pp. 97–8.

view of society, late nineteenth century liberal idealists recognized how the idea of a general will could be interpreted in opposition to elements of a liberal creed. References to a general will were much more rhetorical than substantive: the general will appealed to an inclusive national community in which difference could be minimized. Moreover it supported a moral reading of the state in which the state could be regarded as not only representing but also enhancing those intimations of virtue in its citizens. The general will enlivened the conception of a moral state which was so critical to late nineteenth century liberals.

4. *The Moral State*

When Herbert Samuel defined Liberalism, he highlighted the moral state as its central commitment: 'That it is the duty of the State to secure to all its members, and all others whom it can influence, the fullest possible opportunity to lead the best life'.[62] All Liberal policy, ranging from social reform, franchise extension, freedom of trade, religious equality, and international peace, he argued, stemmed from this principle, for 'the trunk of the tree of Liberalism is rooted in the soil of ethics'.[63] The conviction that the state was dictated by a moral mandate contributed to the increasing call for social reforms, initiated by the state. Protection of the energy and self-reliance of the individual, however, remained paramount.

Again, the idealists gave philosophical form to the notion of a moral state which was so pervasive in late nineteenth-century liberalism. Rather than regarding the state primarily as a neutral instrument for the preservation of order as was the inclination of many earlier liberals, the idealists, to varying degrees, argued for a much more ardent and vigorous conception of the state. Green's authority with a generation of young politicians and civil servants lay particularly in his conviction that the state, and other civic institutions ought to provide a context for the development of individuals and community. Recalling the Kantian principle that moral acts must be willed rather than compelled, Green explained that the state could nourish morality by enabling individuals to contribute to the better well-being of all.[64] Green, however, was cautious in extolling the virtues of an interventionist state. State action which 'would interfere with the growth of self-reliance, with the formation of a manly conscience and sense of moral dignity – in short, with the moral autonomy which is the condition of highest goodness' was not desirable.[65] If the 'real function of government . . . [is] to maintain conditions of life in which morality shall be possible', a strongly paternalistic state would be counter-productive, for it would limit the space for unselfish, disinterested action. While the state ought not to force its citizens to act in a moral manner – defined again by acting towards a common good – the state ought to remove obstacles to moral action. As Green himself realized, this could entail measures which at first glance seemed unduly authoritarian, notably compulsory education and restrictions of the freedom of contract in health, housing, and property.[66]

62. Samuel, *Liberalism*, p. 4.
63. *Ibid.*, p. 6.
64. See Green, *Principles of Political Obligation*, sects. 7–9.
65. *Ibid.*, sect. 17.
66. See *Ibid.*, sect. 207–210.

In his maiden speech to the Commons, A. H. D. Acland, who had been taught by Green, defended government initiatives in adult education by invoking this principle:[67]

> We can open up to them [the poor] many opportunities now denied to them, and that we are engaged in doing, or are hoping to do, in various ways. We can free their paths from many obstacles that now stand in their way; but after all, the intelligence of the people, who, when the obstacles are removed will make use of the opportunities afforded them is the vital matter.

The idealists also argued that the customary discomfort with which earlier liberals had greeted interventionist legislation rested on a misguided belief that state intervention invariably meant impoverishing the liberty of the individual. It was on this point in particular that the idealists had much to contribute to renewing liberalism. Regarding the individual as framed and nurtured by virtue of their membership in a community, governed by a state which sought to increase opportunities for moral action, led the idealists to dispute the familiar antithesis between the individual and the state. While Herbert Spencer viewed the free play of individual liberty as the mark of a progressive nation, Green argued that social progress is measured by the increased development of its citizen's contribution to social good, 'in short, by the greater power of the citizens as a body to make the most and best of themselves'.[68] Ritchie's attack on Herbert Spencer's laissez faire orthodoxies was especially influential for such figures as Sidney Webb who used Ritchie's critique to build a defence of an interventionist state. The idealist theory of the moral state offered a new basis for political obligation. By defining the state as a moral entity and by casting citizenship as a moral endeavour, the idealists diminished the legalistic, retributive character of the state. Instead they emphasized its positive face, while at the same time reminding their audience of the duties of moral citizenship.

The Liberal Party of course reflected many different levels of commitment to social reform. Gladstone in the 1880s was reluctant to see any dramatic increase in state intervention, noting that it was 'dangerous in principle' to make 'the State minister to the poor of London at the expense of the nation'.[69] John Morley too spoke plainly against such measures as the eight hour work day because it threatened to 'weaken[ing] the springs of responsible action'.[70] While those younger Liberals, like Sir Edward Grey, A. H. D. Acland, Asquith and Haldane who felt impatient with Gladstone's disinterest in the new ideas of social reform also maintained the importance of preserving individual self-reliance, they did not tend to regard increased state activity as inimical to this virtue. As Asquith explained in 1892: 'I am one of those who believe that the collective action of the community may and ought to be employed positively as well as negatively; to raise as well as to level; to equalize opportunities no less than to curtail privileges; to make the freedom of the individual a reality and

---

[67.] Hansard, *Parliamentary Debates*, 3rd ser., CCCII, 1787, A. H. D. Acland, 2 March 1886. Acland also carried Green's concern about the drink issue before the Commons: *ibid.*, CCCXXXIV, 1470–1, 2 Apr. 1889.

[68.] Hobson, *Confessions of an Economic Heretic*, pp. 52–3.

[69.] Gladstone cited in Matthew (ed.), *Diaries of W. E. Gladstone*, X, p. XCV.

[70.] Hamer, *Morley*, pp. 158–9.

not a pretence'.[71] This is precisely where the idealists had much to contribute to
political debate. In their account of the positive state, individual independence was
balanced with interventions to lessen those divisions, such as deep poverty, which
were inimical to communal ideals.

5. *Nation and Empire*

Liberals had long regarded the advancement of national self-determination as their
special province; this undertaking was reflected in liberal support for continental
nationalist movements, in Gladstone's own peculiar understanding of nationhood,
and in support among Radical Liberals for Home Rule for Ireland. The attention to
community which cut through late nineteenth-century political culture shaped the
treatment of this central commitment. The idealists carried over the language of moral
union, with which they described society more generally, to define the nation. To
them the nation was a palpable point of connexion, charged with moral purpose. In
an address to Balliol undergraduates, many of whom subsequently held high office
in Parliament or in the civil service, Caird defined the nation as 'not a mere aggregate
of men, nor even an aggregate linked by natural ties and a common history; it is a
unity at once real and ideal, a spiritual body, whose principle of combination lies in
some common direction of activity'.[72] It was through the nation that individuals
were reminded of their links to each other, and of their duty to cultivate these
connections. More precisely, the nation provided the context for service; it enabled
individuals to contribute to a common good.[73] In keeping with the organic analogy
which characterized idealist discussion of society, Caird averred that the nation must
exercise its moral calling or run the risk of atrophy, of becoming 'feeble and unstrung'.
Belonging to a nation entailed the duty to dignified, manly conduct and to the
cultivation of those virtues which animated civic life. Idealist accounts of nation were
characterized by highly gendered injunctions to meet the 'demands of manhood' and
to cultivate vigorous citizenship.[74] England's illustrious past was also invoked as a
way of defining nationalism. Englishness and defence of liberty were one and the
same. Some late nineteenth-century liberals offered a new development on this familiar
elision. The long-standing conjunction between the English and liberalism was used
to endorse, not a minimal state, but an enlarged state which through its interventions
domestically secured greater liberty for its citizens. Thus, in a characteristically idealist
vein, Caird read English history as a narrative about how the English had balanced
collective action with the freedom of the individual.[75]

   Although most idealists, like many of their contemporaries, regarded the nation
as a form of moral community, their judgement on the role of the state in framing
this community was less predictable. By the time of the outbreak of hostilities between

---

71. Asquith, *Memories and Reflections*, I, 113.

72. E. Caird, 'The Nation as Ethical Ideal', *Lay Sermons* (Glasgow, 1907), p. 102; B. Bosanquet, 'The
Teaching of Patriotism', *Social and International Ideals* (1917), p. 3. See also J. Gibbins, 'Liberalism,
Nationalism and the English Idealists', *History of European Ideas*, XV (1992), 491–7.

73. E. Caird, 'On Queen Victoria's Jubilee', *Lay Sermons*, p. 80; Bosanquet, 'The Teaching of Patriotism',
p. 15.

74. See Caird, 'The Nation as an Ethical Ideal', p. 118; Bosanquet, 'Teaching of Patriotism', p. 13.

75. Caird, 'The Nation as Ethical Ideal', p. 110.

Germany and Britain, this had become a critical public issue. James Bryce expressed a widely held opinion when he blamed German militancy on German philosophers who had created a super state which trampled morality underfoot: 'it is this deadly theory which is at the bottom of the German aggression'.[76] The idealists strove to distance themselves from 'German' theories of the state. Expressing this attempt to detach Kant and Hegel from the escalating conflict, F. H. Bradley wrote to Haldane in October 1914: 'Tho' I have not, like you, a personal knowledge of Germany and the Germans, I find it impossible to believe that the present phase really represents the main substance of the German mind and heart, or that they can fail to see sooner or later that their own admirable virtues have been miserably misapplied.'[77] G. D. H. Cole, Harold Laski, Hobhouse and others pointed to Bosanquet's conjunction of the general will and the state as justification for their charge that idealist theories of the state nurtured German belligerence. Although most reviewers of the first edition of *The Philosophical Theory of the State* (1899) were positive, subsequent editions provoked sufficient criticism to move Bosanquet to clarify that he had had no intention of creating a super state.[78] Such a reading, Bosanquet insisted, resulted from blindness to community, from an unwillingness to see that 'the fascination attached to all that is "social" ' is not embodied in the legal and political form of the state.[79] None the less, even though Bosanquet stepped back from collapsing civil society into the state, he regarded the nation-state as the most complete and inclusive embodiment of the 'social'. While individuals might meet in communities or associations defined by the sectional interests of religion, profession or class, the nation state transcended these differences.[80]

The idealists were not so clear on the origin of the collective sympathy which the nation state embodied; the nation state did not create this unity; rather it expressed within national boundaries the much more deeply seated commonalities which bound individual to individual. The nation-state was a community of shared history, language and institutions, but it was also an imagined community which cut across regional, class, religious and sexual divisions. This is exemplified in the view of the station and duties of the individual which F. H. Bradley so influentially expressed in *Ethical Studies* (1876) and which idealists like Bosanquet and Jones expounded much later.[81]

76. J. Bryce in L. Creighton, W. R. Sorley, H. Rashdall, A. D. Lindsay and H. Oakeley, *The International Crisis: The Theory of the State* (1916), p. 2; see C. Deslisle Burns, B. Russell, and G. D. H. Cole, 'Symposium: The Nature of the State in View of its External Relations', *Proceedings of the Aristotelian Society*, XVI (1915–16), 290–325.

77. National Library of Scotland, Haldane MS., 5910, f. 284, Bradley to Haldane, 15 Oct. 1914. See J. H. Muirhead, *German Philosophy and the War* (Oxford, 1915) and 'Recent Criticisms of the Idealist Theory of the General Will', *Mind*, XXXIII (1924), 166–75, 233–41, 361–8.

78. See B. Bosanquet, 'How the Theory Stands in 1919', in *The Philosophical Theory of the State* (4th edn., 1930), pp. LIX–LXI. See P. Savigear, 'Philosophical Idealism and International Politics: Bosanquet, Trietschke and War', *British Journal of International Studies* I (1975), 48–59; P. J. Nicholson, *The Political Philosophy of the British Idealists* (Cambridge, 1990), pp. 221–9.

79. Bosanquet, *Philosophical Theory of the State*, p. XXXIII.

80. See R. M. MacIver, *Community: A Social Study* (1917, 4th edn., 1970), Appendix B. While sympathetic with the cooperative ideals of the Guild Socialists, the idealists disagreed with their view of the state as one of many institutions: J. S. Mackenzie, *Contemporary British Philosophy*, ed. J. H. Muirhead (1924), pp. 244–5; Bosanquet, *Social and International Ideals*, pp. 224–8, 242.

81. See H. Jones, *Idealism as a Practical Creed* (Glasgow, 1909), p. 123; B. Bosanquet, *Essays and Addresses* (1889), pp. 119–20; *The Philosophical Theory of the State*, pp. 191–2.

Rejecting the notion that classes could be in conflict, Bosanquet instead regarded class as the expression of the differences in rank, profession and 'function' upon which social unity was grounded.[82] 'In a well-organized community', Bosanquet wrote, 'people are satisfied'.[83] But idealist metaphysics did not necessarily dictate a seamless or harmonious view of social relations. Other idealists, notably Jones, Ritchie and Haldane, were much more mindful of the economic and sexual inequalities which cut across the national community. By 'class', Ritchie did not understand the functional view of 'station and its duties' but more fundamentally how industrial capitalism had brought with it a system of deep inequity. The idealist theme of 'identity in difference', which posited that difference was incorporated into a shared wholeness, admitted significant divisions and fractures.

None the less, the idealists most often understood 'community' as transcending difference, and numerous examples might be provided of their disinclination to imagine the common good marred by conflict.[84] They tended not to describe the shared identity which presided over this difference as the product of a contest between competing dispositions. The shared good and the common mind were most often regarded as more noble and indicative of moral character than the private considerations which were a necessary preserve of individuality. This hopeful account of social harmony sounded less and less persuasive to an early twentieth-century audience who were much less sanguine that difference could be so easily resolved into a shared identity.

Although the idealists translated their communitarian ideals into an organic, consensual view of the nation, they tended not to subscribe to contemporary endeavours towards an international community or a federation of nation states. While a sense of how the nation state coexisted with other nation states which collectively shared Christian principles – a 'community of Christendom' – was far more characteristic of late nineteenth-century liberals than was a narrow patriotism, the nation state for most idealists remained a more immediate, and much more organic union than an international federation.[85] A world state would promote active citizenship even less than those representative institutions of the modern state, on the grounds that individuals feel even more remote from the state.[86] Caird and Bosanquet was sceptical that an international community or federation of states could overcome the many differences which separated nations, regarding the nation state as the ultimate unity. In the absence of 'common sentiments' and 'common traditions', an international federation could not be a 'genuine community'.[87]

The Boer War proved to be the test of these more abstract deliberations about

---

[82.] Bosanquet, *Social and International Ideals*, pp. 224–8, 242.

[83.] B. Bosanquet, *Social and International Ideals*, 'Patriotism and the Perfect State', p. 145.

[84.] Bosanquet tended to describe society as essentially harmonious, for if 'all the groupings [within society] are organs of a single pervading life, we find it incredible that there should ultimately be irreconcilable opposition between them'. *The Philosophical Theory of the State*, p. 158.

[85.] Caird, 'The Nation as Ethical Ideal', 110. Ritchie, on the other hand, endorsed the prospect of an international federation: 'Another View of the South African War', *The Ethical World* 13 Jan. 1900, p. 20b.

[86.] See Green, *Principles of Political Obligation*, sect. 199.

[87.] B. Bosanquet, 'The Function of the State', *Social and International Ideals*, p. 292.

the nation-state and international politics. Most idealists were Radical Liberals; most were 'strong Home Rulers', and by implication, might be thought to be less ardent imperialists than the Tories, the Fabians or other elements of the Liberal Party.[88] But reactions to the Boer War broke down any easy distinctions; idealist ranks were very much divided on this issue. Bosanquet, Caird, Muirhead and Watson were strongly pro-Boer. In the company of John Morley, Lloyd George and New Liberals like Hobson and Hobhouse, they regarded Alfred Milner's conduct in South Africa as an illegitimate incursion into the national sovereignty of the Boer Republics, motivated by capitalist interests, thinly disguised as the protection of British settlers. Bosanquet more generally was critical of Britain's imperial designs: the British Empire could not be a true community because her colonies remained unequal partners; they were governed by laws framed by an 'external' power 'which leaves their national consciousness unfounded and unreconciled'.[89] In short, they possessed no general will and, therefore, were prevented from being genuine national communities. This reasoning also underwrote Bosanquet's long-standing commitment to Home Rule for Ireland. His sceptical view of imperialist ventures is particularly striking because he has been so often identified as the architect of a super-state. Yet other idealists came to much less sober and much less critical appraisals of the British imperial state.

Haldane, Mackenzie, Ritchie and Jones ranged themselves with Asquith, Rosebery and other Liberal Imperialists in supporting the war.[90] Ritchie was particularly outspoken, even jingoistic; in fact he regarded patriotism as an important social cement, 'a valuable moral discipline in a community'.[91] His denunciation of Hobson's unpatriotic case 'against his country' appealed to an array of evolutionary, idealist and patriotic arguments.[92] Regarding the Boers as an inferior step in the evolutionary ladder, he justified British intervention as protection from 'Boer prejudices or capitalist greed' (though he expressed little concern for native labourers or dismay at the conduct of English speculators).[93] In keeping with his view that social evolution could be facilitated by the guidance of an enlightened *élite*, he defended British intervention against those who argued for Boer self-determination.[94] Echoing Fabian directives, Ritchie invoked the expectation that the state had a moral function to defend Britain's imperial activities. 'The day for laissez-faire has gone by', Ritchie concluded, 'alike in domestic and Imperial politics'.[95] The new moral state which directed social reforms in Britain was the same moral state which ensured the development of its distant colonial subjects.

---

[88] Haldane, *An Autobiography*, p. 101; see B. Bosanquet, *Bernard Bosanquet and His Friends*, ed. R. Latta (1935), pp. 218, 309, 311.

[89] Bosanquet, 'The Function of the State', p. 294.

[90] See D. Boucher and A. Vincent, *A Radical Hegelian: Sir Henry Jones* (Cardiff, 1994), pp. 140–8, for an account of Jones' critical support for the war.

[91] R. Latta, 'Memoir', ed. R. Latta (1905), *Philosophical Studies*, p. 49. See D. G. Ritchie, 'Another View of the South African War', *Ethical World*, 13 Jan. 1900, pp. 19–20; 'The South African War', 3 Feb. 1900, pp. 70–1; letter, 17 Feb. 1900, pp. 110; letter, 3 Mar. 1900, pp. 19–20; 'Mr. Hobson's Book [*The War in South Africa*] and the Coming Settlement', 10 Mar. 1900, pp. 145–6; 'John Brown's Body', 29 Sept. 1900, p. 613.

[92] Ritchie, 'Mr. Hobson's Book and the Coming Settlement', p. 145a.

[93] D. G. Ritchie, 'Ethical Judgments as to the War', *Ethical World* 3 March 1900, p. 142b.

[94] Bodleian Library, Oxford, M. S. Bryce 143, f. 161–3, Ritchie to Bryce, 7 Feb. 1900.

[95] Ritchie, 'Mr. Hobson's Book and the Coming Settlement', p. 146b.

Looking back on the fading fortunes of the Liberal Party, Haldane reflected: 'We Liberals failed to realize in the beginning of 1906 that the spirit was rapidly changing, and that the outlook of Victorian Liberalism was not sufficient for the progressive movement which had set in early in the twentieth century . . . What was needed was a new and enlightened attitude towards social problems, and this in the main we failed to adopt.'[96] He recalled the profusion of ideas – Christian socialist, Fabian, and idealist – which were discussed in some Liberal circles: 'If these ideas had been more studied in the days of Campbell-Bannerman and before that, the fading away of the Liberal Party might, I think, have been averted'.[97] By this account, the waning of the Liberal Party could not be attributed to the absence of a philosophical grounding for progressive legislation. Idealism had entered main stream Liberalism, and with this influx, the individualistic premises of mid-nineteenth-century liberalism had met with a more communitarian understanding of society. But, for Haldane who was seeking to explain the decline of his party, this influx of ideas had not animated public policy as fully as it ought to have.

The profusion of what many late nineteenth-century commentators regarded as new ideas contained a substantial residue of much older arguments. The distinctive emphasis which the idealists gave to re-stating the utilitarian foundations of nineteenth-century liberalism and elucidating a moral theory of the state contained such stalwart themes as individual self-reliance. Apprehension about the disintegrating force of individualism co-existed with a concern to protect that self-reliance which was essential to a vibrant society. Idealist and New Liberal accounts of the general will recalled the Whig theme of representation of public interest as much as they justified a new participatory democracy.

The idealists brought to late nineteenth-century political culture a way of thinking about community. For some, this category enabled them to interpret the divisions in their society as part of a grander harmonious narrative in which disparate elements were drawn together into a coherent peaceable society. For others the attention to community did not overcome the great divisions which stood in the way of real community; community remained then an ideal to govern individual and public affairs. The rhetoric of community resonated with a generation which was peculiarly apprehensive about a perceived disintegration of communal values. Idealism furnished nineteenth-century liberal political culture with a philosophical grounding for its attachment to community. But this was always a partial communitarianism; it was articulated within a liberal framework. It recalled the earnestness of non-conformist liberal traditions; it revived the Whig theme of public interest; it re-animated the virtues of independence; it provided a basis for social welfare initiatives as partnerships between the state and other social institutions. By calling upon communitarian themes, liberal thinkers and political figures sought to balance some of the potentially incongruous commitments of late Victorian and Edwardian liberalism.

[96.] Haldane, *An Autobiography*, p. 228.
[97.] *Ibid.*, p. 123.

Franchise Reform, 'First Past the Post' and the Strange Case of Unionist Ireland

The Queen's University of Belfast

By 1922 James Henry Mussen Campbell,[1] first Baron Glenavy was chairman of the Irish Free State Senate.[2] Even for so blatant a careerist as Glenavy this move might be seen as constituting a bridge too far, particularly in terms of the high standard of the rewards his ambition had formerly brought him. A senior counsel by 1892, Unionist M.P. for the St Stephens Green division of Dublin in the late nineties, for Trinity College Dublin from 1903 to 1916, successively Solicitor General for Ireland, Irish Attorney General, Lord Chief Justice for Ireland and last Lord Chancellor of Ireland from 1918 to 1921, his was a perfect example of a blue-chip career in the last days of British rule in a united Ireland. His former colleague and fellow Unionist activist Edward Carson,[3] the carefully nurtured discovery of Arthur Balfour's Irish years, with a career no less glittering behind him, spent late 1921 denouncing the betrayal of the loyalists of Ireland in the Anglo-Irish Treaty of 1921.[4] He too had been a star of *fin de siècle* Dublin and London's legal firmaments; reluctant defender of the Marquess of Queensberry in his libel action against Carson's boyhood acquaintance Oscar Wilde, crown prosecutor, Solicitor General for Ireland, M.P. for Dublin University, Attorney General and member of the wartime cabinet. While Edward Carson, the Dubliner, ended his career as Lord Carson of Duncairn, Lord of Appeal in London, horrified by a political resolution to the so-called Irish question that he found particularly personally wounding, Glenavy, with a considerable degree of distaste, sat down with the resignation of a southern Irish Unionist and dealt with his sometime hereditary enemies.

[1.] (1851–1931); graduate of Trinity College, University of Dublin; barrister; Q.C., 1892; Unionist M.P. for St Stephen's Green division in Dublin, 1898–1900, and Dublin University, 1903–16; Solicitor-General for Ireland, 1901–05; Attorney-General, 1905, 1916; Lord Chief Justice of Ireland, 1916; Lord Chancellor of Ireland, 1918–21; baron 1921; chairman of Irish Free State Senate, 1922–28. See *D.N.B. 1931–40*, p. 141.

[2.] For an account of Glenavy's senate career see D. O'Sullivan, *The Irish Free State and its Senate* (Dublin, 1940). His son later became secretary of the Irish Department of Industry and Commerce.

[3.] Carson is heavily biographised in rather jarring late accretions to the high Victorian manner. See E. Marjoribanks and I. Colvin, *Life of Lord Carson* (3 vols., 1932–36); T. Montgomery Hyde, *Carson. The Life of Sir Edward Carson, Lord Carson of Duncairn* (1953). For more recent and historiographically current readings of Carson see G. Boyce, 'Edward Carson (1845–1935) and Irish Unionism', in *Worsted in the Game: Losers in Irish History*, ed., C. Brady (Dublin, 1989); A. Jackson, *Sir Edward Carson* (Dundalk, 1993); A. Gailey, 'King Carson: An Essay on the Invention of Leadership', *Irish Historical Studies*, XXX (1996).

[4.] 'I was only a puppet, and so was Ulster, and so was Ireland, in the political game that was to get the Conservative party into power', Hansard, *Lords Debs*, 5th ser., XLVIII, 38–53, 14 Dec. 1921.

Winston Churchill's often quoted lines about the reemergence of the dreary steeples of Fermanagh and Tyrone at the end of World War I accurately expressed an exasperated weariness with the messy leakage of Irish affairs into British politics after the war.[5] By 1921, however, it seemed that a new consensus between the upper echelons of the English parties meant that the issue of Ireland would never again constitute or usefully serve as the crucial ground of conflict between the parties.[6] Signed, sealed and delivered, Ireland was neatly handed back to the rulers of its two constituent parts, to make of it as they pleased. Neither the bloody civil war that followed on the treaty in the new Irish Free State, nor the messy allegations of pogroms and sectarianism in the new jurisdiction of Northern Ireland seriously intruded on the political consciousness of Whitehall or Westminster. The respective pleas by all interest groups to the bar of London opinion that had constituted one of the main fulcrums of nineteenth-century Irish political dealing was at an end, and all relevant parties were left with the less than edifying task of talking to themselves or to one another. Most chose the former option. To an extent, then, the meaning conveyed by Churchill's dreary steeples is all wrong. If he meant that the passions of the past remained emblazoned on the features of the present he was indeed correct. But, by any other standard of change, nowhere in the British Isles was transformed more dramatically in the final years of the long nineteenth century than the island of Ireland. And nobody, perhaps, experienced that change as acutely as the Unionists of Ireland. The slow erosion of the power of Anglo-Irish Ireland, that had begun with Catholic emancipation, had taken less than 100 years to leave Irish Unionists beached, with little more than the rump six counties of the nine county province of Ulster, a quasi-autonomous Belfast Parliament, and the charmless prospect of the options for service in 'the south' delineated by Lord Glenavy's tinny prize.

But the readaptations pointed up by the divergent choices made by Glenavy and Carson were foreshadowed and prefigured in the shaded variations in Unionist self-fashionings, largely determined by geography, in the years from 1886 onwards.[7] The coincidence of franchise reform with Parnellite electoral ascendancy in the mid-

5. W. S. Churchill, *The Aftermath, being a Sequel to the World Crisis* (1941): 'As the deluge subsides and the waters fall we see the dreary steeples of Fermanagh and Tyrone emerging once again. The integrity of their quarrel is one of the few institutions that have been unaltered in the cataclysm which has swept the world. That says a lot for the persistency with which Irishmen on the one side or the other are able to pursue their controversies. It says a great deal for the power which Ireland has, both Nationalist and Orange, to lay her hands upon the vital strings of British life and politics and to hold, dominate and convulse, year after year, generation after generation, the politics of this powerful country'.

6. For the line that Ireland would never again serve as the crucial ground of conflict between the parties see R. Fanning, 'Britain, Ireland and the End of the Union', in *Ireland after the Union*, ed. Lord Blake (Oxford, 1989), pp. 105–20.

7. There is a vast literature on Irish Unionism. For the standard historical works see P. Buckland, *Irish Unionism, 1. The Anglo-Irish and the New Ireland, 1885–1922* (Dublin and New York, 1972); *Irish Unionism, 2. Ulster Unionism and the Origins of Northern Ireland* (Dublin and New York, 1973); *Irish Unionism 1885–1923: A Documentary History* (Belfast, 1973). The most significant recent work on Ulster Unionism is by A. Jackson; see in particular *The Ulster Party, Irish Unionists in the House of Commons* (Oxford, 1989); and *Colonel Edward Saunderson* (Oxford, 1993). For a highly innovative interpretation that attempts to integrate 'the pre-partition debate' between nationalists and unionists see P. Bew, *Ideology and the Irish Question. Ulster Unionism and Irish Nationalism, 1912–1916* (Oxford, 1994).

1880's,[8] or rather their essential concommitance, effectively divided Unionist Ireland in 1886. The first-past-the-post electoral system ensured that the map of Ireland was solidly nationalist outside the province of Ulster, where the division of Nationalists to others was roughly even. Provided, of course, that there was no internal contest between Liberals and Conservatives, the pro-Union vote was maximised and solid in Ulster. This was paid for by the very high price of marginalising what had been Liberal Ulster and of recharting the choppy waters of Orangeism.[9] But, as Unionist pressure groups constantly emphasised, of those who voted outside Ulster a high percentage voted Unionist. These votes were however consigned to the bin of *Notes from Ireland*[10] or other Loyal and Patriotic Union maps, bulletins, propaganda sheets and statistics with which the Irish Unionists so relentlessly bombarded the English parties in these years. The first real fissure in *political* Irish Unionism – it had always been socially, intellectually, culturally and stylistically heterogeneous – was the desire of the geographically scattered Unionists of Connacht, Leinster and Munster to point this up. This was not at all desirable to the geographically concentrated Unionists of Ulster who preferred to ignore the so-called defects of a system that benefited them. So, with the exception of a couple of Dublin members,[11] the Irish Unionist Party became in effect the Ulster Party from 1886. There were however 144 members of the House of Lords who held lands and estates on both sides of the Irish Sea and of these 116 held their lands in the three southern provinces.[12] As Patrick Buckland has

---

8. The definitive work on the Irish franchise before 1885 is K. T. Hoppen's *Elections, Politics and Society in Ireland, 1832–1885* (Oxford 1985). For the franchise and redistribution settlements of 1884–85 see A. Jones, *The Politics of Reform, 1884* (Cambridge, 1972). On the implications of franchise reform see B. M. Walker, *Parliamentary Election Results in Ireland, 1801–1922* (Dublin, 1978).

9. For the marginalisation of Ulster Liberalism in the 1880's see P. Bew and F. Wright 'The Agrarian Opposition in Ulster Politics, 1848–1887', in *Irish Peasants: Violence and Political Unrest 1780–1914*, eds. S. Clarke and J. S. Donnelly (Manchester, 1983). For a recent study that downplays the role of leadership from above in the growth of Orangeism after 1801 see Jackson, *Ulster Party* and *Saunderson*.

10. *Notes From Ireland*, first published on 25 Sept. 1886, professed to be a regular bulletin of Irish affairs, a 'record of the sayings and doings of the Parnellite party in furtherance of the "Separatist policy" for Ireland; and of facts connected with the country, for the information of the imperial parliament, the press, and the public generally'.

11. Two seats were held for Trinity College Dublin, or Dublin University, as it was officially called. These were usually the preserve of lawyers: 'The legal members from Trinity College, Dublin, usually found their election to parliament a stepping stone to higher things and quite frequently a government in its desire to have an Irish Attorney General or Solicitor General in the House of Commons had thrust its candidate upon the only partially willing graduates. Of the twenty MP's elected for Trinity between the Act of Union and Lecky's election in 1895, no less than fifteen passed on to high judicial office and several of the others were barristers, although they did not practice. It can be seen, then, that for the ambitious Queen's Counsel the representation was a very considerable prize'. J. J. Auchmuty, *Lecky, a Biographical Essay* (1945), p. 89. The law officers at Dublin Castle and this legal establishment are fascinating. See V. T. H. Delany, *Christopher Pales, Lord Chief Baron of Her Majesty's Court of Exchequer in Ireland, 1874–1916* (Dublin, 1960) for an insight into the legal world of Ireland in those years. On the question of Dublin Unionist representation generally, in particular the controversial defeats of H. H. M. Campbell and Horace Plunkett in the divisions of St Stephen's Green and South County Dublin in 1900 see A. Jackson, 'The Failure of Unionism in Dublin, 1900', *Irish Historical Studies*, XXV (1989). Walter Long's intrigues in Dublin electoral politics are even more fascinating. See R. Murphy, 'Walter Long and the Conservative Party, 1905–21' (University of Bristol Ph.D., 1984).

12. A full list of these peers, detailing the location of their primary landed interests – Britain, Ulster or the three southern provinces of Ireland – and the ways in which their sympathies lay in 1886 and 1920 shows a strong correlation between geographical location and the adoption of a more favourable attitude towards some form of devolved government by 1920: Buckland, *Irish Unionism, 1*, Appendix B. Among the most politically forceful peers in those years were Abercorn, Ardilaun, Ashbourne, Belmore, Castletown, De Vesci, Dufferin and Ava, Dunraven, Lansdowne, Londonderry, Oranmore, Templetown and Waterford.

pointed out, 17 Irish Unionists sat for British constituencies in 1886, and most of these were not from Ulster.

In a historiographical endorsement of the judgement of posterity neither the rhetoric nor the discourse of the anti-Nationalist party on the ground in Ireland has received much critical attention. One of the reasons for this is the embarrassment that the disjunction between the classic anti-Home Rule[13] position as articulated by English political sympathisers and Unionist intellectuals and the less savoury utterances on the ground can provoke. At the parliamentary level the anti-Home Rule case was made in the language of inalienable historic right in relation to the existence of the United Kingdom, of Irish nationalism as extension of land greed and appropriation on historically dubious grounds.[14] Ironically the intellectual case for the separateness of Ireland had been most widely made by Irish Tories in the previous half century.[15]

13. The classic anti-Home Rule position evolved from a language of rights to a language of Ulster between 1886 and 1912. In the Home Rule debates of 1886 and 1893 Unionists focussed on the illegitimacy of the carving out of 'this arbitrarily selected area' from the United Kingdom, on the connexion between the land war and Parnellite ascendancy, on the absurdity of conceding to the peasantry the right to constitute themselves as the so-called Irish nation in opposition to the weight of property and intellect of loyal Ireland, on the financial havoc that Home Rule would bring, and on the case of Ulster. The unfittedness of the Irish for government was emphasised in the 1893 debates in the light of the 'Parnellism and Crime' findings and the Parnellite split. The argument for Empire was never particularly advanced by Irish Unionists but after 1886 it became a powerful binding-force between Chamberlain and his new allies. Anti-democratic arguments provided one ground of opposition. As Lecky wrote in *Democracy and Liberty*, defending the importance of the Trinity College seats: 'Nothing in the Irish representation is so manifestly wanted as a more adequate representation of loyalty and intelligence in three provinces. Loyal and well-educated men are to be found there in abundance; in nearly every form of industry, enterprise and philanthropy they take the foremost place; but they have no corresponding weight in the political representation, as they are usually swamped by an ignorant and influenced peasantry, . . . we are now told that, in computing the relative strength of parties in Ireland, the University representation must be subtracted "as it does not represent the nation". This dignity, it appears, belongs more truly to the illiterates – more than one in five professedly unable even to read the names upon the ballot papers (1892 election) – who in some remote western district, or in some decaying country town, are driven like sheep to the polling booth by agitators or priests'. Quoted in Auchmuty, *Lecky*, pp. 86–8. See too W. E. H. Lecky, 'Ireland in the Light of History' (1891) in *Historical and Other Political Essays* (edited by his wife Elizabeth Lecky after his death, 1910), pp. 62–81. The classic objections to Home Rule by 1912 are outlined in *Against Home Rule: The Case for Union*, ed. S. Rosenbaum (1912).

14. The Unionist position protested primarily at the acceptance of the notion of Irish nationality by Gladstone. Irish nationalism was, for those who saw themselves as loyal Irishmen, a construction that required repudiation. Franchise reform and the consequent creation of an apparently pro-Home Rule majority on the island, stimulated by 1886 and 1893, strained their arguments into a – from their point of view – undesirably anti-democratic shape. Hence from the late 1880's onwards there is an attempt to re-establish the United Kingdom as the base electoral unit. There is the alternative mirror argument of two nationalisms whereby 'Ulster' – with its internal unionist majority – becomes an essential unit. See W. F. Monypenny, *The Two Irish Nations: An Essay on Home Rule* (1913), p. 3, for an interesting perspective: 'Irish history is a constant tragedy, a tragedy on the deeper sense, not as the clash of right and wrong, but as the clash of two rights'.

15. See J. Hutchinson, *The Dynamics of Cultural Nationalism: The Gaelic Revival and the Creation of the Irish Nation State* (1987). On Irish Tory discontents see J. Spence, 'The Philosophy of Irish Toryism, 1833–52: A Study of Reactions to Liberal Reformism in Ireland in the Generation Between the First Reform Act and the Famine, with especial reference to Expressions of National Feeling among the Protestant Ascendancy', (University of London Ph.D., 1991). The intellectual history of early nineteenth century Ireland awaits its historian. See J. Sheehy, *The Rediscovery of Ireland's Past: The Celtic Revival 1830–1930*, (1980). The articulation of a Celticist awareness of Irishness from the publications of C. Brooke, *Reliques of Irish Poetry* (Dublin, 1789) onwards was linked to a self-articulation as Irish by sections of the so-called ascendancy class. This is particularly marked in circles around the Royal Irish Academy and the Irish Ordnance Survey, and has resonances in the works of Irish unionists like Samuel Ferguson. See R. Foster, *The Story of Ireland, An Inaugural Lecture Delivered Before the University of Oxford on 1 December, 1994* (Oxford, 1995).

The distrust of London that characterized this Ireland was at a high water mark in the years after Catholic emancipation.[16] Isaac Butt was not alone in travelling a circuitous route to a Home Rule position.[17] The land agitation and particularly Gladstone's Land Act of 1881 had concluded that particular trajectory.[18]

The less polite essence of the Unionist case after 1886 was that the nationalists of Ireland were ignorant, illiterate, duplicitous, murderous, unacquainted with the truth, prejudiced, illiberal and violent.[19] This contained some truth. But tolerance, liberality and fair play were scarcely the distinguishing characteristics of certain sections of the Unionists of Ireland.[20] This was to prove ultimately dangerous for the Unionist argument in the case of Ulster. Ironically the stereotype of Irish nationalism prepared so carefully in propaganda in the late nineteenth century was to engulf the self-representation of Ulster Unionism, particularly in the late twentieth century.[21]

The Irish Loyal and Patriotic Union was founded in May 1885, but did not announce its existence until 16 October 1885.[22] Its secretary, Edward Caulfield Houston,[23] worked tirelessly through the 1885 election to ensure that Unionists contested seats in the three provinces outside Ulster and to record the percentage of the vote that they received. Houston is one of the forgotten Unionist activists of these years, scarcely meriting a mention in accounts of the period. It appears that he was crucial in determining the tone and content of Irish Loyal and Patriotic Union publications. From the beginning the I.L.P.U. was widely supported, particularly by Unionist Dublin.[24] Its first public annual meeting was addressed by Lord

---

16. See the early years of the Home Government Association as representing the patriotic impulses of a section of the Anglo-Irish. Liberal reforms of the Irish Church and land further served to alienate sections of opinion. For Gladstone's Irish reforms see J. P. Parry, *Democracy and Religion: Gladstone and the Liberal Party, 1867–1875* (Cambridge, 1986).

17. D. Thornley, *Isaac Butt and Home Rule* (Dublin, 1964).

18. For the falling-away of support for liberalism in Ireland see M. O'Callaghan, *British High Politics and a Nationalist Ireland. Criminality, Land and the Law under Forster and Balfour* (Cork, 1994).

19. See T. H. Ford, *Albert Venn Dicey: The Man and his Times* (Chichester, 1985) for Dicey's role in disseminating pamphlets on Irish violence in association with a new edition of *The Law of the Constitution* in 1886. The only solution to Parnell's attempt to convert agrarian discontent into a political platform for Home Rule was 'to create a nation of peasant proprietors as the French had in Picardy'. See R. A. Cosgrove, 'The Relevance of Irish History: The Gladstone-Dicey Debate about Home Rule, 1886–87', *Eire Ireland*, XIII, no 4 (1978), p. 9. See Bew, *Ideology and the Irish Question*, pp. 52–3, on Dicey.

20. See Jackson, *The Ulster Party* on the notorious Rosslea incident. See too E. Saunderson, *Two Irelands: Loyalty Versus Treason* (London and Dublin, 1884).

21. There has been an intellectual renaissance in contemporary unionism since 1985, which seeks to counter this negative stereotype. New academic work on Ulster unionism seeks to analyse it in a sympathetic manner. See R. English and G. Walker, *Unionism in Modern Ireland: New Perspectives on Politics and Culture* (Basingstoke, 1996). See also James Ferris's forthcoming Cambridge Ph.D.

22. Buckland, *Irish Unionism*, 1, p. 2.

23. Edward Caulfield Houston. See W. D. Bowman, *The Story of 'The Times'* (1931) on Houston's involvement with the Pigott forgeries. See more importantly the official history, *The History of the Times: The Twentieth Century, 1884–1912* (1947) and H. Harrison's response, *Parnell, Joseph Chamberlain and 'The Times'* (Belfast and Dublin, n.d., probably 1947–48). The official history did subsequently amend the section on the 'Parnellism on Crime' episode, including the role of Houston, who Harrison refers to as *Ernest* Caulfield Houston. See too T. W. Moody, '*The Times* Versus Parnell and Co, 1887–90', in *Historical Studies: Papers Read Before the Irish Conference of Historians, VI, Dublin, June 1965* (1968), pp. 147–79.

24. Support fluctuated and meetings tended to be better attended in times of crisis. See the report by executive committee of work done in 1885, quoted in Buckland, *Irish Unionism: Documentary History*, p. 98.

de Vesci[25] in January 1886. The Provost of Trinity College the Rev J. H. Jellett[26] urged[27]

> that you must absolutely for the present sink all minor differences . . . I ask of you all to forget whether you are Whigs or Tories, Protestants or Roman Catholics and only think of yourselves as citizens of a country which is assailed by the greatest danger that has ever threatened its existence, and from which danger it is your duty to save it, and a duty in which, I firmly believe, if firmly, courageously carried out you must be successful.

John Pentland Mahaffy,[28] the most famous academic in late nineteenth century Ireland, joined as did his Trinity peers Edward Dowden[29] and Atkinson. William Hartpole Lecky[30] leant support as did the distinguished Tudor and Stuart historian Richard Bagwell.[31] The existence of the Ulster Loyalist Anti-Repeal Union[32] was a blow to all Ireland unity but the formation of an Irish Unionist Party at Westminster did point up the demographic misfortune of the southern Unionists at least in the House of Commons.[33] In the Lords the Irish Unionist representation was more strongly southern. One of the most active I.L.P.U. members was Thomas Maguire, professor of Moral Philosophy at Trinity College Dublin, first Roman Catholic fellow of the College and from 1869 to the taking up of his Trinity fellowship in 1880 at the age of 49, seven years after the passage of Fawcett's Relief Act, holder of the chair of Latin at the Queen's College in Galway.[34] Maguire was a passionate Unionist and a dedicated pamphleteer and polemicist. One of his more celebrated effusions 'England's duty to Ireland, as plain to a Loyal Irish Roman Catholic'[35] provoked Patrick Pearse's stonemason father into a 20,000 word

---

[25].   *Ibid.* John Robert William Vesey, 4th Viscount de Vesci, devoted his speech to praising the tireless work of Houston, who had been introduced to his employers by Sir Richard Grosvenor, the Liberal Whip. Houston had previously worked as an assistant to Dr Patton of the *Dublin Daily Express.* Dr Patton was *The Times* Dublin correspondent.

[26].   See R. B. McDowell and D. A. Webb, *Trinity College, Dublin, 1592–1952, an Academic History* (Cambridge, 1982) for Jellett.

[27].   *The Irish Times,* 8 Jan. 1886, quoted in Buckland, *Irish Unionism: Documentary History,* pp. 121–2.

[28].   For Mahaffy see W. B. Stanford and R. B. McDowell, *Mahaffy: A Biography of an Anglo-Irishman* (1971).

[29].   See *Letters of Edward Dowden and his Correspondents,* eds. E. D. and H. M. Dowden (1914) and *Fragments of Old Letters E. D. to E. D. W.,* ed. E. D. Dowden (1914).

[30].   See Lecky's biography by his widow Elizabeth for fascinating material on the development of his views in these years. There is no mention of his membership of the I.L.P.U. in her account, though he was active as a pamphleteer and adviser: *A Review of the Rt Hon William Edward Hartpole Lecky by his Wife* (1909).

[31].   For Bagwell's later role as a senator in the Irish Free State Senate see M. O'Callaghan, 'Language, Nationality and Cultural Identity, 1922–27: The *Catholic Bulletin* and *The Irish Statesman* Reappraised', *Irish Historical Studies,* XXIV (1984), 226–45.

[32].   Very short-lived.

[33].   Jackson, *Ulster Party,* p. 55.

[34].   While completing this article, Paul Bew has drawn my attention to a recent study of Maguire. T. P. Foley, 'Thomas Maguire and the Parnell Forgeries', *Journal of the Galway Archaeological and Historical Society,* XLVI (1994), 173–96.

[35].   T. Maguire, *England's Duty to Ireland, as Plain to a Loyal Irish Roman Catholic* (Dublin and London, 1886). Other notable pamphlets of Maguire: *Reasons Why Britons Should Oppose Home Rule* (Dublin and London, 1886), and *The Effects of Home Rule on the Higher Education* (London and Dublin, 1886).

response.[36] The pamphlet that so enraged James Pearse was typical of the torrent of publications emanating from the I.L.P.U. offices between 1886 and 1891 when it reconstituted itself as the Irish Unionist Alliance. As Dudley Edwards quotes Maguire's pamphlet, the Parnellites were 'the most degraded section of the inhabitants of the British Isles . . . The vast preponderance of intelligence and wealth is in the hands of Protestants'. Home Rule would result in the slaughter of Loyalists, the new police force would be made up of whisky drinking corner boys and anybody found in possession of an object of English manufacture would be 'stoned and kicked to death'. Ironically the deployment of stage Irish stereotypes, while the stuff of Unionist propaganda was a double edged weapon.

Alvin Jackson has suggested that Irish unionism 'before 1911 may be described as a parliamentary movement'. It was primarily that but it was also a complex, if divided, propaganda machine that operated informally through a network of landed, political, legal and academic contacts and formally through the dense mass of publications produced by the I.L.P.U. and its successor the Irish Unionist Alliance. Patrick Buckland has delineated this territory clearly, particularly by drawing attention to a massive and underutilized archive in his magnificent *Irish Unionism 1885–1923: A Documentary History* (1973) and in *Irish Unionism 1: The Anglo-Irish and the New Ireland, 1885–1922*, on both of which this essay heavily relies, but that material on the ground remains unintegrated into a wider story. More significant than even the loyalist popular associations were the impressive Irish Unionist intellectuals who shaped high political opinion through the higher journalism and the complex network of Unionist scribblers at its lower levels. Ironically the preponderance of quasi-impecunious journalists in the Irish parliamentary party or the Parnellite party, as it was more commonly known, has obscured the skilled journalistic case made by Irish Unionists up to and including 1922.

More significantly the largely successful nature of Unionist argument and propaganda, certainly up to the time of the outbreak of World War I, is forgotten in a Whiggish preoccupation with the post 1921 position.[37] The neat tragic irony of history is that the case made most forcefully by Unionist Dublin about the violence, murderousness and dangerousness of Nationalist Ireland held the Unionist line up to and including the crisis years of 1910 to 1914. Indeed it is arguably the case that Unionism won the propaganda war of 1880 to 1914 hands down, despite the political outcome of a dominion status Free State and a partitioned Ireland.[38] Such a conclusion is one of the only ways of making sense of Anglo-Irish relations in the twentieth century.

One of the first significant high-profile altercations in which the I.L.P.U. was involved was the question of the so-called Pigott letters. Edward Caulfield Houston made available to the editor of *The Times*, George Earle Buckle, material, mostly

---

[36.] James Pearse's reply said: 'England's duty to Ireland is to give lawful effect to the will of the people, constitutionally ascertained and expounded by those who are legally and by British law chosen to represent them'. Quoted in R. D. Edwards, *Patrick Pearse, the Triumph of Failure* (1977), pp. 9–10. I am indebted to Dr Patrick Maume for this reference.

[37.] See Bew, *Ideology and the Irish Question* for an attempt to remedy this.

[38.] See N. Mansergh, *The Unresolved Question: The Anglo-Irish Settlement and its Undoing* (1991), and R. B. McDowell, *The Irish Convention 1917–18* (London and Toronto, 1970).

letters, purporting to substantiate a view of Irish nationalism as criminal conspiracy since 1879 and subsequently presented him with clinching letters apparently signed by Parnell expressing approbation of the murder in the Phoenix Park in 1882 of the Chief Secretary for Ireland, Lord Frederick Cavendish, and Thomas Henry Burke, the vitally important Under-Secretary in the Dublin Castle administration. The publication of three articles based on a creative integration of this material under the heading 'Parnellism and Crime' by *The Times* coincided with the introduction of Arthur Balfour's Crimes Bill of 1887.[39] It resulted in the sprawling and seemingly endless special commission to investigate the validity of these and other charges. The commission became commonly known as 'Parnellism and Crime'. I have argued extensively elsewhere that despite the vindication of Parnell on the central question of the Pigott forgeries the commission substantively succeeded in establishing the connexion between Parnellism and crime in the minds of all who followed it, however superficially.[40] There is an extensive literature that clearly delineates the complex connexions between the parliamentary party and Land and National League involvement in agrarian violence, often under tacit I.R.B. control. Recent rediscoveries of allegations that Parnell was very possibly sworn into the Fenian movement in the library of Trinity College Dublin in 1882 are plausible, if unproven.[41] The changed political circumstances of the post-1886 political situation meant that Parnell was anxious to distance himself from agrarian violence, land agitation and non-democratic forces and his reimmersion in the narrative of the entrails of the early 1880's was highly politically inconvenient at the very least, and politically disastrous in any long term context.[42] It rallied Liberals to his cause in 1890, but it certainly simultaneously gratified his opponents.

On 30 August 1889 the I.L.P.U. issued a statement refuting utterly the Parnellite allegation that funds of the Union had been used to purchase the Pigott letters either by Edward Caulfield Houston or by Dr Maguire.[43] In evidence before the special

39. For the implications of this coincidence see M. O'Callaghan, 'Parnellism and Crime: Constructing a Conservative Strategy of Containment 1887–91', in *Parnell: The Politics of Power*, ed. D. McCartney (Dublin, 1991), pp. 102–24.
40. O'Callaghan, *British High Politics*, pp. 70–1.
41. P. Maume, 'Parnell and the I.R.B. Oath', *Irish Historical Studies*, XXIX (1995), 363–70.
42. See, for a contemporary informed analysis *Lecky by his Wife*, p. 213: 'The sitting of the Parnell Commission that winter engrossed public attention and their dramatic development drew the bond still closer between Gladstonians and Parnellites; but though the letters attributed to Parnell proved forgeries, the report with the findings of the Commission – which was issued the following winter – severely condemned the methods of Parnellism'. In her footnote (*ibid.*, n. 1) Elizabeth Lecky drew attention to where Lecky wrote to Mr Booth: 'I think the report will do great good when it comes out. It is amusing to see both sides proclaiming their triumph; but only one side prints the report, and it hardly needs a Solomon to draw the inference'.
43. I.L.P.U. circular to 'members and friends', 30 Aug. 1889, refuting accusations that I.L.P.U. funds had been used to purchase the Pigott letters. Public Records of Northern Ireland (D989A/1/4), quoted in Buckland, *Irish Unionism: Documentary History*, pp. 150–51: 'So far was the pretended belief in these allegations carried that the Secretary of the Association was summoned to attend before the Special Commission with the books of the Association, whereupon the Executive Committee gave immediate directions for their production. In accordance with those directions every book of the Irish Loyal and Patriotic Union was in court in charge of the Secretary and Assistant Secretary on the 12th of July last, when Mr Houston, as Secretary, having been examined as to the willingness of the Association to allow the books to be inspected, stated that every book was at the disposal of their lordships for inspection, but that the Committee objected to allow an examination of them by political opponents. The judges were then pressed by Counsel to direct that the books should be open for general inspection, but their lordships refused to make any such order, on the ground that their production had no bearing on any issue before the Commission'.

commission Houston insisted on this, though he did admit to receiving a sum in excess of £1000 from Buckle for the letters.[44] The whole story is tantalizingly revealing of the intimacies of Dublin in the period.

In his fascinating essay, 'To the Northern Counties Station: Lord Randolph Churchill and the Prelude to the Orange Card',[45] Roy Foster has recreated the milieu of urbane anti-landlord professional legal Dublin and its role in speeding Lord Randolph Churchill in the playing of the Orange card in Ulster.[46] The circle around Edward Caulfield Houston was perhaps no less important. Cross-examined by the Attorney General,[47] acting for *The Times* and Sir Charles Russell, Houston stated that his career was as a journalist, but that he had been in full-time employment with the I.L.P.U. since its inception. Asked to describe what the I.L.P.U. was, he said 'A sort of anti-Land League; that is the best way to sum it up'.[48] Houston emphasised that he had taken an interest in dramatic acts of nationalist savagery before becoming secretary of the I.L.P.U. – that may indeed have been one of his qualifications for the job. In 1882 he wrote 'the descriptive account that appeared in *The Times* at the time of the Phoenix Park murders'.[49] He said that he was not however on the staff of *The Times*: 'I was doing special work at the time'. When asked if he attended the murder trials of 1882 and 1883 he replied that he had attended them in full.[50] These were the trials during which members of the Invincibles, a secret gang closely connected to formal nationalist groupings, had been found guilty of the murders of Cavendish and Burke.[51] All of the material that he had produced, apparently through Pigott, centred on these murders. It is at least open to question as to whether Pigott worked as alone as Houston attempted to suggest. Certainly Houston's highly detailed knowledge of the case would have been scarcely irrelevant.

According to Houston Richard Pigott[52] had contacted him about what he – Pigott

[44.] The official record of the commission is published as *Special Commission Act, 1888, reprint of the short-hand notes of the speeches, proceedings and evidence taken before the Commissioners appointed under the above named Act* (12 vols., 1890). Quotations in this article are from one of the three unofficial records of the commission: *Parnellism and Crime: The Special Commission Reprinted from The Times* (4 vols., 1889–90), part XIV, p. 42.

[45.] In R. F. Foster, *Paddy and Mr Punch: Connections in Irish and English History* (1993), pp. 233–61.

[46.] Contemporary unionist historiography tends to underplay the significance of outside intent to 'play the Orange card' and underlines the relative autogenerative internal dynamics of Ulster loyalism. Foster emphasises FitzGibbon's later unease at the potential implications of the Orange card by quoting from FitzGibbon to Churchill in 1888: 'Ulster cannot be made a subdivision of united Ireland, without depriving all congenial inhabitants of the rest of the island of their only hope and support, at the same time exposing the "masses" living in Ulster to the most unbending and to them repugnant rule of the extreme Ulster party, and sacrificing all the "loyalists" everywhere else. On the other hand it can't be kept as an England in Ireland without raising a frontier question of the most utterly unsoluble character, and it can't be forced under the hateful yoke of home rule without destruction of its prosperity, if not without actual force'. *Ibid.*, p. 258.

[47.] Sir Richard Webster, who had attempted to withdraw from the case, as had his second, Sir Henry James: 'Every day I curse Chamberlain and the Unionists for their obstinacy'. Webster quoted in Sir Edward Clarke, *The Story of my Life* (1918).

[48.] *Special Commission*, part XIV, p. 33.

[49.] *Ibid.*

[50.] *Ibid.*

[51.] For the Invincibles see L. O'Brock, *Revolutionary Underground: The Story of the Irish Republican Brotherhood, 1858–1924* (Dublin, 1976), pp. 24–35.

[52.] See Dick Donovan [J. E. Muddick], *The Crime of the Century: Being the Life Story of Richard Pigott* (1904), and Richard Pigott, *Recollections of an Irish Journalist* (Dublin, 1882).

– claimed was John Devoy's connexion with the Invincibles and with further connexions between the Parnellite party and crime in mid-1885. Houston retained Pigott,
a magnificently Balzacian character, at the rate of a guinea a day and published a
pamphlet written by Pigott and published in amended form as 'Parnellism Unmasked'.[53] This was one of the first of a series of pamphlets published by the I.L.P.U.
detailing the criminality of the Irish M.P.s. Pigott, even in 1886, was a notorious
Dublin character whose chequered career had involved running three Fenian newspapers, selling or attempting to sell his organs of record to Lord Spencer, Forster and
Trevelyan, and moving at haste ahead of his creditors from address to address in the
Kingstown and Sandycove areas of south County Dublin.[54] Pigott certainly knew a
great deal about a lot of people, particularly old Fenians, and is in many ways one
of the most fascinating and incorrigible characters in shadowland Dublin in these
years.[55] Pitting his wits in a delicate balancing act between Fenians, Dublin Castle,
Land and National League groupings he was certainly hard-done-by by the Parnellite
party's terms of purchase when they bought his papers and turned them into William
O'Brien's *United Ireland*. In 1885, armed with a guinea a day and the promise of
funds for sufficiently important documents substantiating his stories, Pigott proceeded
to Paris and Lausanne in pursuit of incriminating information from a source called
Eugene Davis. Paris had been used by the Parnellites as the scene of meetings in the
early eighties and had teemed with *demi-mondaine* Fenians before many of them were
expelled in the mid-eighties. Pigott wished to go to New York for some higher
authority to authorise written statements from his sources but had to content himself
going back and forth to Paris where incriminating letters 'had been left in a bag in
the same room in Paris in which Frank Byrne was arrested, and that the letters had
been either in the possession of Frank Byrne or a man named Kelly, a schoolmaster
who was supposed to have purchased the Phoenix Park knives'.[56] By April 1886
Houston was forced to approach Buckle at *The Times* as his funds were, he claimed,
exhausted, and could no longer sustain Pigott's further peregrinations.[57] Pigott duly
proceeded to New York though Buckle declined to finance the trip. In May 1886
Pigott returned with a sealed letter which he told Houston he had obtained from J.
J. Breslin instructing certain people in Paris to hand over 11 letters that ostensibly
implicated Parnell and Egan in directly inciting and ordering murders. Houston and
Dr Thomas Maguire went to Paris in July 1886 and were given the 11 letters, the
first batch of many it was intimated, and they subsequently handed these over to
MacDonald of *The Times*. Maguire had provided the money to purchase the letters
and the cost at that stage of the enterprise was £1,780. Later, in the *coup de grâce*,
the letter condoning the murder of Burke – purporting to be signed by Parnell –
was obtained as late as 1888. Mr Pigott suddenly came across it among his papers.

[53.] R. Pigott, *Parnellism Unmasked* (Dublin, 1885), amended by E. C. Houston.

[54.] Papers in the National Library of Ireland contain detailed accounts of Pigott's circumstances. His
lifestyle is disclosed in embarrassing detail during the course of his cross-examination, during which his
begging letters to William Forster were revealed by T. Wemys Reid. *Special Commission*, part XIV, pp.
118–269.

[55.] There is no study of Dublin journalistic circles in the 1880s.

[56.] *Special Commission*, part XIV, p. 75.

[57.] Money paid by Soames *after* letters procured. *Ibid.*, p. 69.

Further batches arrived in February or March 1888 and July 1888, after the decision to appoint a special commission had been made.[58] Chamberlain had been crucial in pressing a willing Salisbury to appoint it.[59] In many ways its institution sealed their alliance. Soames, *The Times* legal advisor, was a party to some of the early meetings, and on the appointment of the special commission Houston claimed that he decided to conclude the anonymity that had cloaked himself and Pigott as suppliers of the letters and dragged the unfortunate Pigott to the office of Soames to discuss the new 'open policy'. An open policy was the last thing that Pigott needed. Houston, the allegedly innocent dupe, claims never to have doubted the authenticity of the letters. In many ways they merely substantiated what most of Unionist Dublin believed to be true.[60] They were irresistible documentary ballast to the rumour mill. More than that they were a vital potential political trump. In February 1889 Houston was living in London at Cork Street and had been since receiving his original subpoena in 1888. Houston was a Liberal in 1885, so his closest confidantes in the I.L.P.U. were fellow Liberals, by 1886 Liberal Unionists. Monies were lent to Houston by Sir Rowland Blennerhassett,[61] Lord Richard Grosvenor and Mr Hogg of Dublin. In Paris Pigott stayed at the Hotel St Petersbourg while Maguire and Houston stayed at the Hotel du Monde near the Opéra. Houston was not merely responsible for supplying the letters, he had also been engaged by *The Times* to assist them in the conduct of the case and in dealing with Dublin Castle substantiation of the anti-Parnellite position, which is another story.[62] On being asked for corroboration of Pigott's account of events Houston said.[63]

> Information at the disposal of the government which was not utilized in bringing what I consider criminals to justice . . . The impression on my mind at the time was assisted by reports which appeared in the daily press and in private mouths . . . it seemed probable.

Houston said that others were engaged in the production of the 'Black Pamphlet', that his alias in Paris was Wilson and that he constantly refrained from having his name connected with Pigott's by not paying him by cheque. Houston's closest colleague in the whole affair, Dr Maguire, died in London in February 1889,[64] shortly before he was due to give evidence.[65]

[58.] Letters listed in *ibid.*, p. 43.

[59.] Harrison, *Parnell, Chamberlain and 'The Times'*, p. 19.

[60.] 'The impression on my mind at that time was assisted by reports which appeared in the daily press and in private mouths'. Houston's evidence, *Special Commission*, part XIV, p. 76.

[61.] *Ibid.*, p. 81. Blennerhassett was a successful Kerry landlord, a former Liberal and a leading light in the I.L.P.U. He introduced Captain O'Shea to George Buckle at a dinner in Previtali's. Buckle subsequently sent O'Shea to liaise with Houston in preparing for the Special Commission. Harrison, *Parnell, Chamberlain and 'The Times'*, p. 22.

[62.] L. O'Broin, *The Prime Informer – A Suppressed Scandal* (1971) for suggestions of government collusion in *The Times* case. Moody, '*The Times*' versus Parnell and Co, 1887–90', pp. 159–64, largely accepts O'Broin's case. See O'Callaghan, *Pamellism and Crime*, p. 110.

[63.] *Special Commission*, part XIV, p. 76.

[64.] The mystery of Maguire's death seems to be answered in Foley, 'Thomas Maguire'.

[65.] *Special Commission*, part XIV, p. 81.

I was working without the consent and knowledge of my committee, and my position was a difficult one. Several times I had to explain my absence from my work for two or three days, and all that sort of thing. I knew that if it came out that I was pursuing that investigation I might find myself in a very risky position in regard to my continuing in office.

There were 15 or more directors of the I.L.P.U. committee and only two of them had provided him with funds. Of these the most prominent was the Kerry Liberal Sir Rowland Blennerhassett who presided at meetings but was not chairman. Administrative details in Dublin were conducted through William Farquharson, the managing clerk in the I.L.P.U. office, at 33 Leinster Road. Houston also explained his case to Lord Hartington and asked for advice as to how to proceed. Hartington seems to have suggested approaching W. T. Stead of the *Pall Mall Gazette*. Stead subsequently reported the interview in print claiming that Houston insisted that he had sound documentary evidence linking Parnell and other Irish leaders to the murders, in particular Dillon and Sexton. Mr Stead told Houston that he had lost £3,000 over the 'Maiden Tribute to Modern Babylon' and that he did not intend to risk anything more unless he was certain it was going to be a success.[66]

Despite the complicated fall-out from Houston's initiative the basic strategy of pursuing extensive and widely disseminated propaganda on the Nationalist parliamentary party remained the central plank of the I.L.P.U.'s methodology. That this was profoundly distasteful to Irish Tories like Fitzgibbon and Morris was neither here nor there. They were working for a far more sophisticated long term strategy for Irish Unionism through the uncertain instrument of Randolph Churchill that involved a realignment of oppositions in Irish politics through a subtle connexion between local government reform and land purchase locked into an Irish economic and social base.[67] They also had the wit to see the dynamics of democratic politics and their obvious fall-out if forces were not realigned in Ireland. Churchill's intemperate attack on the commission even before it sat was largely influenced by them.[68]

> The tribunal, whatever its decision will not prevent the Irish constituencies from returning as representatives the parties implicated. In such an event the honour of the House of Commons could only be vindicated by repeated expulsions followed by disfranchisement. Does any reasonable person contemplate such a course?

On receiving the commission's final report, and in the light of the judge's decision that the papers and documents of the Irish Loyal and Patriotic Union could not be made open for scrutiny, Salisbury's government represented it as a triumph of a kind for the Unionists of Ireland.[69]

[66.] *Ibid.*, p. 86.
[67.] See R. F. Foster, *Lord Randolph Churchill: A Political Life* (Oxford, 1981), p. 364, for realignment, and Foster, 'Northern Counties Station', p. 280, for FitzGibbon's opposition to bailing out landlords who he believed were being crushed by 'economic forces'.
[68.] T. P. O'Connor, *Memoirs of an Old Parliamentarian, 1885–1929* (New York, 2 vols., 1929), II, 178.
[69.] *Ibid.*, pp. 178–9.

This House deems it to be a duty to record its reprobation of the true charges of the gravest description, based on private and public documentary evidence, which have been proved against members of this House and other persons; and while declaring its satisfaction at twin conspiracies, the one treasonable and the other criminal, to which fifty two members of this House have been parties, this House expresses its profound sorrow for the wrong inflicted and the suffering and loss endured by the loyal minority in Ireland, through a protracted period, by reason of these acts of flagrant iniquity.

While 'Parnellism and Crime' can be seen as a personal embarrassment for Houston, and may have contributed to the organisation's decision to rename itself the Irish Unionist Alliance, in substance that material thrown up by the enquiry was perfectly in line with the story that large numbers of active Irish Unionists wished to tell a British audience. That approach formed the basis of all subsequent unionist propaganda. In 1886 a series called *Notes From Ireland* had been initiated as a record of the sayings and doings of the Parnellite party in furtherance of the ' "separatist police" for Ireland; and of facts connected with the country, for the information of the imperial parliament, the press and the public generally'.[70]

In 1885 the I.L.P.U. had funded almost 50 election contests in the southern provinces of Ireland and right into the 1890's, it was insisted that they should contest all seats where they had a sizeable minority so that the anti-Home Rule vote could be recorded. By the early twentieth century the Irish Unionist Alliance contested only the Dublin and Dublin University constituencies. They subsidised Ulster Unionism financially, provided a London office for what was in effect the Ulster party and provided a massive weight of publications[71] refuting the Home Rule case in series after series of publications. They tirelessly canvassed local supporters to supply stories of priestly intimidation, violent extremism and disreputable behaviour by Nationalists which they duly printed and distributed in massive print runs. They drew up numerous signed petitions highlighting the horrors contingent on local government reform. Morley and Birrell were perhaps the most hated chief secretaries in the history of the Irish administration as they were both alleged to be the willing slaves of Redmond and his place-men, and loomed large in Irish Unionist Alliance demonology.

In 1886 the I.U.A. prepared one million copies of 164 leaflets supplemented by half a million copies of posters, pamphlets and maps and over 90,000 copies of the ubiquitous *Notes from Ireland* with a massive staff of speakers addressing the English, Welsh and Scottish constituencies. In 1892–3 the effort was no less striking. The press committee, in a six month period in 1893, distributed three million leaflets nationally, and 250,000 pamphlets through the polling districts of Lancashire. In the non-Irish constituencies where by-elections took place every individual voter received a selection of leaflets by post detailing the horrors of nationalist Ireland and the

---

[70.] Buckland, *Irish Unionism: Documentary History*, p. xv. *Notes from Ireland*, available in bound volumes at the Public Records Office of Northern Ireland in the series D989A-C. Also published as part of I.L.P.U. and I.U.A. annual publications.

[71.] I.L.P.U. and I.U.A. publications vols I– (published annually by the Irish Unionist Alliance, Dublin, London and Belfast, and Hodges, Figgis and Company Ltd, Grafton St, Dublin).

legitimacy of the opposition to Home Rule. The material, available now in bound volumes, is lurid and dramatic. In June 1893 a staff of 15 speakers attended 90 meetings in England. Irish merchants addressed local gatherings of businessmen.

Meetings were held in Stafford, Walsall, Wednesbury, Huddersfield, Carlisle, Whitehaven, Barrow and Wolverhampton. Linlithgowshire, where the Unionists won, and Pontefract, where the Gladstonians narrowly escaped defeat were concentrated upon, as was West Lothian where the Alliance believed itself to be crucial in the return of Captain Hope. In conjunction with the Ladies' Liberal Unionist Association of England and the Central Conservative Association the Alliance had a number of ladies at work 'spreading the light'.[72] In 1894 the Alliance published a pamphlet on the 'Westmeath Examiner'[73] and Nulty, Roman Catholic Bishop of Meath, subtitled 'Ecclesiastical tyranny in Irish politics upheld in Rome'. Four more pamphlets and a 103 leaflets were published in that year.[74] The leaflets covered a ritualistic range of topics, and were frequently reprints from the local press highlighting Irish horrors: Intellectual freedom and Home Rule; Religious Intolerance in Ireland; a Clare Whiteboy case, jury packing in full swing; Mr Chamberlain on Unionists and Separatists; Lord Rosebery and the justification of the House of Lords (predominant partner speech 12 March 1894); Ulster and Home Rule, a reply to Lord Rosebery; Law and Order under Mr Morley; Characters of the Anti-Parnellite leaders, told by one another; The Recent Acts of the House of Lords Studied; Morley and Balfour: a parallel; Home Rule and Civil Liberty – Are the safeguards sufficient?; The Evicted Tenants, a sample of Nationalist Administration; Nationalist Administration, a sample of Tralee (not good apparently); Mr John Bright and Irish Nationalists.[75]

> The Bill Committee . . . is in constant communication with the Irish Unionist Parliamentary Party, who, it may be stated, hold meetings twice a week at the London Offices of the Alliance, and who are in this way furnished with information upon all the numerous questions which crop up at intervals in the discussion upon the Bill.[76]

From September 1911 to the middle of July 1914 an estimated six million books, leaflets and pamphlets were distributed.[77] The supreme governing body of the Alliance was the council which met three times a year but the executive committee which met twice weekly actually ran it through a series of committees. The executive was described as[78]

[72.] Report of the Speakers Committee from *The Irish Unionist Alliance: An Account of its Work and Organisation* (1893), quoted by Buckland, *Irish Unionism: Documentary History*, pp. 143–7.
[73.] The appalling behaviour of many of the Catholic clergy during the Parnellite split obviously provided fertile ground for propaganda. On priests and the split see F. Callanan, *The Parnell Split, 1890–91* (Cork, 1992) and his *Timothy Michael Healy and the Foundation of the Independent Irish State* (Cork, 1996).
[74.] *Irish Unionist Alliance Publications, Vol IV. Pamphlets and Leaflets, 7th and 8th Series 1894–95* (Dublin, 1895).
[75.] *Ibid.*, leaflets nos. 166, 168–70, 173–81, pp. 1–38.
[76.] Report of bill committee, *Irish Unionist Alliance* in Buckland, *Irish Unionism: Documentary History*, p. 144.
[77.] *Ibid.*, p. 25.
[78.] *Ibid.*, p. 143.

being composed of the most respected leaders in the mercantile and commercial ranks of the country, men occupying high positions in the great banking establishments and in the industrial life of Ireland. This influential and representative body meets twice each week, and they decide questions of policy and finance referred to them by the various sub-committees immediately engaged in the work of the Alliance, which is divided between its departmental committees . . . they have each a secretary who is constantly engaged, under their direction, in the management of his department.

Clearly this was all very expensive,

but the Unionists of Ireland have not grumbled at this expense. They have generously and liberally contributed to the work of the Alliance, and they had – from the fact that men like Lord Iveagh and Lord Ardilaun[79] were willing, nay anxious to guarantee large sums when the Guarantee Fund was first opened – significant assurance that the money would be spent in the way most likely to achieve the best results.

The Dublin-based Unionist campaigners were often critical of what they saw as the supine passivity of the 'Lords of the Soil'.[80] There is a certain churlishness in this attitude of the mercantile and professional classes of Dublin, given that the landlords were those who had endured the rock-face of the Land and National League. The landlords had however provided copy for the Liberal stereotype of reaction and repression. They also pursued their own interests vigorously, often at the expense of their urban allies.[81] From the Ashbourne Act of 1885 onwards the prospect of being bought out on favourable terms remained a possibility. Gladstone said of the abortive Land Purchase Bill of 1886 'the great object of this measure is not to dispose of the entire subject of Irish land, but to allow the Irish landlord refuge and defence from a possible mode of government in Ireland which he regards as fatal to him'.[82] In *The Irish Question*, he said the bill was 'a daring attempt we made to carry to the very uttermost our service to the men whom we knew to be as a class the bitterest and most implacable of our political adversaries'.[83]

He did not deny the charge that it was indeed 'a gigantic bribe'. But for Gladstone such a policy was desirable in tandem with Home Rule, as a means of securing its stability. For Tories, the policy of land purchase was partly a means of rescuing the landlords of Ireland, but more particularly a means of rectifying the anomolous status

[79.] Arthur Edward Guinness, 1st Baron Ardilaun and Edward Cecil Guinness, 1st Earl of Iveagh.

[80.] At a local level landed magnates were often unsupportive. In 1912 the 'Lords of the Soil' were seen to be attempting to break the commitment of the Kingstown and district unionist club in south County Dublin to form drill and rifle sections by refusing to provide them with a hall: 'Lords Longford and de Vesci had been approached both directly on the subject of Corrig School as a club house and through Mr Stewart, their agent, for permission to use Corrig School grounds or house for physical culture and that they had met with a refusal on both occasions'. This left them with nothing but the Orange Hall in York Road, which 'prevented many Roman Catholics from coming'. *Minute Book of the Kingstown and District Unionist Club*, quoted in Buckland, *Irish Unionism: Documentary History*, pp. 153–5.

[81.] As in the Irish Landowners' Convention.

[82.] Paper for Cabinet, 10 Mar. 1886, as quoted in H. C. G. Matthew, *Gladstone, 1875–1898* (Oxford, 1995), p. 247.

[83.] W. E. Gladstone, *The Irish Question*, p. 44, quoted again in Matthew, *Gladstone*, p. 247. See O'Callaghan, *British High Politics* for the historiographical debate on the formation of policy on Irish land.

of property after what they persisted in seeing as Gladstone's ruinous act of 1881. In their eyes this had left the landlords as mere encumberancers, trapped and powerless to exercise the rights of property in a correctly untrammelled way on their own estates. Proposals to rescue professional, non-propertied Unionists appealed to no particular ideological agenda.

Thomas Pim *jr*, director of the highly successful Quaker family mercantile dynasty of Pim and Sons, and a Liberal before 1886 said, on being pressed to attend an Irish Unionist Alliance function in April 1892,[84]

> You should recollect that we businessmen in Dublin live by the Nationalists in the country towns and there is no use in abusing them. Very few businessmen will take any part and, where I am willing to fight, I don't think that your association should ask me to move a resolution which would be brought up against me in every town in Ireland.

By contrast the Irish Landowner's Convention, pursuing their own specific political self-interest, felt in no such way constrained. And Gladstone's assumption that the most difficult-to-reconcile section of the Unionist jigsaw would be the landlords, demonstrated the narrowness of his acquaintance with the newly activated Orange section of what was to conclude as an Ulster Unionist coalition lead by a mercantile class constrained not at all in the fashion laid out by Pim.[85]

The constitution and bye laws of the Irish Landowners Convention were initially drawn up in April 1888. In 1889 the Executive committee held 30 meetings, usually in concentrated batches when the Commons and Lords were in session. Effectively they provided a lobbying and research organisation for the information of the Irish peers in the upper House and for the information and support of sympathetic M.P.s in the Commons. Clearly the landlords did not believe that they could trust their fates to elected representatives alone. Writing to Arthur Balfour on 19 April 1894 Hugh de Fellenberg Montgomery, a cultivated and active landowner from Tyrone, complained to Edward Carson – a member of the Dublin professional classes[86] – for failing to attend diligently to the review of land legislation taking place under the Morley Commission:[87]

[84.] Buckland, *Irish Unionism: Documentary History*, pp. 59–61.

[85.] On Gladstone's Ulster blind-spot see J. Loughlin, *Gladstone, Home Rule and the Ulster Question 1882–1893* (Dublin, 1986).

[86.] Alvin Jackson emphasises the fluidity of Carson's opinions over time and his strong connexions with the landed Lambert family at Castle Ellen in Galway. Jackson, *Carson*, p. 25.

[87.] Morley appointed two commissions, equally repugnant to the landlords. The so-called *Evicted Tenants Commission* was actually appointed by Lord Houghton as Lord Lieutenant and was '*to enquire into and report respecting estates where the tenancy of a holding or of holdings has been determined since the first day of May 1879 and in respect of which holdings claims to be reinstated have been made by the tenants evicted therefrom now resident in Ireland*', H. C. 1893–94, XXXI. The so-called Morley Commission was, in fact, the other one, *Report of the Select Committee to enquire into and report upon the principles and practices of the Irish land commissioners and county court judges in carrying out the fair rent and free sale provisions of the Land Acts of 1870, 1881 and 1887 and of the Redemption of Rent Act of 1891, and to suggest such improvements in law or practice as they may deem to be desirable*, H. C. 1894 (310) XIII. Landlords were particularly exercised by the brief of this commission because it was axiomatic with them that their diminished financial status was due to the disgracefully low levels of rent set by the Land Commissioners. Their propaganda on this point was extremely successful, so any question of reopening the can of worms, officially made them nervous. It is at least arguable, see O'Callaghan, *British High Politics*, pp. 145–52,

Now, as you prevented the Irish landlords from capturing one of the Dublin University seats last election and sending a man to parliament who, though doubtless not so smart as Carson, would have stuck to his post both in the Committee and in the House, as a protector of landlord interests like a leech and is quite capable of asking witnesses very pertinent questions; may I say that I think the least you can do for us landlords and for Dublin University, which both as a Corporation and as a collection of individual Masters of Arts is largely dependent on the Landlords Londowner [sic] interest in Irish land, is to make Carson stick to his post on the Committee, when he can do work for us no one else able to serve on it can do, even at considerable sacrifice of professional business? He owes his position and his cheap seat to you and is bound to do what you bid him.[88]

The chairman of the executive committee of the Landowners Convention was Thomas Butler and the secretary was G. de L. Willis. Their offices were at 4 Kildare Street, Dublin, conveniently close to that bastion of landlord socialising, the Kildare Street Club. When country members flocked in for their conventions they moved to the Leinster Lecture Hall in Molesworth Street. On the committee were substantial landowners: Duke of Abercorn; Lord Castletown; Lord Monteagle from Mount Trenchard in Limerick; James Stronge, Hockley Lodge, Armagh; Frank Watney, Landmore, Londonderry; Col. Charles Tottenham, Ballycurry, Wicklow. In 1895 the Earl of Arran, Castle Gore, Mayo; J. Townsend Trench, Kenmare, Kerry; J. Blakiston-Houston, Orangefield, Belfast; and W. E. Scott, Willsboro', Co. Londonderry, were also among the members. These were the class from whom the lord lieutenants of counties and the non-stipendiary magistracy were usually selected. Even before the dreaded full-blown reform of local government in 1898, under the Liberal interregnum of Houghton[89] and Morley from 1892–95 attempts were made to replace the almost universally Unionist cohort from which selection was made with Catholic Unionists or dubious Home Rulers. Members of the Irish parliamentary party would accept no office under the Dublin Castle administration, but they did contribute names of third-raters from whom nominal Catholic/Nationalists could be chosen. As Morley wrote to Houghton

as long as really distinguished Nationalist Irishmen, for reasons to their credit refuse to serve the crown they forfeit to some extent the claim to interfere in cases such as

---

[87] *continued*   that their economic position was no more reduced than that of their fellow landlords in Britain in those years and that the Land Commissioners were reasonably equitable in their rent setting. To concede this would, however, collapse the whole economic argument for land purchase as a *necessary* measure to save landlords from unjust appropriation and leave only the ideological argument for purchase to remove the blot on the absoluteness of the rights of property implicit in the 1881 act – the potential implications of which on the *other* side of St George's Channel, seriously concerned the Tories.

[88.]   Hugh de Fellenberg Montgomery to Arthur J. Balfour, 19 Apr. 1894, quoted in Buckland, *Irish Unionism: Documentary History* pp. 282–3.

[89.]   Houghton often, however, demurred at some of the more *outré* candidates proposed by the nationalists. For example, the nationalist proposal to appoint a Meath cattle dealer as the lord lieutenant of that county: 'I am much disposed to ask you to tell Healy or whoever it is that if they set their hearts on this appointment they must get a new Lord Lieutenant to make it'. Cambridge University Library, Crewe MS. C/36, Houghton to Morley, 26 May 1895. Morley occasionally inclined to another view. 'Guerre aux chateau, peace to the cattle salesmen and liquor sellers'. *Ibid.*, Morley to Houghton, 7 Nov. 1894.

these in favour of utterly undistinguished followers. I confess on that point the Parnellite position seems to me much the juster.

Lord Mayo,[90] of Palmerstown in Straffan, canvassing for the job of lord lieutenant of Kildare in December 1893 commented, appropos of his potential rivals for the post:[91]

The Earl of Drogheda – does not live in the country; Lord Seaton – lives two or three months in the country; Baron de Roebuck – an excellent country gentleman, lives entirely at home and is great at all county duties; Ambrose O'Farrell – old Roman Catholic whig family, father sat for county for many years. Lives entirely at home; Major Hugh Barton – lives at home, rich, derives his income from the firm of Barton Gultier [*sic*], large wine importers of Bordeaux. Excellent country gentleman. These are the names of the leading county magnates. Lastly there is myself. I live here nine months in the year. I am afraid we have not a Home Ruler of property in the county except one, George Wolfe and he lives in Wicklow.

In pursuing the righteousness of their case through the Irish Landowners Convention the landlords were decidedly unamateurish. Their role in shaping legislation and influencing policy in these years is crucial.[92] Irish landlords had swallowed the 1887 Land Act as the price of Liberal Unionist support. Far earlier than most analysts of the period acknowledge the Irish Landowners Convention had one clear and central policy – the purchase of landed estates through some Treasury mechanism and their sale to the tenants. Chamberlain,[93] in marked contrast to Hartington, was utterly opposed to any plan to buy out Irish landowners with taxpayers money. In fact when the Landowners Convention was pressing most clearly this policy aim he was still mulling over the possibility of some form of devolved local government for Ireland – after a Home Rule Parliament the next nightmare of the landlords, and indeed of other Unionists outside the Howth circle.[94] As Hugh de Fellenberg Montgomery of

90. Dermot Robert Wyndham Bourke, 7th Earl of Mayo.

91. Cambridge Univ. Lib., Crewe MS. C/36, Lord Mayo to Lord Rosebery, 6 Dec. 1893; Morley to Houghton, 23 Dec. 1893. 'It is an ingenious and novel way of making an application. I never heard of G. Wolfe . . . The only question is who is the least obnoxious'.

92. See their published papers, particularly after 1893, for the sheer detail of their application. Irish Landowners' Convention, *Reports of the Executive Committee. Submitted to the Irish Landowners' Convention*, 8th report, Jan. 1893, including appendix, separately published as a pamphlet, *Home Rule and the Irish Land Question*, 10th report, Jan. 1895; 11th report, Feb. 1896; 12th report, Jan. 1897, including appendix containing memorandum submitted to government in March 1896, three weeks before introduction of Land Bill, 'Memorandum Relative to the Land Judge's Report' (late Landed Estates Court); 14th report, Feb. 1899, incorporating appendix entitled 'A Memorandum Submitted for the Relief of Irish Landlords Submitted for the Consideration of Her Majesty's Government'; 15th report, Apr. 1900; 16th report, Apr. 1901; 17th report, Aug. 1902; 18th report, Apr. 1904. Full Collection Reports, 1–29, 1887–1919, National Library of Ireland, 3330941 18. See too, return of the resolutions and statements adopted by the Irish Landowners' Convention on the 10 Oct. 1903; and report of the Irish Land Conference dated 3 Jan. 1903; and minute on the Land Conference Report, adopted on the 7 Jan. 1903, by the executive committee of the Irish Landowners' Convention (H.M.S.O., Dublin, 1903).

93. Chamberlain wanted a system of land purchase funded by Irish credit and administered through Irish local government. In the years from 1887 to 1889 he toyed with such ideas with Randolph Churchill.

94. Lecky saw the Irish landlords as being behind the debacle of the 1900 by elections in Dublin, particularly through the I.U.A. secretary, Elrington Ball: 'as long as Mr Ball remains first honorary Secretary of the Alliance it is inevitable that that body should be associated with the movement of w[hic]h he was the head and front – the avowed and conspicuous leader'. W. E. H. Lecky to H. de F. Montgomery, 26 Nov. 1900, quoted in Buckland, *Irish Unionism: Documentary History*, p. 160.

the Landowners' Convention pointed out in a letter to E. Willis of 26 April 1889 this was being worked upon by former Irish Liberals, horrified by the so-called '*Birmingham Post* Plan' at that time. They were pressing on their Liberal Unionist allies at the Birmingham conference a fully state funded system of land purchase, with an absolute provision that it would not be compulsory to sell. Montgomery, pressing this policy as firmly as possible, wrote to Willis of the Landowners' Convention that he finally spoke very strongly about it to Lord Hartington[95]

> who seemed entirely to agree with me – but said there was the difficulty of the way in which Gladstone's Land Bill [the Land Purchase Bill to accompany the Home Rule Bill of 1886] had been attacked by unionists – to which I said is it not the business of these men [meaning Chamberlain and allies] to do all they can to extricate us from the mess this has got us into, instead of getting us deeper and deeper by going on assuring the British elector he is to contribute no share and take no responsibility in the settlement of the Irish Land Question. Is not the broad distinction between Gladstone's proposal and any Unionist proposal so plain that even the British elector can be made to understand it?

The net result of all this lobbying was that the 1889 Liberal Unionist meeting at Birmingham adopted a resolution that placed them more or less in line with the Landowners' Convention and the Tories on Irish land. Quite why they should have bought this proposal is interesting, but not as interesting why the Irish Landowners' Convention should have had such a policy as early as 1889:[96]

> This meeting, believing that the land question is at the root of Irish disaffection and discontent, respectfully urges her majesty's government to introduce into parliament without delay a measure under which the Irish agricultural tenants generally may become the proprietors of their holdings by methods which do not impose undue burden and responsibility upon the imperial exchequer.[97]

The main aim of the Irish Landowners' Convention, with broad support from Irish Unionist peers in the Lords and sympathetic members in the Commons – amongst whom the Dublin professionals could not usually be numbered – was to demonstrate tirelessly the utter futility of attempting to continue with the rent-arbitrating machinery set up under the 1881 act. Morley's commission of 1894, and his even more irritating Evicted Tenants Commission, represented the high water mark of landlord anxiety in these years. To read in detail through the annual reports, papers, appendices and publications of the Irish Landowners' Convention is to be astounded by the efficiency and sophistication of their operation. Light play is even made of William O'Brien's vilely anti-semitic ravings about the London and Birmingham mortgagers who, *United*

[95]. H. de F. Montgomery to E. Willis, 26 Apr. 1889, quoted in *ibid.*, pp. 268–71.

[96]. The 1886 Land Bill which failed with the Home Rule Bill seems to have concentrated landlord aspirations in this direction building on Ashbourne's Act of 1885. The advancing of British credit for the scheme was novel. See *The Ashbourne Papers, 1869–1913: A Calendar of the Papers of Edward Gibson, 1st Lord Ashbourne*, eds. A. B. Cooke and A. P. W. Malcolmson (Belfast, 1974). There is just one, disappointingly unrevealing, reference to his 1885 act: 'The whole matter was left to me, and I was told by my colleagues that they wanted a Purchase Bill produced at once, and one that would pass and work' (p. 26).

[97]. Buckland, *Irish Unionism: Documentary History*, p. 267.

Ireland claimed, were squeezing the oppressed landlords of Ireland and ensuring that they had little choice other than to oppress their tenants. This charming proposal for a joint repudiation of Jewish oppressors served merely as an opportunity for the landlords to display in novel form their probity.[98]

It is certainly true that the ugly intent of the Land War, and subsequent eruptions from the Plan of Campaign to the United Irish League of William O'Brien and T. W. Russell's Ulster demands, contained a serious agenda to acquire proprietorial rights; a peasant proprietorship had been one of the Land League's defining rallying cries. It is also clear that for much of the eighties and nineties there was little tenant demand for purchase outside Ulster. Many nationalists had designs on the landlords' estates, but it is difficult to see Redmond or Healy after 1891 as full-blooded pursuers of the appropriation of landlord property. From the results of the Irish Landowners' Convention survey it appears that by as early as 1887 the bulk of the Irish landlords were committed to having their estates, in the sense of their rented-out land, bought out.[99] Most of them expressed a desire to remain on their demesnes, presumably living on invested income and protected from the weapon of tenant power over their assets. Perhaps as a class they believed after 1886 that the writing was on the wall and that, if there was a short or medium prospect of a Home Rule Parliament, they had better cash in on favourable terms before the Land Commission revised judicial rents to laughably low levels. Every ostensibly neutral commission on Irish land in these years was no more than a cypher for the political intent behind its construction, so it is difficult to get behind the conflicting authoritative conclusions to a reasonable assessment of the economics of the situation.[100] It seems to be the case that as far as landlords were concerned, in an unstable political situation their land was an unrealisable

---

[98.] 'Mortgages and Other Land Chargeants', Appendix C, *Irish Landowners' Convention Report* (1893), p. 29.

[99.] On 23 Dec. 1887 the committee 'issued a series of 30 queries, with the view of ascertaining, as accurately as possible, the opinions held upon the principal aspects of the question (i.e. purchase) among Irish landowners in every part of the country. In response to this appeal the Committee received between 80 and 90 manuscripts, including replies from the County Committees of nearly three fourths of the Irish Counties'. Cowper's Land Commission was designed to consolidate argument for purchase. The Landowners' Convention piously noted in 1889: 'The majority of Irish landlord desire to continue to reside and spend their incomes in their native country, and to discharge their duties there as residents. In the interest of all classes in the country, legislation on the Irish land question should promote the retention and establishment in Ireland of a body of country gentlemen, such as is found in most countries'. *Irish Landowners' Convention, 4th Report of the Executive Committee to be submitted to the Irish Landowners Convention on Wednesday, 18th December 1889* – a detailed purchase scheme as desired by the landlords, pp. 1–35. The Cowper Commission provided the required analysis, and all interested parties were referred to the following publication: *Peasant Proprietors in Ireland: A Series of Letters on Lord Ashbourne's Act: By 'The Times' Commissioner Reprinted by Permission* (London, William Ridgway, 169 Piccadilly W; Dublin, Hodges Figgis and Co, 104 Grafton St, 1888). Interestingly Hodges Figgis were also the Dublin publishers of I.L.P.U. and I.U.A. collections.

[100.] See the frenzied communications on the Evicted Tenants Commission, set up at the instigation of nationalists and first revealed in a letter to Justin McCarthy; letters between Lister Drummond, secretary to the Commission, and G. de L. Willis. The landlords main concern was the thought of raking over the history of evictions. 'That the landlords in such circumstances should oppose the League and resort to the only weapon they had for their protection, viz., eviction, is not to be wondered at'. This statement from the report of the Cowper's Commission was vital for landowners. See *Irish Landowners' Convention. 8th Report of the Executive Committee to be Submitted to the Irish Landowners Convention on Thursday, 21st January 1893*, pp. 15–28, O'Callaghan, *British High Politics*, passim.

asset except through sale to the tenantry, since nobody else would want to, or indeed could, buy it, and since it was increasingly difficult to borrow against. It is at least partly true that a decline in landed income was common to the British Isles as a whole in these years, particularly a reduction in rental income. That was obviously not the context for self-comprehension or the predominant reality for Irish landlords. They lobbied for the appointment of commissions and they lobbied to have the terms of commissions' findings – particularly those of the Fry Commission – widely politically disseminated. They attended or sent observers to and participated in all debates on Irish land, tirelessly moving to have expunged from the record any references deemed hostile or unsympathetic to landlords as a body.[101]

There is a tendency to read the last decades of the nineteenth century and the first years of the twentieth through the lenses of democratic politics. This is clearly ruinous for any understanding of Victorian or Edwardian Ireland. The foundation of modern mass democratic politics was the 1884–85 reform and redistribution debate; this was exceptionally contentious in the case of Ireland. Indeed the first blow Irish Unionism received in these years was from the Tories, on the redistribution issue. Their great white hope, Northcote, was outmanoeuvred by Salisbury, who sold the pass of Irish Unionism. 1884 to 1885 made 1886 possible. Irish nationalist electoral power paved the way for Gladstonian action, and in many ways his motives are irrelevant here. If all political groupings were attempting to come to terms with what the new mass politics would mean then Ireland provided merely one of the first sick answers to that question.

Irish Unionist popular representation outside Ulster was wiped out by the nature of the new electoral deal. A first-past-the-post system was obviously absurd for the political situation of Ireland. But, as so frequently in the past, measures ideal or potentially ideal for a homogenous society were imposed there. The self-image, sense of identity and structures of Irish Unionism did not change overnight merely because democratic politics were inaugurated. Irish Unionism, under the forcing pace of franchise reform, became an alliance of very different interest groups – landowners, urban professionals, passionate hibernophiles, old Liberals, died-in-the-wool-Tories, radical Ulster Presbyterians, learned Kerry classicists, long time waiting Catholic fellows of Trinity College Dublin, Orangemen, brilliant historians, cranky bigots, old Catholic Whigs, working class Dublin, the Belfast docks, the O'Callaghan Westropps of Clare – the list is endless. After 1886 they could barely muster a Commons seat outside Ulster, despite being a significant minority in the rest of Ireland. Irish Unionism was, from 1886 to 1910 a shifting kalaediscope of overlapping and sometimes conflicting alliances and organisations. The Irish Loyal and Patriotic Union, the Irish Unionist Alliance, the Irish Landowners' Convention, the Irish peers in the House of Lords, the Irish Unionist members who sat for English constituencies and the largely Ulster parliamentary party – this was Irish Unionism. The power of the Lords may have been in decline in the eighties and nineties, but it was not broken until 1910. Irish Unionism was far more than the number of M.P.s it returned to the House of Commons. In the Irish Landowners' Convention the landlords of Ireland acted as

---

101. See annual reports already cited. Very detailed accounts of strategy are contained in these reports.

one. Ironically their successful achievement of the ill-advised goal of state-aided land purchase destroyed that formidable base. The next knell of the democratic age, the dismantling of the power of the House of Lords, finished it.

For the transition from the politics of property to the politics of the franchise had graver consequences in Ireland where the divide between the propertied and the propertyless was about more than just that. And the failure of the transition to democratic politics to make provision for electoral equity by anything more sophisticated than first-past-the-post system in a complexly differentiated society denied democratic rights to the Unionists of Leinster, Munster and Connacht and in time to the Catholics of Ulster *manqué*. Irish Nationalists and Irish Unionists were both dramatically skilled at using the transition to democracy in the best possible way to maximise their own strengths – the Land and National League with their propaganda that paved the way to 1886, and the Unionists of Ireland as managed from Dublin. There were two conflicting sets of political rights at issue and in opposition, but the political structures did not allow of their expression. Hence, for the Unionists of Ireland, Irish nationalist electoral ascendency could be countered only by rendering their opponents criminal conspirators and unfit persons; to allow anything else was to concede the defeat of their own case. The other possibility was to insist on Ireland as a mere fragment of the United Kingdom thus requiring an overall United Kingdom electoral majority for any change. Even up to 1914 this was not entirely ruled out as a line of argument. But the alliance that constituted the high game of Irish unionism collapsed as first the landlords settled on their own terms and then the Lords lost their day; it was not surprising that Edward Carson chose to go down the line against his old ally Balfour on this. Irish Unionism was rolled back to the point at which only seats in the Commons and old ties counted. When some form of Home Rule for Ireland became increasingly inevitable after 1910 the appeals against it on the grounds of Irish barbarism and the democratic unit of the United Kingdom gave way, under Carson's direction, to the trump case of Ulster. While Carson took up the cause of Ulster as the most effective last stand against Home Rule for all Ireland, the effect of this choice was to be that by 1914 at the level of high political debate, what constituted Irish unionism was deemed to be nothing more than that area you could safely carve out of the province of Ulster with the certainty of a majority – four, six or nine counties?[102] Certainly, Ulster had always been different but it scarcely adequately represented Irish unionism, in all its rich diversity.

[102.] See M. Laffan's lucid and succinct *Partition of Ireland 1911–1925* (Dublin, 1985) for the best account of this discussion.

Protests From Behind the Grille: Gender and the Transformation of Parliament, 1867–1918

CLAIRE EUSTANCE

University of Greenwich

Women's associations with parliamentary government in Britain have always been complicated. A contemporary indication of this is evident in the current Parliament where there are only 63 women out of a total of 651 M.P.s. Yet even this figure is in sharp contrast to women's position vis à vis Parliament in the nineteenth and early twentieth centuries. The annual editions of Dod's *Parliamentary Companion*, published from the 1880s until 1918 emphasised women's lack of political rights: 'Ladies are excluded from the House of Commons, but there is a gallery above that of the Reporters from which, concealed by a grating in front, they are allowed an imperfect view of the House'.[1] The language used in this extract is revealing: women were allowed to view proceedings in the Commons, but it was made clear that they should be neither seen nor heard. The grille was a symbol of the distinction of sex, the embodiment of the belief that politics was a male domain, and that any interest shown by women was marginal, or to quote Dod, 'imperfect'.

The campaigns leading up to the 1867 Reform Act signalled the beginning of a significant and organized challenge by women to their exclusion from British national politics. It was not until 1918 that women over 30 were allowed the parliamentary vote. The 50 years in between were marked by prolonged, diverse and increasingly militant campaigns for women's admittance to parliamentary politics. These campaigns have been the subject of different historical studies exploring the nature of women's demands; the variety of women's suffrage organizations and tactics which emerged between the 1860s and 1920s, the diversity of demands and ideas, as well as conflicts and similarities between them.[2] These studies have been framed in consideration of the development of feminism as a means of understanding and challenging women's lack of equality in political, economic, sexual, and cultural areas of society.[3]

[1] Dod's *Parliamentary Companion* (1906), p. 131.

[2] See E. S. Pankhurst, *The Suffragette Movement. An Intimate Account of Persons and Ideals* (reprint of 1st edn., [1931], 1984); R. Fulford, *Votes for Women, The Story of a Struggle* (Readers Union edn., 1958); L. Garner, *Stepping Stones to Women's Liberty. Feminist Ideas in the Women's Suffrage Movement 1900–1918* (1984); L. Parker Hume, *The National Union of Women's Suffrage Societies, 1897–1914* (New York, 1982); S. S. Holton, *Feminism and Democracy: Women's Suffrage and Reform Politics, 1900–1918* (Cambridge, 1987); J. Liddington and J. Norris, *One Hand Tied Behind Us. The Rise of the Women's Suffrage Movement* (2nd edn., 1984); A. Rosen, *'Rise Up Women!' The Militant Campaign of the Women's Social and Political Union, 1903–1914* (1974).

[3] See C. Dyhouse, *Feminism and the Family in England, 1880–1939* (Oxford, 1989); P. Levine, *Victorian Feminism, 1850–1900* (1987); S. Jeffreys, *The Spinster and Her Enemies. Feminism and Sexuality, 1880–1930* (1985); and S. Kingsley Kent, *Sex and Suffrage* (Princeton, 1987).

Running parallel, but rarely touching upon the above issues, a great volume of work has been produced on the development of a parliamentary system of government in Britain dating from the 1832 Reform Act. In these 'orthodox' histories the emphasis has been, to varying degrees, on the changing role and power of the Lords and the Commons, the development and growing centrality of the party system, the processes by which the Cabinet came to dictate and control much of the legislation discussed in the two Houses, and lastly the changing role of the state whereby greater intervention in the lives of the populace was introduced through legislation.[4]

This article sets out to explore the connexions between these developments in parliamentary government and what has often been projected as the less significant issue of the campaigns for equal political rights between men and women. Specifically, it proposes an interpretation of this period in Parliament's history as one in which gendered interests, assumptions and practices were central to the developments in the ideal and reality of government. Moreover, by looking at the campaigns for women's inclusion into national parliamentary politics, and the responses to them from men within Parliament, and sections of the national press, it will identify the scope and limitations of challenges by women, and some men, to the male exclusivity of the franchise, government and the legislation produced.

Women's concealment behind the grille not only demonstrated women's exclusion, it also emphasised how Parliament before 1918 was an exclusively male environment. This situation was explicitly and implicitly reinforced by successive male Parliaments and it was something that many M.P.s, in all parties, identified as their right, and as an embodiment of their masculinity. Consequently, male M.P.s would not easily concede this all-male environment, indeed, many could not conceive of Parliament in any other way.[5]

On one eventful day in October 1908 the male domain of the Commons' chamber was invaded by a woman. Mrs Travers-Symons, an advocate of women's suffrage, managed to enter the chamber and interrupt the debate taking place, and called out to the assembled M.P.s her demand for 'votes for women'. Newspaper reports noted that she was quickly seized by an attendant and carried away.[6] References to such protests by women by a variety of historians have dwelt (with varying degrees of condemnation and admiration) on their actions in so far as they were a manifestation of the militant women's suffrage campaign of the early years of the twentieth century.[7]

---

[4] See articles in *The House of Commons in the Twentieth Century. Essays by Members of the Study of Parliament Group*, ed. S. A. Walkland (Oxford, 1979); *The Politics of Parliamentary Reform*, ed. D. Judge (1983), and early chapters in P. Norton, *The Commons in Perspective* (Oxford, 1981). The exception to this separation between women's suffrage and parliamentary reform is the more recent work of Martin Pugh. See M. Pugh, *State and Society. British Political and Social History, 1870–1992* (1994).

[5] Attitudes towards women's political equality and access to political government are also pertinent to the House of Lords, where peeresses did not gain entry in their own rights until 1959 (although this change in the law was not fully implemented until 1963). However, throughout the period covered in this article the most concerted issues centred on the House of Commons and it is here that I concentrate my considerations. See also note 86, below.

[6] For an account see *Daily News*, 14 Oct. 1908, p. 5, c. 1.

[7] See Fulford, *Votes for Women*, pp. 117–26; and *Suffrage and the Pankhursts*, ed. J. Marcus (1987), pp. 2–9. Marcus also critically summarises the views in G. Dangerfield, *The Strange Death of Liberal England* (Paladin edn., 1970).

Yet what is not considered in any detail is *why* Mrs Travers-Symons's brief presence in the Commons was so disturbing to M.P.s and newspaper reporters watching from the press gallery. The lobby correspondent of the Liberal *Daily News* evoked confrontation and conflict in his report, commenting, 'The Suffragettes have won. A member of their body has entered the House of Commons while legislators were engaged in business'.[8] Apparently the very presence of a woman attempting to speak in the House of Commons shook the foundations on which the post-1832 'modern' Parliament had been established.

2

A re-reading in terms of gender of the transitions of parliamentary government in the nineteenth century is revealing. The 1832 Reform Act significantly increased the male electorate, while inscribing in specific legal language women's exclusion from the parliamentary franchise. By the 1890s, after subsequent extensions in 1867 and 1884, two-thirds of men in Britain were entitled to vote. The changes produced by such increases in the male electorate have been sufficient to warrant a description of the years up to 1884 as 'the golden age of Parliament'.[9] The role of M.P.s took on greater significance under the principle that they were elected to represent the beliefs and interests of their constituents. Other important developments were the formalization of party politics, and the tightening of controls exercised by the parties over their elected M.P.s.

In addition there was a process of regimenting political interest outside Parliament through the formation of political clubs, registration societies, and party organizations like the National Liberal Federation and the Conservative National Union.[10] Another important product of the extended franchise and party control was that by the latter decades of the century the Cabinet was firmly entrenched as the controlling agent in prioritising and dictating legislation passed by Parliament.[11]

These changes both inside and outside Parliament occurred solely and explicitly in reference to male citizens and therefore served, although not necessarily exclusively or uniformly, the interests of both the male electorate and the men seeking to represent them in the House of Commons. Jeff Hearn has characterised the years after 1867 as 'a brief period of men's relative democracy'. They were, he states, 'an interlude characterised by complex public political coalitions of men'.[12]

During the 1880s, the exclusively male orientation of the political organizations outside Parliament was modified somewhat after women were admitted to existing and newly formed political parties. However these moves cannot be seen to herald a new equality between the sexes, nor was women's entry couched in such terms by the majority of nineteenth-century male political activists. Rather, women were admitted to Liberal and Conservative party organizations in order to harness their

[8] *Daily News*, 14 Oct. 1908, p. 5, c. 1.
[9] P. Norton, 'The Organisation of Parliamentary Politics', in Walkland (ed.), *The House of Commons*, p. 7.
[10] *Ibid.*, pp. 7–9.
[11] See *ibid.*, and P. Norton, *The Commons in Perspective*, pp. 16–18, S. A. Walkland, 'Government Legislation in the House of Commons', in Walkland (ed.), *The House of Commons*, pp. 247–60.
[12] J. Hearn, *Men in The Public Eye. Critical Studies on Masculinities*, (1992), pp. 128–9.

usefulness as canvassers and voluntary workers in the aftermath of the 1883 Corrupt Practices Act which set firmer controls on the conduct of electioneering. Only the new socialist parties, the Independent Labour Party and the Social Democratic Federation admitted women on equal terms with men.[13] These changes were also prompted by women's growing interest in politics, and many new female party members took these opportunities to develop and refine their political concerns and interests, and to develop women's organizational strength.[14] However these developments did not appear to directly alter the majority of party members' and male M.P.s' beliefs that the process of governing Britain and framing legislation was primarily and ultimately a male preserve. As Linda Walker and Karen Hunt have indicated, women's presence in the parties did in some cases emphasise gender distinctions and heightened divisions in views concerning men and women's relative relationship to politics.[15] Moreover, the reality of women's continued exclusion from voting and sitting in the House of Commons remained.

It is a gross simplification to explain men's domination of party politics and parliamentary government as being motivated by some inherent, or unchanging desire for power over women. In considering the impact of gender on the development of systems of government it is essential to consider changing social constructions of masculinity in the nineteenth-century. According to John Tosh, dominant ideas about masculinity by the latter half of the nineteenth century were only secondarily about men's relationship with women. Primarily these ideas were geared towards affirming men's status through displays of the following 'manly' traits: 'self-control, hard work and independence'.[16] Tosh identifies three key areas through which masculinity was expressed in social terms: through authority in households, dignified employment and all-male associations.[17] Extending this, I would argue that manliness was also represented in enfranchised men's status as voters. It distinguished these men from voteless men, and was a public expression of their status as heads of households, and overseers of private life, as well as public politics.

Specifically, if we consider the attitudes of male M.P.s towards other all-male associations, it is possible to argue that in the 1880s and 1890s a majority sought to maintain an exclusively male environment in national politics as way of expressing and confirming their manliness. By 1900 the greater majority of M.P.s belonged to at least one metropolitan club, and the impact and influence of clubs in general were at their height.[18] In exclusively all-male surroundings crucial parliamentary matters

[13] L. Walker, 'The Women's Movement in England in the Late Nineteenth and Early Twentieth Centuries', (University of Manchester, Ph.D. 1984), pp. 12–51.

[14] L. Walker, 'Party Political Women: A Comparative Study of Liberal Women and the Primrose League, 1890–1914', pp. 165–91; and J. Hannam, ' "In the Comradeship of the Sexes Lie the Hope of Progress and Social Regeneration": Women in the West Riding ILP. c. 1890–1914', pp. 214–38; both in *Equal or Different. Women's Politics 1880–1914*, ed. J. Rendall (Oxford, 1987).

[15] L. Walker, 'The Women's Movement in England', pp. 52–103; and K. Hunt, cited from conference paper, 'Making Socialist Woman: Politicisation, Gender and the SDF, 1884–1911', University of York, 26 Apr. 1993.

[16] J. Tosh, 'What Should Historian Do With Masculinity? Reflections on Nineteenth Century Britain', *History Workshop Journal*, No. 38 (1994), 183.

[17] *Ibid.*, pp. 184–7. Tosh notes that the scope for dignified employment for working-class men was limited, and suggests that working-class masculine values associated with work tended to be expressed through 'celebration of physical strength'.

[18] M. Rush, 'The Members of Parliament', in Walkland (ed.), *The House of Commons*, p. 118.

of the day were discussed and alliances made and actions endorsed. It was no coincidence, as Brian Harrison points out, that the clubs were the core of M.P.s anti-suffrage networks and attempts to prevent women from obtaining access to parliamentary politics.[19] The clubs reinforced and extended the all-male privileged atmosphere of the House of Commons.

What complicates any straightforward association of dominant masculinity with male domination of government and politics is the presence in the House of Commons, in the political parties (and in metropolitan clubs), of male supporters of both women's suffrage and other reforms affecting women's familial, sexual and economic lives. Among them were John Stuart Mill, Jacob Bright, Keir Hardie, Willoughby Hyett Dickinson and Charles Dilke. Yet it does not follow therefore that ideas about masculinity and patriarchal relations between the sexes were not factors in the development in parliamentary government. On the contrary, it raises important issues concerning competing and changing codes of manly behaviour and values in the latter nineteenth and early twentieth centuries.

Understanding the relationship between gender and Parliament extends beyond exploring those factors that produced an all-male or male-dominated environment. Jeff Hearn has shown that it is also possible to identify how male power and interests – or what were perceived to be male interests – directly related to the legislation enacted in the course of the nineteenth century. Hearn uses the term 'public men' to mean not only male public figures, but any man who had a presence in 'public domains'.[20] He traces how patriarchal power in the second half of the century was enforced through a model of 'fatherly' state intervention by public men into the private lives of families. A series of acts, including the 1861 Offences Against the Person Act and the Custody of Children Act confirmed and enforced divisions between man as breadwinner and public figure and woman as child rearer and private figure.[21] Crucially, Hearn demonstrates that it was not simply men enforcing control over women, but *public* men (including M.P.s and government ministers) intervening in the *private* lives of men and women. It is this construction that contradicts assumptions that nineteenth-century parliamentary government fundamentally or straightforwardly reflected the wishes of the entire male electorate.

It is also important to consider the legislation which resulted from pressures exerted by those societies, often dominated by women, which demanded changes in the conditions under which women lived. From the 1860s, campaigners, in particular Josephine Butler and members of the Ladies' National Association for the Abolition of the Contagious Diseases Acts, had notable success in forcing M.P.s to consider the effects on women of legislation that failed to acknowledge the dangers for women of male immorality. The repeal campaign not only brought sexual issues into public politics, it also marked some change in attitudes to female intervention in politics at a national level.[22] As Mort states, while restrictions were still apparent that defined

[19] B. Harrison, *Separate Spheres. The Opposition To Women's Suffrage in Britain* (1978), p. 103.

[20] J. Hearn, *Men in the Public Eye*, pp. 3, 95. In this article I am specifically concerned with those 'public men' who were M.P.s, and a number of pro and anti-suffrage public figures Parliament, including journalists, and members of men's societies formed to campaign for women's suffrage.

[21] *Ibid.*, pp. 108–15.

[22] Jeffreys, *The Spinster and Her Enemies*, pp. 6–26; and F. Mort, *Dangerous Sexualities. Medico-Moral Politics in England since 1830*, (1987), pp. 86–99.

the types of women who could articulate political concerns, there were moves towards acknowledging women's political involvement.[23]

Over the course of the century, there was support in Parliament not only for the repeal of the Contagious Diseases Acts, but also for reforms in marriage laws and women's access to the municipal franchise and local government posts such as Poor Law Guardians and School Boards. This situation presents a number of interesting areas that illustrate how attitudes towards the state provided possibilities for coalitions between predominantly middle-class men and women.

A connected issue relates to the extent to which some M.P.s were increasingly supportive towards women in public life, particularly parliamentary politics. By the latter part of the nineteenth century, some appeared to be reconciled to ending exclusive male involvement in national politics, whilst others were organising increasingly strenuous opposition to women's demands for parliamentary representation. This raises questions about what the differing attitudes towards women in politics meant in terms of ideas and constructions of masculine identity. As Hearn states, 'Movements to public patriarchies were dialectical, contradictory, historical.'[24]

Masculine identity as it was constructed in the late nineteenth and early twentieth centuries was not automatically experienced in a uniform way. Masculinity and expressions of manliness were affected by class, sexuality and ethnicity, and this was true for M.P.s and ministers as much as for society outside Parliament. Among the law makers in Parliament, there were clear differences of party interests, experiences of work and the relative power of the Members, both in terms of their family networks and their influence in the House. Importantly, from 1867 the representation of working-class voters and the election of working-class M.P.s from the 1880's, fractured any aristocratic or middle-class professionals' monopoly in Parliament. This was most clearly emphasised by Keir Hardie after his election in 1892, when he entered the Commons wearing tweed trousers, serge jacket and cloth cap.[25]

The types of M.P.s elected after 1867 reflected broader social, economic and political developments. Feuchtwanger records that in 1865 there was a family connexion between over half of M.P.s and 30 of the most powerful aristocratic families. By the end of the century this bias had shifted with the election of Members from the business and commercial world and a small number of working-class men. By 1914 the domination of *élite* family networks had changed in every aspect except the most powerful, namely, in the Cabinet.[26] It has been shown that these changes in the personnel of ordinary Members, particular radical Liberals, had an important effect on the emphasis given in the House of Commons to the issue of social and constitutional reform.[27] It is equally valid to assume they had an effect on attitudes towards women's access to democratic citizenship.

Interpretations of Parliament as male defined, identification of differing connexions

[23] Mort, *Dangerous Sexualities*, p. 98.
[24] Hearn, *Men in the Public Eye*, p. 113.
[25] E. J. Feuchtwanger, *Democracy and Empire, Britain 1865–1914* (1985), pp. 207, 210.
[26] *Ibid.*, pp. 2–3.
[27] See D. Sutton, 'Liberalism, State Collectivism and the Social Relations of Citizenship', in *Crises in the British State, 1880–1930*, eds. M. Langan and B. Schwarz (1985), pp. 63–79.

between masculinity and exercising political rights, exploring the manifestations of 'public patriarchies'; and attitudes towards women's demands for access to public politics, provide starting points from which to explore how government, Parliament and legislation have been constructed in reference to gender. Specifically, they can be applied to the question of female enfranchisement in the period from the 1890s to 1918.

From its inception women's suffrage activists in the National Women's Suffrage Society could count on a core of support from a number of pro-suffrage M.P.s. Co-operation between them and women campaigners led to women's suffrage bills being debated in Parliament on many occasions in the 1870s and 1880s.[28] Yet the occurrence of these debates can lead to misleading assumptions that male support for women's suffrage was straightforward and unproblematic. It remained the case that support *per se* could not automatically result in legislation. Equally, numerous discussions in the Commons were accompanied by scathing slights on women's capabilities and desultory laughter. Moreover, there were, of course, both ardent supporters and confirmed opponents within Conservative, Liberal and the growing Labour party ranks, which resulted in a lack of systematic backing from any of the political parties in Parliament until 1912.

A closer consideration of the 1892 debate on women's suffrage reveals a complex series of attitudes towards women's suffrage among male M.P.s and significant party figures which relate once again to the identification of Parliament as a male domain. Rather than there being any straightforward change in favour of political equality between men and women, evidently there was an explicit attempt from some quarters to clarify gender boundaries. Moreover, even among those in favour of some extension of the franchise to women, there was a desire to legislate and formalise an inequality between male and female political involvement.

In 1892 A. J. Balfour, one of the leading Conservative ministers in the Commons, made a speech in favour of extending the parliamentary franchise to women. In it he dealt with the objections of anti-suffragist M.P.s, many of which had changed little since the 1870s. Interestingly his speech was constructed around denials: he denied that enfranchised women would control the policy of the country. He rejected that women would all vote in the same way. He denied that women had not shown that they wanted the vote, and that women were somehow not able to fulfil the duties of active citizenship. He denied that encouraging women to take an active part in politics and in framing the policy of the Empire was 'degrading to the sex'.[29] Yet his investment in the ideal of male control over government was all too evident in his further denials that such legislation would lead to women been admitted to the House of Commons as M.P.s:[30]

> In my opinion women could not with advantage to themselves, or to the community, take part in the labours of a great deliberating assembly like this. That is a reason

[28] Fulford, *Votes For Women*, pp. 71–8.
[29] A. J. Balfour, *Speech in Support of The Parliamentary Franchise Extension to Women, House of Commons, April 27th 1892* (n.d.)
[30] *Ibid.*

for not giving them a seat in this House, but is it a reason for not giving them an opportunity of expressing an opinion and giving a vote every four or five years?

What Balfour did *not* deny was the belief that women were less capable than men to govern, thus indicating how sexually defined boundaries remained a concern, even among supporters of female enfranchisement. It can also be seen that Balfour enforced the belief in an innate manly aptitude to government. Moreover, the tendency in his arguments was to undermine both the impact of the vote and also ideals of democratic representation more generally. His words tacitly implied that extending the franchise to include women would have no impact on either an exclusively male-legislature, and particularly a Cabinet constituted of aristocratic *élites*. Equally significant was Balfour's reference to 'framing the policy of the Empire'.[31] Although he made the point that the British Empire would not be harmed by women's votes, underlying this statement is the whole issue of nationalism and imperialism in this period.

3

Since the 1870s, issues of empire and nation had taken on renewed significance to political leaders, and in public sentiment. Underlying this upsurge in nationalism was an imagined natural superiority of British men and women, cemented in the belief that Britain was a superior civilization.[32] The concomitant identification of Britain as the leading nation across the globe meant that the Houses of Parliament in London represented not only the centre of British national politics, but also the core of Britain's empire. As such, Parliament was characterised as a revered institution where dignity and superiority were paramount. Maintaining the status of this 'Mother of Parliaments' was a serious preoccupation for male M.P.s, large sections of the press, and as Antoinette Burton's work indicates, for many women suffrage activists in the early twentieth century.[33] However, *how* Parliament's dignity would be maintained and improved formed the crux of debates over women's suffrage.

Taking into account the identification of Britain's Parliament as the core of the British Empire, gives added impetus to the view that senior *élite* politicians like Balfour were concerned to preserve or re-emphasise the constituency and male-exclusivity of Parliament because it was deemed to represent supremacy, security and stability. Such representations took on even more significance in the light of increasing attacks towards the end of the century from some quarters on the decadence of M.P.s and civil servants.[34] The description of Parliament as 'the best club in London', was not only indicative of its male exclusivity, but also of the view that politicians were not exclusively dedicated to ensuring effective government, but relished in the *élite* status granted to them. Thus, a complex web of retrenchment and reforms were apparent in the turn-of-the-century Parliament, and at its centre were interconnected issues of gender, class, nation and empire.

[31] *Ibid.*
[32] See Pugh, *State and Society*, pp. 101–2; and Feuchtwanger, *Democracy and Empire*, p. 4.
[33] A. Burton, 'The Feminist Quest for Identity: British Imperial Suffragism and Global Sisterhood, 1900–1915', *Journal of Women's History*, III (1991), 46–81. Burton demonstrates how women suffragists attitudes towards the British Empire were grounded in their belief in British women's superiority.
[34] Pugh, *State and Society*, p. 39.

An example of moves to redefine gender distinctions in favour of male interests can be found in the preface written by the Irish Nationalist M.P., Justin McCarthy, to the published memoirs of William White, the Houses of Parliament doorkeeper between 1850 and 1875. McCarthy's apparent intention in his preface was to compare his experiences in the Houses of Parliament with the earlier Parliaments witnessed by William White. The framing of many of his comments in a nostalgic tone said much about McCarthy's' anxieties about the current position of Parliament in the eyes of the (male) public.[35] However, many of his most sarcastic comments were reserved for the crowds of ladies who covered the terrace of the House on summer evenings, with some lingering in the lobby 'to see what is going on'. Evoking an image of upper-class privilege he makes it clear that he saw women's presence in Parliament as entertaining, but rather absurd. In his view it was inconceivable that women could have any true interest or insight into the serious business being conducted there. Rather, they used the outer environs of Parliament merely as an extension of their social entertainment. Recreating an evening sitting of the Commons, McCarthy wrote[36]:

> when the division-bell suddenly rings . . . every member jumps up and makes for the one available staircase . . . Down this same staircase a stream of ladies is pouring; most of these ladies have not the faintest notion why members should come rushing like madmen up the stairs, and they never think of flattening themselves against the wall or the balustrade to allow the struggling members to get to their division-lobby.

In McCarthy's writing there was a deliberate, yet also obscured preoccupation with establishing boundaries between men and women in political terms. Underlying his portrayal of Parliament was an attempt to deflect the uncertainties and criticisms facing many male politicians by stressing their fundamental distinction from ignorant women.

It was this environment of a totally male defined, *élite*-dominated Parliament, with challenges from new breeds of politicians representing socialists and new liberalism reforms, as well as campaigns by women for a greater stake in politics, that characterized British parliamentary 'democracy' by the first decade of the twentieth century. Ironically, McCarthy also made reference in his preface to White's memoirs to the disorganised and patchy system by which the public gained entry to the public galleries in the Commons. His comment that any unknown ladies might 'be carrying neatly done up packets of dynamite under their skirts' was prophetic given the actions of militant woman suffrage activists a few years later.[37]

4

It is important to stress here how women's history and feminist historiography have made an impact on studies of women's suffrage. Since the 1970's there has been a welcome and necessary deflection from accounts of the progress of suffrage debates and manoeuvres in Parliament and activities in London. Disinvesting in such standard

[35] W. White, *The Inner Life of the House of Commons*, with a preface by J. McCarthy, M.P. (3rd edn., 2 vols., 1904) I, p. xviii.
[36] *Ibid.*, p. xix.
[37] *Ibid.*, p. xviii.

historical approaches has produced ground-breaking studies of suffrage activities in other areas and districts, notably in the North West of England and Scotland.[38] This body of work has sealed the lid on narrow interpretations of the campaign as a London-based phenomenon, undertaken solely by middle-class leisured women. Equally, enquiries into the ideas and concerns of activists have emphasised women's broader challenges to the sexual, social and economic disadvantages they faced. These developments, in addition to new studies of masculinity, make it possible to look once again at the campaigns women suffrage activists directed at the Houses of Parliament and parliamentary politics, and to provide a thorough gender analysis.

At the heart of studies of the women's suffrage campaign is an emphasis on the diversity, distinctiveness and connexions among suffrage activists and feminists. These were expressed, though not exclusively, in membership of the various women's societies active in the late nineteenth and early twentieth centuries. In terms of attitudes towards Parliament, distinct approaches are apparent in the policies of the largest and most active women's suffrage societies active by the first decade of the new century (although this was not necessarily a direct reflection of the varied personal views of the membership). The oldest suffrage society, the National Union of Women Suffrage Societies (N.U.W.S.S.), an amalgamation dating from 1897 of the various regional suffrage societies, was firmly locked into campaigning in Parliament. The N.U.W.S.S. constitution emphasised this policy in its declaration of methods as the 'promotion of united action in Parliament and the country'.[39]

The N.U.W.S.S.'s policy of generating support among M.P.s in the House of Commons remained an integral feature of its work right into the 1920s. The ties between the N.U.W.S.S. executive and members of the Parliamentary Committee for Women's Suffrage in the House of Commons were particularly strong.[40] They endorsed a shared belief that it was at the heart of government that women's demands for the vote would, and must be met.

In this period, despite the anxieties expressed by many anti-suffrage M.P.s that full adult suffrage would result from female enfranchisement, the demand of the women's suffrage movement was for votes for women on the same terms 'as it is or may be given to men'. Less emphasis was placed on the inequalities in the current male franchise, as activists concentrated on ending discrimination by sex. Another related thrust to their arguments was the belief that women had particular qualities they could bring to politics, often concentrating on issues related to the home, education, and welfare.[41] While there were a number of important alternative stances, notably in relation to demands for universal adult suffrage, broadly speaking, votes on the same terms as men was the key demand of the N.U.W.S.S., the Women's Social and Political Union (W.S.P.U.) and the Women's Freedom League (W.F.L.) formed in 1903 and 1907 respectively.

---

[38]   See Liddington and Norris, *One Hand Tied Behind Us*; and L. Leneman, *A Guid Cause. The Women's Suffrage Movement, in Scotland* (Aberdeen, 1991).

[39]   N.U.W.S.S., *Annual Report* (1907).

[40]   *Ibid*. This Parliamentary Committee was chaired by Charles McLaren.

[41]   See D. Rubinstein, 'Millicent Garrett Fawcett and the Meaning of Women's Emancipation, 1886–99', *Victorian Studies*, XXXIV (1991) 365–80; and notes 2 and 3, above.

The complicated and sometimes contradictory attitude towards principles of democracy among women suffrage activists, reflected the ambivalence in Liberal and Conservative attitudes towards full adult suffrage. Frequent arguments made by women suffrage advocates against the demands of adult suffragists claimed that ending the sex distinction was the first priority, or that full adult suffrage was too great a step to be taken, and something that the government would never concede to in the short term.[42] Such arguments indicate that at the beginning of the century there was a relatively more sympathetic attitude among women suffragists to the principles of Liberalism. Conversely, the Labour movement's attitudes towards women's suffrage were nothing if not divided among a range of different opinions.[43] Moreover, the relatively greater numbers of middle-class activists in the women's suffrage societies undoubtedly had some bearing on Labour's attitude to women's suffrage. Nevertheless both middle and working-class women suffragists did develop a more complementary relationship with the Labour party during the early twentieth-century suffrage campaigns, which perhaps reflected increasing support among women for full adult suffrage, as well as a recognition of the problems of sex inequality among sections of the Labour Party[44] This relationship was confirmed in 1912 when Labour's annual conference finally agreed to endorse women's suffrage. In return the N.U.W.S.S. and the W.F.L. agreed in certain circumstances to work for Labour candidates in elections.

One of the most significant developments in the twentieth century women's suffrage campaign was the adoption of militant tactics, not least because of the impact it had on Parliament and M.P.s. The first militant action in October 1905 represented a direct assault by woman suffrage campaigners on the unquestioned power and integrity of parliamentary government. It signified a break in the trust these women had previously displayed that Parliament was prepared to act on women's demands. As a number of historians have argued, Christabel Pankhurst and Annie Kenney's interruption of speeches at the Liberal meeting in the Free Trade Hall in Manchester represented a growing impatience by employing new publicity seeking tactics of interrupting political procedures.[45] Presenting an important alternative perspective, Jane Marcus has identified their actions as an 'interruption of male political discourse'.[46] The concentration on Parliament and its representatives remained as in previous non-militant campaigns, but instead of pleading to be let in, militant women became directly confrontational and challenged many of the ideals and attitudes that kept all women excluded.

It is instructive to examine the extent to which suffrage agitation by women and men was an acknowledged attempt to *demasculinize* parliamentary politics in order to reform a corrupt political system and so generate a reformed environment where both sexes could work together for an equal and improved society. Therefore, I shall consider a number of protests by suffrage activists, and a range of responses by

[42] For further discussion see Holton, *Feminism and Democracy*, pp. 53–75.

[43] M. Durham, 'Suffrage and After: Feminism in the Early Twentieth Century', in Langan and Schwarz (eds.), *Crises in the British State*, p. 180.

[44] See Garner, *Stepping Stones to Women's Liberty*, pp. 16–19, 34–8, 41–2, 82, 86–8.

[45] Harrison, *Separate Spheres*, p. 177; and Pugh, *State and Society*, p. 134, have concentrated on the negative implications of militancy.

[46] Marcus (ed.), *Suffrage and the Pankhursts*, p. 9.

politicians to women's protests. Lastly, I shall consider the factors integral to women's suffrage activists' beliefs that constrained their challenge to male hegemonic power.

From 1906, militant tactics concentrated on using Parliament, its Members and parliamentary procedures to their own ends. Early demonstrations that were designed to invade the inner precincts of Parliament were forceful challenges to male privilege and female exclusion. The petitions of previous years and the presence of a small number of campaigners behind the grille in the Ladies' Gallery, albeit not always quiet or anonymous, were nevertheless eclipsed by the new direct actions that were backed up by force of numbers.[47] After the W.S.P.U.'s first London meeting in February 1906, between 300 and 400 mostly working women marched to the Houses of Parliament demanding to see their newly elected M.P.s. Eventually they were allowed in 20 at a time, a practice rapidly stopped as subsequent demonstrations in the vicinity of the Houses of Parliament became larger and more frequent.[48]

Attempts to confront politicians with women's suffrage demands were not confined to Westminster. The process of concentrating on government figures was a country-wide phenomenon: Churchill faced protesters in Dundee, and Asquith in Edinburgh. Moreover, campaigns by suffrage activists at by-elections and general elections were an important thrust of the work of regional members and paid organisers in all three main women's suffrage societies.[49]

M.P.s holding any opinion on suffrage found it increasingly difficult to distance themselves from the issue, as W.S.P.U. members, after being refused audiences, intensified their criticisms and confrontations by interrupting speeches at political meetings, particularly those of Cabinet ministers.[50] When the W.F.L. was formed after a split in the W.S.P.U. in September 1907, its members agreed to discontinue this action amid anxieties that it interfered with free speech.[51] This was a somewhat ironic step considering the lengths that were by then being taken to silence women suffrage activists, nevertheless it does emphasise the extent to which some militant women continued to invest in liberal political principles.

As an alternative method of protest, members of the W.F.L. began calling at M.P.'s London residences to demand that their views be considered. It was on occasions like the morning call on Asquith at Downing Street in May 1908, when 20 women

[47] For details of women suffrage actions in Parliament before 1906 see Fulford, *Votes for Women*, pp. 27–83.
[48] Pankhurst, *The Suffragette Movement*, p. 199. See other chapters for her account of other W.S.P.U. protests in the vicinity of Parliament.
[49] There was a great deal of scope for such activities in the period. In addition to the two general elections in 1910, between December 1910 and the outbreak of the First World War, there were 102 by-elections in Britain. See F. W. S. Craig, *Chronology of British Parliamentary By-Elections, 1833–1987* (Chichester, 1987). Examples in this article have a London bias because it was here that the most consistent and concentrated attacks on parliamentary government took place, and it was these attacks, particularly on the Houses of Parliament which produced the greatest diversity of reactions. I do recognize that regional studies of campaigning during by elections and general elections make significant contributions to the issues explored in this article.
[50] For detailed accounts of W.S.P.U. militancy see Rosen, *'Rise Up Women!'*, and Pankhurst, *The Suffragette Movement*.
[51] For further details of W.F.L. policies see C. Eustance, 'Daring To Be Free: The Evolution of Women's Political Identities in the WFL, 1907–1930', (University of York, D. Phil., 1993), Chapters 1 and 3.

refused to move on, that mass arrests became more widespread.[52] In addition to the tactical issue underlining W.S.P.U. and W.F.L. protests at M.P.s, there is *also* the publicity aspect. It soon became apparent to protesters that their actions received unprecedented press attention – often entire front pages of newspapers were devoted to images of protesting women, as well as countless columns. Obviously the links between publicity and protest were recognized and used by suffrage activists, but this should not detract from the sophisticated and well thought out critique underlying the focus on Parliament. Moreover, women had found ways to circumvent their lack of political power by using the media. Thus they challenged the exclusivity of male dialogue in the media and publicized their demands across Britain. There is no doubt that the actions directed at Parliament and M.P.s were considered threatening and disturbing given the extreme reactions. Harsh sentences were meted out to arrested women who refused to pay the fines levied against them. They were, as a rule, refused status as political prisoners and subjected to the tighter regimes in lower prison divisions.

Another strategy women suffrage activists used to challenge male-dominated politics drew on ancient rights as a means of highlighting how women had been left out of developments in systems of government. Actions included attempts to petition the King, which were backed up by claims that before the right to vote had been extended in the nineteenth century, it had been the right of every citizen to appeal to the sovereign through their elected representatives in Parliament.[53] Members of the W.F.L. pointed out in detailed pamphlets and letters in 1908 that because both the vote and the right to appeal to Parliament were being denied to them, they were forced to appeal directly to King Edward VII.[54] Similarly, the right to present petitions to Parliament was used by Emmeline Pankhurst in her defence after being arrested outside the Houses of Parliament in 1911.[55] In both cases the grounds claimed by activists were rejected.

These emphases on the progress of men's political rights, compared to women's lack of rights were not confined to political issues. The W.F.L. in particular made a point of targeting its protests at the courts and 'man-made law'. This was prompted by the ideas of a leading member of the W.F.L., Teresa Billington-Greig, a self-defined feminist, whose interests and ideas constantly led her to push for diverse and provocative sites of militant protest. Initiatives that emphasised the invalidity of man-made laws moved from the police court trials of arrested suffrage activists, towards attacks on attitudes and laws which punished women while displaying leniency towards male offenders, particularly those guilty of sexual crimes against women and children.[56] Moreover, women in all the societies began to resist paying taxes in protest at their inability to have a say in decisions on how their taxes were

[52] *Daily Graphic*, 22 May 1908, p. 6, c. 2.
[53] See copy of letter to King Edward VII, B. L., Maud Arncliffe Sennett Collection of Press Cuttings, Pamphlets, Leaflets and Letters on Women's Suffrage (hereafter cited as M.A.S.), Vol. 8, pp. 22–3.
[54] W.F.L., 'Why We Petition The King', (n.d.), M.A.S., Vol. 8, pp. 12–13.
[55] E. Pankhurst, 'Defence', 21 May 1912, reprinted in Marcus (ed.), *Suffrage and the Pankhursts*, p. 133.
[56] See Eustance, 'Daring To Be Free', Chapters 1, 3, and 4.

spent, and in 1909 the Women's Tax Resistance League was formed to co-ordinate these protests.[57]

Such protests emphasize the ways in which militant and constitutional activists questioned in organized and sophisticated ways *both* male privilege and female exclusion and inequality in Parliament and wider society. It is equally significant that challenges to women's parliamentary exclusion were framed in reference to the development of democratic traditions in Britain. Their actions indicate that women were demanding integration (they described it as reintegration) into their place in the history of British democracy. Thus, while activists might challenge male privilege, this did not appear to extend to challenging the basic foundation of parliamentary institutions themselves. Women suffrage activists wanted access to Britain's national parliamentary democracy in order to bring their concerns and interests into politics, they did not want to destroy it.

In 1909, Alison Neilans unequivocally articulated this distinction in her defence against the charge of unlawfully interfering with a ballot-box, following a W.F.L. planned exercise designed to invalidate an election. This protest in Bermondsey was reported in the *Pall Mall Gazette* as the most 'outrageous' and 'unparalleled' action to date in the women's suffrage agitation.[58] Drawing on past struggles, Neilans declared:[59]

> We have won all our rights by fights and struggles against constituted authority.
>
> To-day, why do we reverence Cromwell, Pym, Hampden, and other who have fought and made England what it is and who gave us such liberties as we enjoy? . . . Gentlemen, I would submit to you that the spirit which makes us fight for freedom is the same whether it breathes through women or men.

Neilans concluded that she felt so strongly precisely because she had the 'deepest respect' for the process of elections, and wanted a part in them. Despite her words, the jury remained unmoved and Neilans and Alice Chapin, her partner in the Bermondsey protest, were imprisoned for three and four months respectively.[60]

Arguments such as those articulated by Neilans had been used by women campaigners before 1909. Nevertheless it is apparent that they were perceived as more threatening in the context of women's physical presence in political arenas during the heightened tension of the militant campaign. Whatever women claimed, it appears that the dominant belief among anti-suffragists, whether in the media or in Parliament, continued to be that Parliament's heritage belonged to men, and that it was in men's hands to preserve and continue the imperial government that had developed. A resolution passed by the Committee for Opposing Female Suffrage conveyed this with the comment that extending the franchise to women 'would be contrary to the best interests of the country and the Empire'.[61] However, apparently running counter

---

57   See M. Kineton Parkes, *Why We Resist Our Taxes* (n.d.).

58   *Pall Mall Gazette*, 28 Oct. 1909.

59   A. Neilans, *Ballot Box Protest. Defence at the Old Bailey* (n.d. [c. 1910]), p. 6.

60   *Ibid.*

61   Fawcett Library, 2/WNA Box 281, resolution passed by Committee for Opposing Female Suffrage, Dec. 1908.

to these declarations in the 1900s were those made by male politicians who were demonstrating their support for women's enfranchisement. Arguably, it was precisely the increased urgency generated by the militant suffrage campaign which brought these divergent strands of thought to the centre of parliamentary politics.

Reaction to one protest in late 1908 in particular is an indication of the diversity of opinion among male M.P.s. On 28 October 1908 in a pre-planned action, two W.F.L. members, Muriel Matters and Helen Fox, entered the Ladies' Gallery and proceeded to chain themselves to the infamous grille. Matters then began to make a speech as attendants desperately tried to remove them. An extract from her speech indicates the sense of outrage many women felt at their exclusion:[62]

> we have listened behind this insulting grille too long. Get to the women's question and get the domestic side of legislation represented. We have sat too long and listened to the illogical utterances of men who know nothing about it . . . For forty years we have sat behind this grille and we are going to do so no longer.

Matters's speech was finally brought to an end when a part of the grille was wrenched free and she and her accomplice were unceremoniously escorted away with sections of the grille still attached to them. In the commotion that ensued Asquith, who was in the chamber at the time, was one of those who demanded a recess. Following this incident and another staged by two male supporters in the Strangers' Gallery, the Speaker of the House announced that both galleries would be closed.[63]

Attitudes among the press were scathing. *The Times* remarked critically that it was a 'childish and unseemly exhibition', and the *Daily News* reported in minute detail the damage to the grille. Another correspondent commented that the protest 'violates the decency with which it is the custom in this country to conduct public business'. Further censorious remarks, which nevertheless managed to convey sensationalist undertones, were made about the simultaneous protests by other members of the W.F.L. in the lobby of the House and around the statue of Richard Coeur de Lion.[64]

The W.F.L.'s executive were delighted with the action which subsequently went down in their history as one of the great militant actions.[65] However, not all sections of the suffrage movement were comfortable with so blatant a violation of Parliament's status. This was particularly true of the executive of the N.U.W.S.S. who were prompted to write a letter to all M.P.s, placing on record their 'strong objections' to the W.F.L.'s protest and other 'similar disturbances'. Nevertheless even though the N.U.W.S.S. leadership was eager to indicate their respect for Parliament, they did point out to M.P.s that the continued refusal to respect the justice of women's demands made militancy more likely. As Millicent Garrett Fawcett commented, 'it must be remembered that the refusal of justice has often led to methods of violence and disorder'.[66] Her words demonstrate how the constitutional N.U.W.S.S. had

[62] *Daily News*, 29 Oct. 1908, p. 5, c. 2.
[63] *Vote*, 30 Dec. 1909, p. 118.
[64] *The Times*, 29 Oct. 1908, p. 10, c. 4; *Daily News*, 29 Oct. 1908, p. 5, c. 1–3.
[65] Mrs Gerald, *Hats Off To The Past. Coats Off To The Future* (n.d. [c. 1932]), p. 2. Remnants of the chain used in the protest were kept as a reminder at the W.F.L. headquarters until the society disbanded in the 1960's.
[66] Fawcett Library, N.U.W.S.S. Archives, Box 303, letter to M.P.s from M. Garrett Fawcett, 9 Nov. 1908.

become radicalized during the militant campaign, and had strengthened their condemnation of the Liberal government's refusal to act on women's demands.[67]

Not all M.P.s reacted to the 'Grille Protest' with the virulence and excess shown by some ministers and sections of the press. Willoughby Hyett Dickinson was one of those M.P.s who demonstrated in the House and at suffrage meetings his firm support for women's enfranchisement. His diary entry on the day of Matter's and Fox's protest presented an alternative interpretation:[68]

> although few members were present and the actual disturbance was not great the House as usual lost its head . . . at the request of Asquith and Balfour, the Speaker announced that both galleries would be closed. A most foolish decision in my opinion . . . To shut out all the public from our debates is perfectly monstrous and will only serve the purpose of the women.

Dickinson's reaction is particularly interesting because it indicates how he failed to fall into line with the outraged reactions of the leaders of his party and the Liberal press. Rather, he expressed more concern about the decision to close the galleries to the public. Dickinson's comments need to be put into a broader context of his opinion of the House of Commons generally.

Frequently Dickinson recorded his dissatisfaction with the 'sharp manoeuvres' inherent in the conduct of Commons business, his dissatisfaction with Asquith as Prime Minister, and his frustrations in making effective speeches there.[69] Such sentiments, together with his belief that women's suffrage was a question of justice, suggest that Dickinson did not feel threatened by women in parliamentary politics, but crucially, that he felt a far greater alienation from the environment of an exclusively male, hierarchy-ridden Parliament than he did from women's enfranchisement. Apparently Dickinson was managing to reconcile his masculine identity with the prospect of women in parliamentary government, and this in turn brought him into conflict with his political associates. It is evidence of such conflicting attitudes which demonstrates how women's suffrage was an important factor in bringing competing ideas about manliness into focus.

While Dickinson may not have experienced any conflict between his interests and women's suffrage, others were not so accommodating to those men who supported women's demands for equal voting rights. On the same day as the 'Grille Protest', Victor Storr and Thomas Bayard Simmonds staged a related protest in the Strangers' Gallery, and threw leaflets into the Commons. *The Times* correspondent reacted by casting aspersions on their manliness, commenting on male supporters' apparent delight in the 'nickname of "lambs" '.[70] Nor did the virulence of the attacks in sections of the media towards male supporters lessen over the years of the campaign. In 1913, Dickinson, a consistent supporter throughout, was subjected to ridicule in a com

---

[67] See Holton, *Feminism and Democracy*, pp. 29–52, for further discussion on early links between the constitutional and militant branches of the suffrage movement.

[68] H. C. White, *Willoughby Hyett Dickinson, 1859–1943. A Memoir*, (Gloucester, 1956), p. 118. An appendix includes edited extracts from Dickinson's diaries.

[69] *Ibid.*, pp. 111–34.

[70] *The Times*, 29 Oct. 1908, p. 10, c. 4.

mentary printed in the journal, *Truth*. The following extract is indicative of the aspersions cast upon his abilities as an M.P., as well as the mockery directed at women's suffrage activists:[71]

> Unfortunately for the Empire, it so happens that Mr Dickinson believes in Women's Suffrage. Having spare time on his hands, he amuses himself with balloting for bills and drafting amendments . . . Nobody has paid much attention to this hobby, but at one time it was quite the fashion for members who liked seeing well-dressed deputations to promise that they would 'Vote for Dickinson'. All that this formula meant was that the ladies, and the name of Dickinson became a symbol for democracy and pretty hats.

In the years between 1907 and 1914, the parliamentary debate about women's suffrage continued, but debate also diversified into the many distinct extra-parliamentary organizations and societies that were formed. Male and female anti-suffragists, including hostile M.P.s were initially organized into separate anti-suffrage societies, but merged in 1910 under the presidency of the Earl of Cromer. A plethora of societies supportive of women's suffrage emerged, some based on professions, others with a mixed male and female members, and still more that were men only. Of the latter the two biggest societies were the Men's League for Women's Suffrage (M.L.W.S.), formed in 1907 and the more militant Men's Political Union for Women's Enfranchisement (M.P.U.W.E.), that followed in 1910. In addition to numerous small business men, professionals and local councillors from across Britain, these organizations could count among their members well-known figures like Henry Woodd Nevinson and Laurence Housman, and M.P.s including Philip Snowden, Sir Alfred Mond, Edward Goulding and Walter MacLaren.

It is apparent that there was a certain preoccupation among the men's societies with emphasising the manly status of their members. The Men's League occasionally published lists of 'all the eminent men who have declared themselves in favour of the cause'.[72] These were used both to demonstrate backing for women's demands, and also to refute attacks and slights on the manliness of male supporters made by hostile sections of the press. The headings used were: Legal, Official and Parliamentary, Army and Navy, Churches, Education, Scientific Professions, Literature and Drama, the Stage, Music and Arts, Athletics, Labour, Commerce and Finance.[73] While all members of the men's societies were in favour of women's enfranchisement, different arguments were used to make their claims. Among the most prevalent were direct associations with justice, articulated as a need to correct an anomaly in current franchise laws, and investments in ideals of progress.[74] Martin Durham has suggested that notions of 'fair play', and 'chivalry' underlined the motivations of these men, and this was certainly apparent in some members' arguments and actions.[75] Nevertheless a closer study of such bodies

---

[71] White, *Willoughby Hyett Dickinson*, pp. 53–5. His biographer fails to identify any veiled insults in the piece.

[72] *The Suffrage Annual and Women's Who's Who*, ed. A. J. R. (1913), p. 54.

[73] M.L.W.S., *A Declaration of Representative Men in Favour of Women's Suffrage* (n.d. [c. 1909]).

[74] See articles in *The Men's League Handbook on Women's Suffrage* (1912).

[75] Durham, 'Suffrage and After', p. 183.

would undoubtedly reveal the extent to which dominant manliness was questioned, and whether alternative formations were explored. One factor that is immediately apparent, is the lack of direct references to how women's suffrage would affect men's role in politics, or ideas of manliness and chivalry. On the contrary, supportive men appear to have sought to reinforce their political status through championing women's demands.[76] Yet, whatever male supporters' agendas were, there is no doubt that a sense of instability was apparent in relation to male support, particularly support of militancy. Given the nature of the treatment of some male protesters, it is apparent that anti-suffrage men were profoundly uncomfortable with male supporters' actions because they perceived them as a threat to manly identity. This seems to have been the case, even though there were no widespread or clearly explicit challenges by the collective membership of men's suffrage societies to dominant codes of masculinity.[77]

Against these concerns about redefinitions of, and perceived challenges to dominant masculinity, the campaigns of women activists and male supporters did result in developments in the women's suffrage issue in Parliament. In 1910, an all-party parliamentary conciliation committee was formed under the presidency of the Earl of Lytton in order to bring a bill before Parliament that would enfranchise women on the same lines as the local government householders franchise. In response, the militant suffrage societies agreed to refrain from militancy as the bill proceeded through the Commons. Yet, again and again, even after successful second readings in 1910 (by a majority of 110) and 1911 (by a majority of 167), the bill was sidelined by the government. The condemnations from suffrage activists – both men and women – against the deceitful government became ever more strident.

A government sponsored Reform Bill with its promised concession on women's suffrage, finally came before the House in 1912, but failed after the Speaker's ruling that a women's suffrage amendment changed the legislation so profoundly that it would have to be brought before the House again. Shortly after yet another Conciliation Bill was presented, but on this occasion failed to pass a second reading. Certainly, W.S.P.U. militancy (resumed at the end of 1911) appeared to influence the reversal of the balance of support in the Commons. Nevertheless, the apparent willingness of some M.P.s to rescind promises and to dwell on the actions of a few suffrage activists, at the expense of the arguments of the majority, revealed much continuing uncertainty about female involvement in parliamentary politics. Clearly, the root of such reservations lay both in fears about the impact that extending women's political rights would have on their own political positions and also in their investments in the ideals of manly independence and integrity. Comments in *The Vote* that 'first rule of modern masculine statesmanship seems to be never to yield until you must, and then to yield the minimum' were apparently borne out.[78]

---

[76] This and other issues relating to male support for women's suffrage are explored in *The Men's Share? Masculinities, Male Support and Women's Suffrage in Britain 1890–1920*, eds. A. V. John and C. Eustance (1997).

[77] I have specified *widespread* and *collective*, as distinct from the interests and actions of individual male supporters. For example, the writer Laurence Housman, who was homosexual, does appear to have connected his challenges to dominant heterosexual constructions of masculinity and domesticity with his interest in women's rights.

[78] *Vote*, 15 Jan. 1910, p. 133. The Men's League criticised the government's actions in an 'open letter' sent to the Prime Minister in November 1911.

The 'modern masculine' Cabinet had a framework for parliamentary business, and it was apparent that the direct involvement of women in political decision making came a long way down the list of priorities. The confrontation with the House of Lords confirmed the Commons' formal primacy in parliamentary government, the welfare reforms embodied the Liberal's ideological agenda, and the Irish Home Rule issue concerned Britain's imperial future. No amount of words or conflicting messages from the government could disguise the fact that parliamentary politics, however unstable, continued to be framed by concerns defined by men, be they Liberals, or indeed Irish Nationalists or Labour Members, who after 1910 held the balance of power. Even though there may have been support for these issues among women, they were still legally excluded from expressing their opinions.

However, if the women's suffrage campaign had shown the extent to which female campaigners were prepared to go in challenging exclusively male government, it also demonstrated its limitations. Teresa Billington-Greig who had left the W.F.L. in 1910, disillusioned with what she saw as the short term aims of the militant suffrage movement, was one of very few feminists articulating criticisms about the underlying limitations of Britain's parliamentary democracy.[79] Yet although she outlined her belief that voters' concerns and demands were not represented by the current parliamentary system, she noted herself that she was not offering any 'substitutive for the political machine'.[80] Far more prevalent in suffrage activists' beliefs were the arguments put forward by Alison Neilans in her speech at the Old Bailey, and by Maude Royden in her pamphlet *The True End of Government*. Royden appealed to the men of Britain to act on democratic principles and admit women, so that the entire nation could decide on all political issues, including those of particular interest to women, for the 'well-being of all'.[81] It is apparent that the majority of suffrage campaigners failed to acknowledge how successfully the very essence of British politics had become intertwined with masculine dominance and imperial ideologies.

Nevertheless, for male politicians resisting women's admittance to Parliament, their investments in dominant constructions of masculinity had been shaken by the challenges of women's enfranchisement. A fracturing of the belief that men were naturally and exclusively responsible for national politics had become increasingly apparent in the words and actions of the male supporters of women's suffrage both inside and outside the House of Commons. As Holton has indicated, the principle of women's right to vote had been conceded before the outbreak of the First World War.[82] However it was the war that served both as a focus for apparent changed attitudes towards women's capabilities, an also as a means of reaffirming vigorous manliness. This situation gave added impetus to the still prevalent beliefs in male supremacy over women in the matter of democratic government and this was clearly apparent in the terms of the 1918 Representation of the People Act.

[79] See T. Billington-Greig, *The Militant Suffrage Movement: Emancipation in a Hurry* (1911), and 'Women and Government' in *The Freewoman*, 21 Dec. 1911, reprinted in *The Non-Violent Militant. Selected Writings of Teresa Billington-Greig*, eds. C. McPhee and A. FitzGerald (1987).

[80] Billington-Greig, 'Women and Government', p. 237.

[81] M. Royden, *The True End of Government. An Appeal to the Men of the United Kingdom of Great Britain* (n.d.), p. 12.

[82] Holton, *Feminism and Democracy*, pp. 116–33.

The exclusivity of male citizenship and male control over national politics was breached by the decision to enfranchise women over 30, followed shortly, with little apparent resistance, by legislation allowing women to stand as M.P.s. Yet the decision to set an age limit for women, contrasted sharply with the unequivocal granting of the vote to all adult males over 21. Further indications that the 1918 Representation of the People Act was overwhelmingly concerned to enhance male citizenship were apparent in the moves to equalize the power of the vote among men, through the virtual abolition of plural voting.[83] Inasmuch as it conceded voting rights to some women, the 1918 Act affirmed *all* adult males' rights to be voting citizens.

The grille in the Ladies' Gallery of the House of Commons had been removed in 1917.[84] Events in the following year marked the official end of exclusively male dominated parliamentary government. However, it marked only a stage in demasculinizing it. Those who had overwhelmingly invested in the belief that women in Parliament would signal the beginning of the end of women's subordination were to be disappointed. It became apparent in the 1920s that gender inequality was much more ingrained in society and in politics than had been acknowledged by the majority of suffrage activists. Women faced backlashes in terms of their employment opportunities, and concerns about their roles as mothers, and not least, fundamental difficulties in actually getting selected for winnable Commons seats. During the 1920s the feminist activists who had previously had such high hopes of women's enfranchisement, diversified their challenges and turned their attention to the practical inequalities which continued to restrict women.[85] One such campaign, spearheaded by Lady Rhondda, for the right of peeresses to sit in the House of Lords, was also a telling indication of a continuing intransigence over women's presence in the Houses of Parliament.[86]

The women's suffrage campaign emphasized diverse attitudes among men both inside and outside Parliament to equality between men and women. It also brought into the foreground conflicting and developing ideas about masculinity, in relation to both power over women, and men's status in society. However, following the First World War and the 1918 Representation of the People Act, the issue of women's enfranchisement, which had served as the focus for public anxiety and private consideration of masculine identity, was marginalized.[87] Although concern about, and challenges to dominant constructions of masculinity was still apparent, the crucial relationship between masculine identity and political domination had not been severed. Parliamentary government remained a profoundly gendered construction.

---

[83] M. Pugh, *The Evolution of the British Electoral System* (1988), p. 9. Pugh notes that after 1918 only 159,000 business votes and 68,000 university votes remained compared to over half a million previously.

[84] Dod's *Parliamentary Companion* (1918), p. 180.

[85] There is a growing body of work on feminist organisations and campaigns relating to the 1920s. For example see J. Alberti, *Beyond Suffrage. Feminists in War and Peace, 1914–1928* (1989); M. Pugh, *Women and the Women's Movement in Britain, 1914–1959* (1992); and D. Beddoe, *Back to Home and Duty, Women Between the War, 1918–1939* (1989), pp. 132–47.

[86] See D. Spender, *Time and Tide Wait For No Man* (1984), pp. 33–45.

[87] The number of suffrage societies declined after 1918. In particular, men's societies that had supported women's suffrage disbanded relatively rapidly after the 1918 Representation of the People Act.

Index

Computing Parliamentary History: George III to Victoria

Parliamentary History
Special Issue One (1994)

Edited by John A. Phillips,
University of California, Riverside

Available • 146 pages • 0 7486 0488 X • £12.95

Parliament and the Atlantic Empire

Parliamentary History
Special Issue Two (1995)

Edited by Philip Lawson,
University of Alberta

Available • 102 pages • 0 7486 0628 9 • £12.95

The Scots and Parliament

Parliamentary History
Special Issue Three (1996)

Edited by Clyve Jones
Institute of Historical Research,
University of London

WILLIAM FERGUSON
Introduction

JULIAN GOODARE
The Estates in the Scottish Parliament, 1286–1707

ALAN R. BORTHWICK
Montrose v. *Dundee* and the Jurisdiction of the
Parliament and Council over Fee and Heritage in
the Mid-Fifteenth Century

JOHN SCALLY
Constitutional Revolution, Party and Faction in the
Scottish Parliaments of Charles I

DAVID HAYTON
Traces of Party Politics in Early Eighteenth-Century
Scottish Elections

DAVID J. BROWN
'Nothing but Strugalls and Corruption': The Commons'
Election for Scotland in 1774

J. I. BRASH
The New Scottish County Electors in 1832:
An Occupational Analysis

Available • 160pp • ISBN 0 7486 0823 0 • £12.95

Parliament and Locality
1660–1939

Parliamentary History
Special Issue Five (1998)

Edited by David Dean
Carleton University, Ottawa

and

Clyve Jones
Institute of Historical Research,
University of London

This forthcoming issue will include articles by
Stephen W. Baskerville, J. V. Beckett, Matthew Cragoe,
David Dean, Barry Doyle, David Eastwood,
Stephen Farrell, Perry Gauci, Joanna Innes,
John A. Phillips, and John Prest

Available March 1998

HOW TO ORDER
These special issues are available from bookshops
or can be ordered direct from our distributor:
Marston Book Services
PO Box 269, Abingdon, Oxon OX14 4YN
Tel: 01235 465500, Fax: 01235 465556

EU Authorised Representative: Easy Access System Europe Mustamäe tee 5
0, 10621 Tallinn, Estonia gpsr.requests@easproject.com

Printed and bound by CPI Group (UK) Ltd, Croydon, CR0 4YY
16/04/2025
01846981-0002